DATA RULES

Acting with Technology

Bonnie Nardi, Victor Kaptelinin, and Kirsten Foot, editors

Tracing Genres through Organizations: A Sociocultural Approach to Information Design, Clay Spinuzzi, 2003

Activity-Centered Design: An Ecological Approach to Designing Smart Tools and Usable Systems, Geraldine Gay and Helene Hembrooke, 2004

The Semiotic Engineering of Human-Computer Interaction, Clarisse Sieckenius de Souza, 2005

Group Cognition: Computer Support for Building Collaborative Knowledge, Gerry Stahl, 2006

Acting with Technology: Activity Theory and Interaction Design, Victor Kaptelinin and Bonnie A. Nardi, 2006

Web Campaigning, Kirsten A. Foot and Steven M. Schneider, 2006

Scientific Collaboration on the Internet, Gary M. Olson, Ann Zimmerman, and Nathan Bos, editors, 2008

Acting with Technology: Activity Theory and Interaction Design, Victor Kaptelinin and Bonnie A. Nardi, 2009

Digitally Enabled Social Change: Activism in the Internet Age, Jennifer Earl and Katrina Kimport, 2011

Invisible Users: Youth in the Internet Cafés of Urban Ghana, Jenna Burrell, 2012

Venture Labor: Work and the Burden of Risk in Innovative Industries, Gina Neff, 2012

Car Crashes without Cars: Lessons about Simulation Technology and Organizational Change from Automotive Design, Paul M. Leonardi, 2012

Coding Places: Software Practice in a South American City, Yuri Takhteyev, 2012

Technology Choices: Why Occupations Differ in Their Embrace of New Technology, Diane E. Bailey and Paul M. Leonardi, 2015

Shifting Practices: Reflections on Technology, Practice, and Innovation, Giovan Francesco Lanzara, 2016

Heteromation, and Other Stories of Computing and Capitalism, Hamid R. Ekbia and Bonnie A. Nardi

The Good Drone: How Social Movements Democratize Surveillance, Austin Choi-Fitzpatrick, 2020

Virtually Amish: Preserving Community at the Internet's Margins, Lindsay Ems, 2022

Data Rules: Reinventing the Market Economy, Cristina Alaimo and Jannis Kallinikos, 2024

DATA RULES

REINVENTING THE MARKET ECONOMY

CRISTINA ALAIMO AND JANNIS KALLINIKOS

FOREWORD BY MICHAEL POWER

The MIT Press
Cambridge, Massachusetts
London, England

The MIT Press would like to thank the anonymous peer reviewers who provided comments on drafts of this book. The generous work of academic experts is essential for establishing the authority and quality of our publications. We acknowledge with gratitude the contributions of these otherwise uncredited readers.

This book was set in Stone Serif and Stone Sans by Westchester Publishing Services. Printed and bound in the United States of America.

Library of Congress Cataloging-in-Publication Data

Names: Alaimo, Cristina, author. | Kallinikos, Jannis, author.
Title: Data rules : reinventing the market economy / Cristina Alaimo and Jannis Kallinikos ; foreword by Michael Power.
Description: Cambridge, Massachusetts : The MIT Press, [2024] | Series: Acting with technology | Includes bibliographical references and index.
Identifiers: LCCN 2023032432 (print) | LCCN 2023032433 (ebook) | ISBN 9780262547932 (paperback) | ISBN 9780262378437 (epub) | ISBN 9780262378420 (pdf)
Subjects: LCSH: Electronic commerce. | Social media—Economic aspects.
Classification: LCC HF5548.32 .A356 2024 (print) | LCC HF5548.32 (ebook) | DDC 658.8/72—dc23/eng/20231101
LC record available at https://lccn.loc.gov/2023032432
LC ebook record available at https://lccn.loc.gov/2023032433

10 9 8 7 6 5 4 3 2 1

CONTENTS

FOREWORD   vii
Michael Power

ACKNOWLEDGMENTS   xi

1   INTRODUCTION   1

I   FOUNDATIONS

2   THE EPISTEMIC FOUNDATIONS OF DATA   21

3   THE DIGITAL DATA REVOLUTION   41

4   THE DATA LIFE CYCLE   61

5   TECHNOLOGIES OF DIFFERENCE: EXCURSUS ON
    SURVEILLANCE   89

II   SOCIAL AND ECONOMIC TRANSFORMATIONS

6   DECENTERING ORGANIZATIONS: DATA, KNOWLEDGE, AND
    INSTITUTIONAL CHANGE   111

7   PLATFORMS AND ECOSYSTEMS   131

8   DATA AND ECOSYSTEMS   149

9   EPILOGUE   171

NOTES   183
REFERENCES   191
INDEX   217

FOREWORD

The very idea of "data," of that which is given to us in experience, has preoccupied many philosophers, from David Hume's naturalistic notion of impressions as unmediated sense data to cruder versions of twentieth-century positivism that contend that data are just "out there." There have also been multiple reactions to these positions and their shared commitment to the "myth of the given." Commonly understood under the umbrella concept of "postempiricism," these reactions argue that, even though feedback from natural reality constrains what we can say about it, observational data and the instrumentation through which data are visible, is irredeemably theory and value-laden. Indeed, at the extreme, some postempiricists point to the self-referential, self-reproducing and closed world of scientific theories and their data—particle physics being especially amenable to such claims. Yet notwithstanding these and other nuances within postempiricism, it is united by a broad consensus that data are a matter of construction and organization. Furthermore, what count as data depend on notational and other, often invisible, practices of carving the world into elements that might be compared, aggregated, and processed. So while it may be too much to say that "anything goes," data are nevertheless not a given but are themselves an outcome and a matter of organized human construction and demarcation.

Given the wider influence of these reactions to positivism on sociological and managerial theories, it is all the more striking, as Cristina Alaimo and Jannis Kallinikos remind us in their study, that data in digital form have not yet been fully subjected to similar critical and constructivist sensibilities and analyses. While the technical reach and transformative nature of the digital age have understandably received considerable attention from scholars— big data, surveillance, blockchains, and algorithms are continuing objects of fascination and extensive debate—the foundations of these developments in digital data have been more or less unproblematized within mainstream theorizing of platforms and ecosystems. Accordingly, Alaimo and Kallinikos develop an explicit manifesto for an interdisciplinary approach to digital data that deconstructs the positivism of the raw click in order to understand how it is an outcome of subtle and understudied datafication processes. They set themselves and others the task of turning data making into an area of inquiry in its own right, which reverse engineers the seeming hardness of digital data. This analysis matters because data encode reality in specific ways, with formative implications for meaning, cognition, and communication. Furthermore, Alaimo and Kallinikos suggest that the construction of digital data provides the underlying infrastructural conditions of possibility for the entities that we call "networks" and for the problems addressed by network economics. In this way, they show us how data are deeply implicated in rewiring the market economy.

Critical accounting scholarship is closely aligned with Alaimo and Kallinikos's project. It is now widely accepted that the data that are used to produce organizational accounts are an outcome of conventions about what to make visible and what remains invisible, and therefore unaccounted. Reductive forms of quantification have played a key role in generating the distinctive facticity and performativity of accounting, which comes to appear natural to human actors and which gets hard-wired into systems, both manual and digital, such as for enterprise resource planning. The critical accounting project can be defined in terms of challenging this naturalism and technicism, exposing its institutional and political foundations, and proposing new representations and counter accounts informed by different values and data constructions.

Yet for all these parallels between Alaimo and Kallinikos's present study and the history of accounting, record keeping, and practices of monitoring, they show how the stakes for digital data constructivism are much higher. They argue that the speed and accumulative character of digital data, as well as the manner in which they pile up, have explosive organizing potential in two important ways. First, they have led to architectures of control that decenter the traditional organizational form largely assumed by critical accounting and require a more ecological approach. Second, and as a consequence, they blur the distinction between transactional and social relations that have been important to studies of corporate social reporting, financialization, and social impact. Hence, much more is at stake than the role of digital data as a reality filter; they underpin and drive new organizational forms, which in turn overflow traditional regulatory and governance frameworks. Digital data do not only accumulate; in doing so, they create forms of connectivity and capabilities for traceability, tracking, and surveillance that did not exist before—food supply chains and social credit systems being much discussed in empirical settings. In turn, these capabilities generate new practices of performance measurement and organizational orders that demand further articulations of digital data. Hence, as Alaimo and Kallinikos show, data do not have a life entirely apart from all their many applications; they are recursively related and mutually formative.

In sum, *Data Rules: Reinventing the Market Economy* demonstrates how digital data have their own semiautonomous sociology of formation, which is as important for understanding the forces shaping our contemporary world as the major and more visible technological developments. It is a sociology that cuts across these developments and interrogates their material conditions of possibility, which might otherwise be overlooked, ignored, or underestimated.

Cristina Alaimo and Jannis Kallinikos are leading scholars working at the intersection of information systems and organizational studies. Their distinctive genre draws extensively on many intellectual currents in sociology, science studies, and social theory. In this compelling book, which brings together many themes from their prior work, they provide us with the untold story of digital data, their making, and their performativity. They also open our eyes to a new cross-cutting agenda that should engage scholars across a wide range of disciplines, as well as the reflective public, since all of us are touched in one way or another by the issues that they raise.

Michael Power
London, July 2023

ACKNOWLEDGMENTS

We have written this book against the echo of ideas concerning the economic and social importance of data, reflected in a variety of academic contexts but also social discourses and considerations. Many people, a variety of settings, and many occasions have helped us make our arguments more coherent and, hopefully, relevant for several stakeholders, including academics, policymakers, and a wider and educated public concerned with the directions that current economy and society are taking. In this regard, a book is always a collective achievement.

We would like here to single out a few colleagues to whom we feel particularly indebted. Ole Hanseth and Eric Monteiro have been travel companions along the journey of this book, read and commented on parts of the book manuscript, and challenged us to make our ideas crisper. So did Aleksi Aaltonen, Carmelo Cennamo, Hans Hasselbladh, Kalle Lyytinen, Attila Márton, and Burt Swanson. We are grateful to all of them. We would also like to extend our gratitude to Ioanna Constantiou, Hamid Ekbia, Samer Faraj, Jonny Holmström, and Youngjin Yoo for sharing their ideas with us and helping us on several occasions. While the writing of this book has a long history, part of it was shaped during our recent years at Luiss University, which we joined in 2020. We would like to take the opportunity to thank Andrea Prencipe, the rector of Luiss University, Henry Chesbrough, Luca Giustiniano, Luigi Marengo, Ian McCarthy, Maria Savona, Mark Thatcher, Alessandro Zattoni, and other colleagues at Luiss for receiving us with such an open mind, providing us ample opportunities for continuing our research and rehearsing our ideas on a few occasions. Great thanks go to Katie Helke at the MIT Press for her support and patience, and Bonnie Nardi and Victor Kaptelinin, series editors at the MIT Press, for having given us the opportunity to publish this manuscript. Writing a book requires a protracted intellectual effort, but also a quiet daily environment. We have, in the last three consecutive summers, been writing chunks of this book in the beautiful and serene summer house of Cristina's parents, Giuseppe Alaimo and Cinzia Cittadino, on the Mediterranean island of Pantelleria, free of the disturbances of daily living. We are deeply indebted to them for their support and encouragement.

1 INTRODUCTION

DATA AND SOCIOECONOMIC TRANSFORMATIONS

The primary objective of this volume is to analyze the forces that install data at the center of contemporary life and reinforce the functions that they perform in the economy and society.[1] Such an objective differs from the widespread understanding of data as technical items that can be technologically amassed and computed to address social, economic, and business issues. Our focus is on something other than the techniques and models which use big data to carry out managerial, economic, and societal interventions. Here, we deal with the long-standing developments in social cognition and communication that have converged to make data critical media for such interventions, a fundamental means through which social situations are read, instrumented, understood, and acted upon. From this perspective, we examine the social and economic transformations associated with the unprecedented diffusion and increasing socioeconomic relevance of data.

Data undoubtedly moved to the forefront of social and economic life thanks to the digital revolution that brought, gradually but inexorably, the *rendition* of a bewildering array of facts and life situations to *data* that are possible to manage apart and beyond the contexts in which they are generated (Couldry & Mejias 2019). A close inspection of these changes suggests that they are more profound than what is usually acknowledged. The *datafication* of life and its accompanying sociotechnical machinery infrastructure social interaction (Alaimo & Kallinikos 2019; Weick 1979) and relax a variety of constraints that, over the course of modernity, have shaped the prevailing modalities of work and communication and the enterprise forms that commanded the production and consumption of goods (Beniger 1986; Castells 1996; Luhmann 2002/2017, 1995; Polanyi 1944/2001). Well-established boundaries of modern societies, such as those between work and private life or between the economic and the social spheres, are less clearly demarcated from one another in the data age. The effects of such profound transformations are already in place. The diffusion of digital platforms as organizational arrangements, the erosion of traditional market practices by platform-based business ecosystems, and the transformation of the contemporary workplace are all closely associated with the functions that data perform as semiotic (sense making), epistemic (knowledge making), and communicative means. These developments, we suggest, are instrumental in rehearsing the relationships of individuals to collective entities (e.g., communities, organizations, and the state) and rebuilding economic institutions (Alaimo & Kallinikos 2021, 2022; Lyytinen 2022; Power 2022).

The digital revolution, however, has deeper and more diverse roots. The interlocking of data with socioeconomic institutions has a line of descent that stretches back to venerable commercial and administrative practices of data management and record keeping (Bowker & Star 1999; Cline-Cohen 1982; Muller 2019; Power 2007; Quattrone 2009). The American business historian Alfred Chandler (1977) traces the emergence of modern corporations in the first half of the twentieth century to the systematic generation of a variety of internal records (e.g., operations, sales, accounting, and financial data) through which management came to monitor and assess corporate performance across functions, production sites, and periods. Chandler's historical outlook is crucial, as it retraces the links that tie together the production and use of records to the birth of institutions (e.g., corporations), a theme that we feel has been largely overlooked in recent discourses on data. A closer reflection on the structural and economic transformations in modern times reveals the strong bonds modern institutions have maintained with broader sociocultural shifts in modes of cognition and communication, the diffusion of technologies such as the printing press and the spread of literacy and, later, numeracy (Beniger 1986; Cline-Cohen 1982; Eisenstein 1979; Hoskin & Macve 1986; Ong 1982; Porter 1995; Yates 1989). Changes of this sort have marked modern life irreversibly along several frontiers and shaped what prominent scholars recognized as the modern institutional order (Goody 1986; Heller 1999; Luhmann 1982; Weber 1947/2012, 1978/2019).

Awareness of the practices by which data as systematic records have been made a vital element of the modern social and economic fabric helps put current trends into broader perspective. Among other things, it contributes to avoiding a narrow and widespread misperception of data as just technical inputs to standardized computations, reinforced by the diffusion of digital technologies and the recent advance of *data science* as a scientific field. Approaching data as records conjures up their image as tools of cognition and institutional memory (and thus knowledge) and means of communication (Borgmann 1999, 2010; Bowker 2005; Eco 1976, 1986, 2000, 2014). Much as they become digital tokens in a technological world where they are regularly piled up and computed along standard lines, data retain their constitution as diffuse epistemic and semiotic elements and communication media. A "like" on social media is a computational token and a way of communicating approval or agreement that is often read as a mark of preference and profile building (Alaimo & Kallinikos 2017). Only as a mark of individual preference can a like become the kernel around which a novel "like economy" operates (Gerlitz & Helmond 2013). Mere clicks do not build complex market exchanges. Clicks make sense only against assumptions, practices, and beliefs in which they are unavoidably inserted and from which they emerge as meaningful pursuits. Similar claims can be made about data generated in manufacturing and service industries, health care, and education (Alaimo & Kallinikos 2021; Bowker & Star 1999; Espeland & Sauder 2007; Leonardi & Treem 2012, 2020; Timmermans & Berg 1997, 2010).

Their formal and technological makeup notwithstanding, digital data continue to work as instruments of reality marking, as complex artifacts of cognition that encode facts (or what pass as facts; see Poovey 1998), and record and transmit information and knowledge. Therefore, assessing the critical role that data assume in the current, predominantly digital world calls for rediscovering their semiotic and epistemic foundations (Bowker 2014; Leonelli 2014, 2015; Strasser & Edwards 2017). It is vital to link these foundations to the new forms of interaction that data promote and the new economic practices and institutions that they establish (Mennicken & Salais 2022). We find it a fascinating intellectual challenge to explore whether and how the technological nature of digital data renews, expands, modifies, challenges, or annuls long-established semiotic and knowledge conventions, and also reweaves the institutional fabric in which data qua records have traditionally been embedded.

The discourses that have been associated with the ongoing data revolution tend to overlook the origins of data as artifacts of cognition and knowledge and media of communication. The narratives of big data (Ayres 2006; Kitchin 2014; Pentland 2014), surveillance through data, and control (Clarke 1988, 2019; Zuboff 2015, 2019) do not make data the objects of their concerns. They are primarily interested in how data might become involved in shaping contemporary events through their technological affordances (e.g., data mining, tracking, and computation), and how their use may serve specific political or economic interests. They leave much of the data dynamics that shape the direction and character of current socioeconomic transformations virtually unexplained. Wittingly or unwittingly, the prevailing accounts of big data, surveillance, and control sidestep the dense communicative fabric into which data are embedded and overlook the variety of cognitive (semiotic and epistemic) and communicative functions they perform (boyd & Crawford 2012; Ekbia et al. 2015).

User tracking and surveillance are widespread in current societies while big data analytics has over the last decade or so grown to become a pervasive exercise. Nevertheless, the recognition of these practices by no means exhausts the many other things that people and institutions do with data. A fuller appreciation of the rising relevance of data and the socioeconomic implications of their diffusion, therefore, requires rediscovering the functions that data perform. This translates to deconstructing and analyzing the texture of details by and through which data work as encoding devices and reality filters, instruments of knowledge, and media of exchange and communication. Such a task becomes imperative as one moves from the neat world of big concepts to the impressive variety of details that underlie the ways that data are involved in rehearsing and rebuilding social and economic practices (Alaimo & Kallinikos 2021, 2022; Edwards 2010; Monteiro 2022).

These broader concerns provide a glimpse of the background against which we seek to approach the social and economic transformations underlying the diffusion of data. We associate these developments with the establishment of new enterprise configurations and novel social and economic practices emerging from data-shaped patterns of living and forms of organizing (Bailey, Leonardi, & Barley 2012; Faraj, Pachidi, & Sayegh 2018; Turow & Couldry 2018; Von Krogh 2018). The picture is complex, quickly shifting, and challenging to describe in definitive terms. Yet it is shown in the diffusion of digital platforms and the formation of large, often global, and platform-gravitating value networks or ecosystems (e.g., Ciborra 1996; De Reuver, Sørensen, & Basole 2018; Iansiti & Levien 2004; Jacobides, Cennamo, & Gawer 2018; Phillips & Ritala 2019; Shipilov & Gawer 2020). Many of these arrangements and the practices underlying them cluster around tasks and exchanges that are, in most essential respects, instrumented, conducted, and assessed by recourse to data and the services that data enable (Kornberger, Pflueger, & Mouritsen 2017). While characteristic of commercial platforms and social media, these developments have lately spread across a wide range of fields, including agriculture and traditional manufacturing, whose obstinate materiality once seemed to evade their rendition into digital bits (Alaimo 2022a; Greenfield 2017; Monteiro & Parmiggiani 2019). It is in this broader sense that the title of this book should be interpreted.

DATA, TECHNOLOGY, AND ALGORITHMS

The observations that we have advanced here suggest that the perception of data as technical items does not do justice to the semiotic, epistemic, and communication functions that data perform in economy and society (Turow & Couldry 2018). It is reasonable, though, to wonder to what degree the technological nature of digital data and the formalized operations embodied in software systems and devices by which they are produced and managed shape these functions. This is, no doubt, an intricate question that echoes vexed issues of content versus form or medium, recurrent in the history of communication, in arts, semiotics, and cognition more widely (Ahonen 1993; Goodman 1976, 1978; Ong 1982; Sontag 1966/2009; Tomasello 1999). The medium is never an innocent carrier of the content that it conveys; rather, it is variously involved in shaping it, a condition that has found its most memorable expression in Marshall McLuhan's hyperbole "the medium is the message" (McLuhan 1964).

The facts that digital data mediate are undeniably shaped by the technical prescriptions by which they encode the life incidents they capture, the formal rules and principles of large data repositories (databases), the standards and protocols required for their transmission, the metrics that make specific data visible, and the hardwired functionalities of software systems through which they are produced and shared (Dourish 2017; Ekbia & Nardi 2017; Lyytinen 2022). These operations, furthermore, are contingent on the inexorable logic of bitstrings and how lower-level computing operations support higher-level, semantic functions (Borgmann 1999; Faulkner & Runde 2019; Hanseth & Lyytinen 2010; Yoo 2010; Yoo, Henfridsson, & Lyytinen 2010).[2] All these formal prerequisites compromise content specificity or detail (context) for recognizability, retrieval, and other similar cognitive benefits. In addition, data are often generated on the assumption that they matter in conjunction with other tokens in a large enough scale to disclose novel configurations of similarities and differences (usually expressed as metrics) (Desrosiéres 1998). As the practice of recombining and repurposing data across domains diffuses, the variety of circumstances that these massive data volumes bring about necessitates additional formalization and standardization. The growing institutional immersion of artificial intelligence (AI) applications and emerging technologies further reinforce these trends (Bailey et al. 2022; Iansiti & Lakhani 2020).

All these conditions are undoubtedly responsible for the widespread perception of data as mere technical elements, at a remove from the fields in which cognition, action and knowledge, and communication unfold. A closer reflection on these conditions nonetheless indicates that the production of digital data is inescapably associated with the establishment of a semantic layer that is not reducible to the underlying technological principles and operations, no matter how much it is contingent on them (Alaimo, Kallinikos, & Aaltonen 2020; Beyes et al. 2022; Gitelman 2013; Mingers & Willcocks 2014). Whether in the form of social data produced by online interaction and communication or sensor-generated data, the incidents of life that pass through the lenses of digital data unavoidably embody operations of filtering, describing, or otherwise, positing a meaningful reality and acting upon it. Traffic monitoring, user whereabouts on social media, machine utilization metrics in industrial platforms, and patient records in health care all transcend the formal (logical, computational) and material (digital, electrical) underpinnings of data qua technological elements. In other words, the production and use of digital data are related to meaning creation, knowledge development, and management (Iliadis 2023). In most of their technological incarnations, data still furnish the means for bringing about distinctions that help lift areas of social and economic reality out of the dense background to which they belong and make them the objects of social and economic interference.

Digital data grow at the crossroads upon which computation encounters signification, the mechanics of data processing turn upon meaning, and technological affordances fuse with communication modes and practices (Alaimo & Kallinikos 2019, 2022; Borgmann 1999, 2012; Buckland 1991; Kittler 1997; Zuboff 1988). There is, no doubt, a steady friction but also an interpenetration between data as technological items on the one hand and data as signifying, representing, and communicating tokens on the other. The diffused practice of combining digital data across diverse domains and regularly repurposing and reusing them (Markus 2001) indicates the mutual implication of their technological and semantic qualities. Even if amenable to machine processing and management, data remain instruments of communication, cognition, and representation (Kittler 1996; Swanson 1999, 2022; Tuomi 1999). This hybrid makeup grants digital data their distinctive and fascinating character and renders them a ubiquitous companion of contemporary socioeconomic life.

While offering a vivid contrast to the widespread misperception of data as technical items, these observations also qualify the impact that algorithms have been claimed to have upon persons, work patterns, and institutions (Kellogg, Valentine, & Christin 2020; Orlikowski & Scott 2014). The variety of functions that data perform as reality filters, instruments of knowledge, and media of communication are hardly reducible to the computational procedures that algorithms (even learning algorithms) embody. Some time ago, the computer scientist Peter Wegner contrasted algorithms with interaction. His argument is complex, but it can be summed up by the claim that interaction is critical to the performance of many computational systems, as it provides the data input and learning capabilities that the adequate functioning of these systems require, a task that cannot be accomplished by algorithms alone (Wegner 1997). The acumen of this observation, advanced long before algorithms acquired the traction that they currently have, is unambiguously manifested by the history of computing technologies. A quick reflection on the transition from large, centrally controlled, computationally intensive, and yet interaction-dumb mainframes to desktop computing, the development of the Internet, and the diffusion of tablets and smart phones along with the Internet of Things

(IoT) provides a forceful reminder of the evolutionary trajectory of digital technologies (Arthur 2009; Aspray 1990; Mumford 1934/2010; Winner 1986). The immersion of computing technologies and devices in the context of daily living and the interaction of machines with other machines and with heterogenous users (Zittrain 2008) are the most revolutionary developments of computer technologies after their invention as universal machines of computation (Agar 2017; Ceruzzi 2003; Cortada 2011). These conditions bespeak the ongoing importance of data and the broader mindscape in which the uses of current technologies and devices are embedded. To equate these processes to algorithms amounts to mistaking "multipart complex systems for simple, singular ones" (Bogost 2015).

While vital to current forms of cognitive automation, algorithms are only one (albeit pervasive) element of far more complex technological and institutional machinery (Kallinikos & Constantiou 2015). The black boxing of the workings of this machinery and the dependence of algorithmic outputs on the scope, semantic variety, and quality of data upon which algorithmic operations are predicated risks compromising the complexity and subtlety of the bigger picture. It is important not to lose sight of the fundamental fact that algorithms maintain the connection with their surroundings through the data that they are fed. Data are, as it were, the "sensing arms" of algorithms, the means through which algorithms transcend their operational closure as procedures of calculation (i.e., mechanical operations) and link and interact with reality. Through data, algorithms communicate with their environments and get to "know about" and "learn from" what is happening around them. Algorithms without living data are no more than sheer mathematical exercises (Gillespie 2014). Contrasting data with algorithms may ultimately be pointless. It is, though worthwhile, against the background of the widespread, reified use of algorithms to stress their mutual implication and underline the patterns by which they presuppose and reinforce one another. The impact of algorithms on work, management, organizations, societies, and economic practices (Barrett et al. 2012; Lebovitz, Lifshitz-Assaf, & Levina 2022; Waardenburg, Huysman, & Sergeeva 2022) is heavily shaped by the life situations that data mediate, and thus by the scope, size, and quality of these mediations upon which algorithms operate (Alaimo & Kallinikos 2017, 2021; Dourish 2016, 2017; Glaser, Pollock, & D'Adderio 2021).

DATA AND SOCIAL INQUIRY

The tension and interpenetration of the formal nature of digital data with the semiotic, epistemic, and communicative functions that they perform is a fundamental motif of this book and a critical frontier that we explore in its pages. Given this, it takes only a small step to realize that *data making* and *data use* constitute essential *areas of social inquiry*, distinct from contemporary data science and the framing of data in predominantly technical terms. Data making and data use are areas of social inquiry as far as data serve several semiotic and knowledge functions and shape interaction and communication; and by the same token, as far as the terms by which things and life situations are first marked and then transcribed to data are bound up with the social values, cultural schemes, and institutional predilections of the settings in which data are generated and made a widespread cognitive currency and communication medium (Borgmann 1999, 2010, 2012; Turow & Couldry 2018). Put differently, data are political artifacts (Winner 1986) that become objects of social inquiry insofar as they serve a variety of social and economic ends and are involved in the making of social institutions and society.

Several insights ensue from these observations. To begin with, the social and cultural foundations of data challenge their widespread perception as *hard facts* and contest the status of data as inevitable, "out there," or objective in the sense of physical entities. Although there is significant variation in the conditions and methods by which data transcribe things and life incidents and relate to other data, these operations (transcription and relatability) and the content that data carry are never inevitable. The facts that data records convey might have been otherwise (i.e., different facts might have been reported) had the specifications, cultural values, and assumptions of their making been of another kind (Hacking 1999). This applies as much to the encoding of user behavior or opinions into data (e.g., how social media encode interaction) as to the recording of commercial transactions or to the transcription of physical things and processes to data (e.g., sensor data encoding signals from vehicle traffic, body functions). It takes much hard work to unpack these predilections and reverse engineer the process of data generation. In a good deal of cases, predilections are hardwired into the operations of institutions and serve the prevailing orders. Accordingly, contesting the inevitable status of data does not make data negotiable and the terms by which they have been produced malleable. It may nonetheless open a vista of intriguing questions along which the social impact of data can be contemplated, unpacked, understood, critiqued, and eventually changed (Couldry & Mejias 2019, 2020; Grisot et al. 2019; Hildebrandt 2015; Iliadis & Russo 2016; Lindgren & Holmström 2020).[3]

As in all systems of signs and notation, data become marks (semiotic tokens) only on the tacit assumption that the things they mark (or represent) could have been marked in other ways (Eco 1976, 2000). The fact that data are not inevitable, therefore, suggests not simply that they could be otherwise, but also that the semiotic, epistemic, and communication functions that they perform are part and parcel of a plural ecosystem of knowing (Bateson 1972/2000; Knorr Cetina 1999; Star 1995; Star & Griesemer 1989). The noninevitable nature of data is a consequence of the cultural roots of human cognition and the perception and interpretation of reality along multiple avenues and from alternative perspectives (Searle 1995, 2010; Tomasello 1999). Data are the outcome of operations that encode or translate facts and relations out there that could have been encoded and translated in other ways. But data also are the result of a variety of strategies of cognition that make the world knowable and expand, as it were, its confines (Kallinikos 1999, 2010; Latour 1986, 1987). This complex ecosystem of knowing and the variety of communication and signification functions that it allows grant data their signifying potency and the importance that they acquire in the socioeconomic transformations that characterize our time. These ideas provide a first approximation of the complex fabric of social and economic relations into which data are embedded. Data are essential and pervasive artifacts of cognition and knowledge that are deployed to mark off areas of social and economic reality and establish the practices that develop around the mastery, exploitation, and use of these areas.

The systematic production and use of data lead to the establishment of social entities or objects that would hardly exist apart from the data that target, delimit, describe, and manage them. Unemployment rates, credit or reputation scores, and health records are all examples of objects made of data. Studying these objects is an essential pursuit of a social science of data. Through data, social and economic areas are marked, separated from others, and given ontological independence and stability through the standardized descriptions and metrics that various forms of data enable. Thus objectified, these areas (e.g., health, education, productivity, innovation, and criminality) become central reference points around which social, economic, and institutional practices and relations develop. Similar claims have earlier been made, in the aftermath of Michel Foucault's writing, by diverse scholars such as Desrosières (1998) (in the areas of statistics and social objects); Hacking (1990) and Porter (1995) (statistics, social welfare, psychiatry); Espeland and Sauder (2007) (university rankings); Miller and O'Leary (1987); and Power (2007) (accounting, economics), among others.

The far-reaching significance of social objects, engineered out of data, underscores the need to study them in ways that respond to their social and economic complexity and the challenges raised by the technical developments we briefly referred to earlier, which we expound in more detail in the pages of this book. A good deal of the social objects that populate our lives these days and pervade the operations of organizations and institutional actors are brought into being, revised, expanded, and eliminated through the objectification of things and life situations that digital data afford (Alaimo & Kallinikos 2022; Leonelli 2014). Thus conceived, social objects unravel the stability and institutional embedment of social practice (see, e.g., Knorr Cetina 1999, 9; Lounsbury & Crumley 2007) and help circumvent a good deal of the hyperbole and undue simplifications that perceive it as just the local accomplishment of situated actors.

These ideas indicate that the diverse and dispersed constitution of digital data, along with the methods and techniques by which they are produced, shared, repurposed, aggregated, and commercialized, require the establishment of new *structural arrangements* or *enterprise forms* that can host or accommodate novel social practices. The digital rendition of things and life situations occurs on a much larger scale than earlier forms of disembedment (such as writing or counting; Giddens 1990) and brings about new forms of interaction and exchange. It also exhibits frequent and recursive feedback loops in real time between local events and global conditions that would have been beyond reach, without the technological affordances upon which data management practices rely (Lyytinen 2022). Consider the work of music or film recommender systems and how they connect individual users to standardized global infrastructures in interacting feedback loops. These developments provide a good deal of incentive for revising traditional *architectures of control* underlying economic organizations. In fact, the dispersion and heterogeneity of data and the institutional fragmentation underlying the ways by which they are procured or repurposed, aggregated, and commercialized call into question the foundation of organizations as concentrated systems run predominantly on data derived from internal operations, well fenced off from organizational surroundings (Chandler 1977).

These transformations signal a change of paradigmatic import associated with the *decentering of organizations*. The notion of firms (and formal organizations more broadly) as centered systems makes sense when these systems can keep an external world at arm's length and obtain a relative operational independence from it. This partition into an internal set of contingencies that could be paid heed to and managed on a continuous basis and an external world that is attended to only periodically is increasingly undone by the machinery of digital data, their dispersion, heterogeneity, uncertain origin, and steady reproduction and renewal. We analyze these epochal transformations in considerable detail in part II of this book (chapters 6, 7, and 8), in connection with the advent of digital platforms and digital ecosystems.

As these observations suggest, our take on digital platforms and digital business ecosystems takes stock and yet diverges in several respects from the quickly mushrooming body of literature on these subjects (see, e.g., Adner 2017; Brynjolfsson & McAfee 2014; Jacobides, Cennamo, & Gawer 2018; McIntyre & Srinivasan 2017; Brynjolfsson & McAfee 2014; McIntyre et al. 2020; Parker, Van Alstyne, & Choudary 2016; Van Alstyne, Parker, & Choudary 2016). We connect the emergence of platforms and ecosystems to the diffusion and institutional embedment of data, conceived along the lines briefly described in this introduction. The overwhelming majority of research on platforms and ecosystems overlooks the functions of data as artifacts of cognition and knowledge and media of communication, remaining oblivious to the far-reaching role that data play as agents of social and economic engineering. Digital connectivity and the affordances of digital technologies alone do not establish links among social and economic actors, nor do they shape their interactions. To achieve these goals, digital technologies rely upon the variety of functions data perform as semiotic, epistemic, and communicative elements.

It hardly comes as a surprise that the prevailing research on these matters fails to observe the social and institutional repercussions of the diffusion of platforms and ecosystems. A central argument of this book is that digital platforms and digital business ecosystems are not only novel organizational forms and arrangements, but also vehicles for transgressing the institutional separation of *transactions* from *social relations* upon which the operations of markets and organizations have been predicated in modern times (Luhmann 1982, 1993). This transgressing could occur only with the massive rendition of facts, relationships, and life situations into data. The reading and commercialization of the biological *body*, the domestic *room*, and the *public space* (Greenfield 2017, 32) achieved by sensors and IoT constitute a case in point. Far from being simply novel organizational arrangements, platforms and ecosystems are institutional expressions of far-reaching socioeconomic changes. Their diffusion points to the fact that the separation of the economy from society and the reservation of a private space, distinct and apart from institutional operations that have defined the modern social order (Giddens 1990; Luhmann 1982, 2002), are no longer as relevant and operative as they once were.

OUTLINE OF THE BOOK

After this introduction, chapter 2 retraces the epistemic foundations of data and unravels the multiple ties that data have maintained with cognition and social action. The chapter reconstructs some of the modalities by which data, through various material means and across widely different historical contexts, have been constitutionally intertwined with collective knowledge dynamics and novel institutional forms. We briefly recount the use of clay tokens and show how the structure of clay-based systems of record making supported the rise of general concepts and complex practices such as the economic exchange of goods and the social structures that developed around them. We then move on to tracing the function of data as statistical quantities connected to the development of the modern state. In conjunction with furnishing the means for constructing novel *social objects*, such as crime and unemployment rates, data came to be widespread instruments of intervening upon and governing social life. The chapter further outlines the role that data records have played in the development of modern corporations and the establishment of management control practices.

Chapter 3 investigates the patterns through which the mechanization of records and the emergence of computational science have changed the makeup and the epistemic functions of data. The technological rendition of data introduced an artificial separation between data and their informative and communicative content, which has been further reinforced but also modified by the advent of personal computers and the Internet. With the arrival of the web, data emerged both as a key medium of interaction and the cognitive infrastructure through which a good deal of organizational processes and everyday chores take place. Despite these path-breaking developments, the prevailing mindset sees data as solely algorithmic input, factual data points, or economic resources. Drawing on a variety of social science contributions, we advance an alternative conception of digital data as multilayered technological artifacts that are *agnostic,* in terms of the content that they mediate; *homogenizing,* in that they transcend the intrinsic qualities of things encountered across regions of the real; and *non-neutral,* in the sense of embodying a variety of social and technical predilections. Taken together, these conditions make data potent medium of social encounters, economic orchestration, and exchange.

Chapter 4 delves further into these details and examines the processes by which data are made and become standardized and aggregated into objects that can take on novel social and economic lives. We analyze and illustrate how the making of data always entails a series of predilections on what things, incidents, and social relationships to capture and encode into the medium of data. This is followed by the exposition of the patterns underlying the piling of data into aggregate objects used to circumscribe and manage organizational tasks and processes. Such novel data objects become the center stage upon which organizational knowledge and practices unfold. The core of these ideas is that the making of data is a complex interactive and nonlinear process whereby individual data tokens reflect wider social and technical conditions while remaining vital elements that renew and expand these conditions. Moving further along this road, we reflect upon and analyze how data become commodities (i.e., are packaged and traded across a variety of situations). Making data into commodities entails a few critical operations whereby their validity, facticity, and economic value are constantly held in check, reinforced, and expanded.

Chapter 5 is an excursus into surveillance and some of the issues raised by user tracking and monitoring. Our objective is to draw on the ideas put forward in the preceding chapters to reappraise the quest for regulating the terms by which data are generated and used. We first outline the difficulties of separating data tracking and monitoring from the background of technological, social, and institutional relations in which they occur. These difficulties, we suggest, are aggravated by the diffuse nature of the cognitive and communicative functions that data currently assume in the lives of people and the operations of organizations and institutions. This is followed by our effort to reapproach surveillance in ways that go beyond the "Big Brother" deadlock of watching and being watched. We contrast the Big Brother approach to modern forms of surveillance (e.g., Foucault 1988; Hacking 1999), which, we claim, make up a complex relational game where those subjected to it are required to be active and (critically) capable game participants. Approaching surveillance in these terms allows us to obtain a critical yet more inquisitive account of the risks and opportunities associated with the centrality of digital technologies and the generation and use of digital data across most walks of life. Most important, it allows us to move the discussion forward by reconsidering how the diffusion of data, of which data-driven tracking and monitoring are conspicuous manifestations, is both a cause and an expression of a major, underlying social trend whereby the distinct spheres characteristic of the modern social order (e.g., economy, politics, and personal and domestic lives) increasingly lose their sharp outlines. We conclude with a few reflections on these path-breaking developments and a call to ground regulation in an adequate understanding of what data are and how they work as agents of social and economic change.

Chapter 6 sets out to explore the implications of the developments outlined in the preceding chapters for organizations and the emerging systems and practices of producing and trading goods. None of these objectives can be pursued adequately, short of the appreciation of the position that the modern business enterprise has occupied in the production machinery of industrial and early information economy. We accordingly retrace the principles that have made the modern business enterprise the diffuse institution of the resource conversion and value creation process in modern times. Revisiting key versions of the theory of the firm in economics and the prevailing conceptions of organization in the decades that followed World War II in organization theory, we show how the modern business enterprise has essentially been instrumented as a bounded and concentrated system, whereby the conversion process and the development of organizational capabilities occur under relatively controlled environments and with reference to largely internal circumstances (i.e., assets, technologies, people and professions, and their relations). The diffusion of digital data and their involvement in personal, public, and economic lives, as analyzed in the preceding chapters, challenge most of the presuppositions on which the modern business enterprise has been predicated. The dispersed, heterogeneous, and shifting matrix of relations out of which data are currently generated and made economically relevant reorders the significance that internal exigencies have assumed in the structuring of organizational operations and challenges the relatively self-contained nature of firms and organizations. The cumulative upshot of these developments is the *decentering of organizations* and the diffusion of economic arrangements and organizational forms that increasingly rely on data to organize a much wider, dispersed, and steadily shifting range of tasks and contingencies than it has been the case. These transformations are evidenced by the rise and ongoing diffusion of digital platforms and digital business ecosystems.

We further explore these developments in chapter 7 by first tracing the origins of the concept of the digital platform in product architecture and the management and innovation literature in which platforms have been construed as configurations of a stable core and variable peripheral components that promote market adaptation, cost reduction, and ultimately innovation (design rules). We then consider a populous research strand that approaches platforms as multisided markets and virtual exchange systems made of several types of participants, whose platform relationships are governed by the dynamics of network effects (market rules). We reconstruct this dynamic and show how network effects are essentially measures of the sociality of goods (e.g., recommendation and personalization systems and other similar items) that are systematically captured in the form of data and further used in aggregate form as the basis for reinforcing network effects and the vital role that they play in platform establishment, takeoff, and dominance. This is followed by a brief review of the literature on digital business ecosystems. We revisit the notion of business ecosystems and outline how ecosystems differ and are linked to platforms. In particular, we focus on the importance that the concept of complementarities has assumed for ecosystem formation, retrace the origins of the concept in the interlacing of production systems, and outline the ways that complementarities work in comparison to network effects. At the end of the chapter, we make a summative assessment of the key propositions and perspectives of this rather miscellaneous body of literature and show how reflection on data and data technologies is virtually absent from the mainstream theorizing and empirical research on platforms and ecosystems.

In chapter 8, we further explore many of the ideas developed in the preceding chapters. The importance of *design rules* and *market rules* notwithstanding, we show the significance *data rules* have acquired in shaping ecosystem dynamics. A key point that we make is that cast in the digital medium, the *structure of relations* that lead to ecosystem emergence and evolution is essentially a structure of relations constituted and managed by data, whereby different data types are brought to bear on each other in ways that fashion value-reinforcing complementarities. As distinct from interdependencies formed from physical resources, activities, or output, data-derived complementarities are revocable, and thus shifting and opportunistic. With looser bonds to specialized knowledge, sector-based procedures, or established industrial relations, ecosystem participation, and the data interdependencies it features, posits several coordinative dilemmas that must be addressed in new ways that respond to the hypertechnological context in which they are embedded. In such data-pervaded or data-made ecosystems, formed by heterogeneous tasks, relations, and actors, such dilemmas are regularly addressed by the structuring of participation via data objects (chapter 4) and other technologies such as application programming interfaces (APIs). Data objects work as the cognitive and behavioral scripts that can orient user actions and execute ecosystem exchanges. By furnishing the prevailing modalities by which relations are continuously constructed and maintained and novel socioeconomic interdependencies are forged, data objects shape the various actors' roles and positions within the ecosystem. We conclude the chapter with a broader reflection on data and the nature of relations that lead to digital ecosystem structure and behavior and the implications that these developments have for data and ecosystem regulation.

Finally, in chapter 9 we retrace our journey through and with data and summarize the implications. We reassert the semiotic, epistemic, and communication functions that data perform and link these functions to the foundations of a new economic order in which platforms and ecosystems figure prominently. We also state that platforms are novel enterprise and organizational forms engaged in the mediation of the contribution of platform participants as distinct from the focus on the resource conversion process, characteristic of traditional firms and organizations. In an analogous fashion, we portray ecosystems as arrangements of collaboration and competition that develop around the pursuit of complementarities that often cross the boundaries of traditional products and industries. Taken together, platforms and ecosystems both extend and challenge the functions of organizations as major sites of the resource conversion process and of markets as coordinative arrangements. It is a central attribute of the performative order of the current economy that it draws social interactions into the circuit of its operations. For the first time in history, social interactions as distinct from economic transactions are made a straightforward productive force and the management of the whereabouts of large populations an essential quality of the economic machinery that rules the current world. These ideas make imperative the analysis of data and the ways that they are involved in weaving the socioeconomic fabric from a point of view that captures their importance as pervasive forces of economic restructuring and social engineering. We conclude with a call for a *social science of data* distinct from data science, which does justice to this importance, as well as the variety of functions that data perform as filters of perception, instruments of knowledge, and media of communication.

1 FOUNDATIONS

2 THE EPISTEMIC FOUNDATIONS OF DATA

The interlocking of data with socioeconomic practices and institutions has a long line of descent that stretches back to record keeping and the invention and use of several notation technologies. During the Upper Paleolithic (20,000 years ago), people used marks on cave walls or portable sticks to record observations or count events.[1] Clay tokens in the Near East have been used to record and represent possession of goods and transactions carried out by merchants or regulated by the state already around 8500 BC (Goody 1986). Despite many profound differences across epochs and civilizations, record keeping has worked for more than 20,000 years as the steady foundation for developing complex systems of knowledge, shaping social practices, and building institutions (Cline-Cohen 1982; Power 1997, 2007; Quattrone 2009).

In this chapter, we retrace the cognitive and communicative foundations of data and the practices by which data in the form of systematic records have been made a vital element of modern economy and society (Mennicken & Salais 2022). Linking digital data to the cognitive and communicative foundations of all data helps to reestablish their connections to a broader history of signs and notation systems and the development of various technologies of data making and record keeping. Data are cognitive and communicative artifacts insofar as they encode events in an agreed-upon format on physical supports of some kind (Borgmann 1999; Buckland 1991). Thus encoded, data can be used to enhance memory, extract lessons from experience, and identify indicators for foreshadowing future events. However, what constitutes a record—what can be considered data—changes over time (Leonelli 2015; Strasser & Edwards 2017). Such changes are seldom due to technological shifts alone. In all their formal qualities and functions, data are closely bound up with the signifying and representing conventions of human cultures and their institutions. In the following sections, we pull out some of the threads that connect data to culture by reexamining their cognitive and communicative constitution, the technologies by which they have been underlain, and the evolution of the functions that they have performed in structuring organizations, social practices, and institutions.

To recognize and analyze the degree of innovation that digital data bring to contemporary society, it is necessary to identify what they inherit from antecedent record-keeping traditions and how they differ from them. The novelty of digital technology notwithstanding, data have not become necessary to societies and organizations all of a sudden. While recognizing the relevance and necessity of a historically informed understanding of data,[2] what we do, it should be made clear, is not history. We do not intend to reconstruct the historical trajectories of data but rather to look back at the foundational role of data and record-keeping processes in fostering cognition and socioeconomic action, detect their distinctive contribution to the birth of institutions, and identify how the cognitive and communicative functions that they perform have been conducive to novel practices (Eisenstein 1979; Goody 1986; Hacking 1990).[3] Such an account is sought with a view to assessing the novelty of digital technology in spinning the threads that tie data to socioeconomic life (as discussed in chapters 3 and 4).

In the current world, digital data are the pervasive media through which several aspects of social reality are made visible, understood, and acted upon. Such prominence has not come to pass as the outcome of recent technological developments alone. The cognitive and communicative foundations of data can hardly be dissociated from the evolution of tools and systems of recording, storing, classifying, indexing, filing, and archiving (among others) that have shaped the logic and practices of data and record keeping and contributed to placing data at the core of many social undertakings. Yet looking solely at the material or technological substrata of these changes tells only one side of the story (Leonardi, Nardi, & Kallinikos 2012). The comparison with previous formats of record keeping exemplifies the point. The decisive role that clay tokens have played in the development of commerce, writing, and bureaucracy over the 5,000 years that they remained in use cannot be explained by recounting the history of clay or pottery alone. To address questions such as "How can a simple mark on a wood stick enable a contract?" or (as we will see in later chapters) "How can a simple site click be sold as a taste preference?" we need to approach data from a social science perspective and consider them neither as technical items nor as situated outputs, but rather as knowledge and cognitive artifacts that can pull things together and build worlds. The materiality of data tokens (in this case, clay) is essential, and learning about the context of exchange is crucial, and yet neither of the two aspects alone can enforce a clay token as a loan.

Rather than taking for granted the role of technology, we explore to what extent it modifies the nature of the links that data maintain with the pursuits of socioeconomic actors and the emergence of institutions. This chapter reconstructs three historical episodes to display the modalities by which data have always been constitutionally intertwined with collective knowledge dynamics and novel institutional forms. We detect a few common and recurring elements across these episodes. In the first, we retrace how the record-keeping system of clay tokens has been associated with the emergence of protobureaucracies that facilitated the establishment of complex socioeconomic exchanges. Supported by the interplay between the characteristics of the token's format, the logic under which they were organized, and the social practices they established, the widespread use of clay tokens helped institutionalize general concepts such as economic exchange.

In the second episode, we explore the modalities by which institutional forms, data practices, and epistemic paradigms are linked. Out of the avalanche of numbers produced by modern statistics (Porter 1995), novel social objects emerged. The inquiry into social objects is fundamental to comprehending the politics of data; that is, the ways by which systems of data, social practices, and institutions maintain reciprocal, dynamic relations with the reality they record, order, classify, and operate upon.

In the third episode, we illustrate the role that data have played in the emergence of novel institutions and organizational structures. Modern corporations were established at the crossroads of data and objects with certain epistemic orientations (the quest for efficiency later translated into the principles of scientific management) and practices (administrative work). These ideas indicate that record keeping and data in general perform their epistemic and social functions by virtue of being in a constant, close-knit dialogue with technologies, broader knowledge paradigms, and social structures.

COGNITIVE ARTIFACTS

The invention and use of clay tokens—small clay pieces in simple geometric shapes—represents a foundational episode in the history of record making. They work as examples that illustrate the power of data and the different cognitive and social practices that develop in conjunction or around it.[4] Clay tokens supported a sophisticated record-keeping and exchange system that continued to be used even after the invention of writing, working as an essential component of a complex administrative apparatus (MacGinnis et al. 2014).[5]

As records, clay tokens filled a specific cognitive function and were organized under distinctive principles and technologies. For instance, they were easier to use than written clay tablets, which were later adopted as writing tools. Also, their formats—small units that could be exchanged individually or gathered in groups—made clay tokens more readily manipulable and flexible; they could be used to keep track of transactions more promptly than records engraved in clay tablets that were hard to modify, rearrange, or erase. Their flexibility and manipulability and the fact that their system did not require reading and counting, and yet was highly standardized, made clay tokens widespread tools for the establishment and diffusion of commerce, bookkeeping, contract enforcement, and credit and debit transactions across the whole eastern Mediterranean and Near East for more than 5,000 years (Schmandt-Besserat 2010). Clay tokens "offered a path for contemporary data storage prior to more permanent recording" (MacGinnis et al. 2014, 290), allowing illiterate merchants or semiliterate bureaucrats to work at enforcing record keeping, monitoring transactions, and developing advanced social practices that served centrally administered taxation.

Despite the simple materiality (clay) and technology supporting them, clay tokens show an impressive closeness to many of the organizational principles and rules of other forms of data. The standardized simplicity, flexibility, and manipulability of clay tokens favored their usage in specific socioeconomic practices. Record formats and the logic under which they are organized in broader systems stand out as two of the most relevant characteristics of data fostering cognition and social action. Ordered data collections laid out the organizing principles of a database—namely data, a data structure, a medium, and routines to sort and access that data— much before digital technologies (Sepkoski 2017).[6] As the episode of clay

FIGURE 2.1

Clay tokens were very simple artifacts made in standardized shapes (e.g., cones, cylinders, spheres, ovoids, disks, pyramids, and tetrahedrons) and sizes (ranging from 1 to 3 cm). Each shape represented a particular kind of good. Clay tokens either referred to standard measures of goods (e.g., cups, baskets, and granaries, a workday) or units (one cylinder represented one sheep). Meanwhile, their size represented quantities. *Source*: Wikimedia Commons (https://commons.wikimedia.org/wiki/File:Clay _accounting_tokens_Susa_Louvre_n2.jpg); photo by Marie-Lan Nguyen licensed under CC-BY 2.5 (https://creativecommons.org/licenses/by/2.5/deed.en).

tokens illustrates, the primary functions of record keeping (to aid memory and provide evidence) are closely associated with standardizing, storing, and sorting practices whose modalities rely on but are not overdetermined by technologies.

Record keeping is first and foremost a technology of memory and of distance. Once an event, fact, or observation is fixed into a record—which means formatted under some rules and anchored to some physical devices— it becomes something else, acquiring an independent reality of its own. As such, the token, a newly made entity, unavoidably works as the basis for further cognition and action. A record takes an event (or an object) and, using tools, a set of arbitrary conventions, memory practices, and institutions separates it from its context and transforms it into something that can travel across time and space. Because of its abstractedness from context, records-as-things confer to the content that they carry a "thingness-like nature" (Buckland 1991). The primary epistemic function of records thus coincides with the objectification of life situations. This affords other vital cognitive and social practices (the arrangement of several records together, indexing, filing, archiving, and pattern making) that have over time forever changed the production of knowledge and the organization of society, leading, among other things, to the establishment of professions and institutions (Goody 1986; Bowker & Star 1999).

There is yet another fundamental or primary function that records fulfill. As clay tokens are set to record events happening prevalently among individuals, their systematic use "marks a first move towards an economy based on a generalized media of exchange that we may refer to as money" (Goody 1986, 53). Clay tokens built a general concept of exchange out of a situated event (known as "an exchange"). Without the physical support and semiotic or signifying properties of clay tokens, it would have been unlikely to understand and make the abstract notion of exchange a generalized social practice. Clay tokens provided the standard basis for recording exchanges and objectifying transactions. In this process, they ended up establishing a disembodied idea of exchange that was made physically and cognitively manipulable, thanks to the thingness-like nature of records. Working with clay tokens allowed comparisons among past exchange records, calculating ratios, and averages; or estimates of future exchanges, which are essential for taxation. From a simple situated interaction among individuals, a more complex idea of social exchange was born, along with the possibility of institutionalizing its occurrence. Cast in this light, records are linked to knowledge and institutions that have historically helped to establish the social practices that developed around the notion of a generalized exchange and came to be associated with the use of standardized media such as numbers, money and prices, information, or letters of credit (Porter 1995; Varian 2010).

Some archaeologists support the view that the establishment and diffusion of such complex practices, together with the corresponding development of urban settlements and their institutions, led to writing. Nonetheless, "at the emergence of cities, about 3,500 BC, the token system underwent profound changes" (Schmandt-Besserat 1980, 358). Clay tokens started to be marked on their surfaces and to be gathered and enclosed in specific clay envelopes shaped like empty balls, which were then sealed and often pressed on their surfaces with marks similar in shape to those of the tokens that they contained (see figure 2.2). These envelopes have been identified as "data storage"[7] units and "accounting devices" (Oppenheim 1959) that were used, for instance, as bills of lading accompanying shipments of merchandise from centers of production in the countryside to administrative centers in the cities (Schmandt-Besserat 1980, 360). Sometimes these envelopes presented more detailed inscriptions, which provided additional information on their content, other times instructed officials on how to handle the envelope, and still, on other occasions, served only the purpose of officially sealing a transaction or a contract.[8] Even though the technology and the materials used have been somewhat different, the practice of clustering data tokens together into newly created objects, accounting or calculating devices with further inscriptions (often metadata or data about data) has indeed been characteristic of stable exchange and data practices that have traversed millennia (see also Sepkoski 2017).[9]

If the assumptions of prominent archaeologists are correct, then writing emerged out of the devices, practices, and institutions of record keeping.[10] Record keeping in this case meant quite specifically that the use of clay tokens and clay envelopes and the practices of ensuring their content were official and institutionalized. This motivated and established schematic forms of writing and its conventions, such as using formulas and omitting verbs. Inscriptions on clay tablets later used formalized conventions such as lists and repetitions, a sign that early forms of writing on clay envelopes fed back into language and its rules (Goody 1986, 55).[11] Writing, as Walter

FIGURE 2.2
Globular envelope with a cluster of accounting tokens. Clay, Uruk period. From
the Tell of the Acropolis in Susa. *Source*: Wikipedia (https://it.m.wikipedia.org/wiki
/File:Accountancy_clay_envelope_Louvre_Sb1932.jpg); photo by Marie-Lan Nguyen
licensed under CC-BY 2.5 (https://creativecommons.org/licenses/by/2.5/deed.en).

Ong claims, "initiated what print and computers only continue" (Ong 1982, 78).[12] If the beginning of bookkeeping and writing originated from the administrative needs of temple management in urban settlements, the establishment of record-keeping systems (together with their records, tools, devices, and early forms of writing) served as the cognitive and material bases for the further development of bureaucracy and administration.[13]

For some eminent scholars, the most pervasive innovation brought about by writing is processual and categorical thinking—the capacity to think abstractly about concepts and, among other abilities, to order ideas in broader abstract categories (Havelock 1963).[14] In this sense, the example of clay tokens shows that writing continues what clay records and record keeping first established. Categorical thinking is both the result of the distance that written records acquired from the contexts in which they originated or used and of the spare processing capacity that the human brain gained by not having to remember entire chunks of information. As previously mentioned, general concepts, represented with tokens, become amenable to handling and manipulation that further develop into complex systems of knowledge. Freed from the burden of memory and context and equipped with the right technologies and institutions, literate people effectively started to process data, ordering, classifying, and intervening in the ideas and concepts carried by signs, marks, and tokens and further developing and assembling more complex representations and constructs.

As they became things-like, records opened a space of freedom and interpretation for the concepts that they carried. Facts, events, and ideas could be copied, ordered into collections, and integrated into broader views about knowledge. Records and their acquired status as data meant that knowledge grew endemically or endogenously—out of records rather than out of contexts. Gradually, it became ordinary to write about writing, to refer to the content of books and tables as facts, and to take for granted their existence outside the tokens into which they were encoded. Written records became placeholders within systems of knowledge that did not need references outside their communication system to build meaning and cumulate practices that could survive context and the passage of time.

THE POLITICS OF DATA

The life of data took another epistemic turn with the advent of modernity. In a sense, modernity itself emerged out of a more general epistemic shift that reinforced the notion of objectivity and linked its meaning to science, whereby scientific objectivism provided the ground for rebuilding institutions and society (see Daston & Galison 2007). Empiricism, the rationalization of knowledge, and the rush toward measurement practices and standardized observations changed the entire knowledge apparatus and its institutions, contributing to the rise of new actors such as the modern state (Desrosières 1998; Foucault 1970).

The word "data" started to be used more frequently and became the empirical basis upon which novel rational systems of knowledge and disciplines were established (Hacking 1990). Even today, the meaning of "data" preserves some of the ambiguities that arose during early modernity. The Latin etymology of "datum" is "something that is given." Yet the interpretation of what is given as a (given) fact existing out there that can be discovered or collected is the inheritance of the project of rationalization, which has its roots in modernity. A datum, for the Romans, was a rhetorical device to initiate an argument or debate (Rosenberg 2013, 2018). The use of formulas such as "given this . . . then that" was relevant as a formal initiator of an oral contest with specific social and institutional functions.[15] Even when the term "datum" was used in scientific arguments, it preserved its rhetorical function and by no means denoted something existing out there. Still, it indicated things taken for granted and not inquired after. The interpretation of the concept of data (as what is given) shifted from being a cultural artifact serving a function to something that was believed to exist independent of the reality of conventions of which it was part. Somehow ironically, as it signaled a complete overturn of the original meaning, the term came to signify a "particular sort of representational entity upon which one could operate through systems of calculation, classification, and communication, while holding the question of referential truth in abeyance" (Rosenberg 2018, 566). The shift has been the outcome of a long and tortuous sociocultural process that reached its peak during modernity and holds sway even today, as the advent and diffusion of data science attests.

Starting with the Enlightenment, the meaning of data as *facts*, existing outside the conventions of the communication system by which they are conveyed, was carefully crafted by the invention of quantification techniques, the modern idea of scientific, economic, and technological progress, and aided by the birth of the modern, rational state (see, e.g., Poovey 1998).[16] Thanks to the development of statistical tools and their application in public affairs, the notion of data took on a new meaning. It was gradually accepted and institutionalized as existing out there (given), even when the data were collected and used to describe nominal entities such as averages of suicides, unemployment rates, gross domestic product (GDP), or popularity indexes.

Alain Desrosières (1998) and Ian Hacking (1990) described these socio-cultural turns with acumen and considerable detail. The rise and use of statistics that occurred during modernity brought the identification and institutionalization of areas of social life (e.g., demographics, distribution of diseases, and urban and rural dynamics) that had until then been vaguely perceived or even barely acknowledged. The systematic measurement of newly discovered facts and more rationalized methodologies of record keeping allowed several scientific practices that established the contours of the discipline of statistics, rational state administration, and the authority of experts. The efficient documentation of facts over time, their grouping and classification, and the constant monitoring applied to newly coined concepts brought the discovery of regularities and the study of their occurrence. The development of knowledge as a prediction of social facts and the laws behind their occurrences allowed institutional control and intervention.

It is characteristic of measurement and recording practices, Desrosières claims (1998), to reinforce the semantic coherence of the facts that they measure and record and lend them identity and, crucially, stability. In doing so, measurement and recording help establish *social objects*, abstract entities that become frequent targets of institutional practices. Examples include unemployment rate, GDP, and crime rate. Independent of what these objects represent or help detect or discover, these observations indicate that social objects are as much real as the resourceful outcome of the measurement systems and recording conventions that sustain them. Despite the factual aura that their institutional embedment conveys, social objects always develop out of the constant negotiation of the ways the world is and how this world is fashioned by laws, measuring innovations and techniques of the disciplines and recording systems (here statistics) with which the production of these objects is associated. Modernity then is inextricably bound up with the project of rationalization (Heller 1999; Weber 1947/2012) and the fashioning of an intricate apparatus of technologies, quantification, rules, measurement, experts, and institutions that became centrally involved in bringing forth the reality that such an apparatus measured and recorded.

The shift in the epistemic role of data and the relatively tight coupling between measurement, expertise, and institutions advanced a novel idea of society and social institutions that was partly determined by the social objects that they established. Entities such as crime, suicide, and unemployment rates were granted an existence as independent givens, as attributes of a concept of society that they constructed (or summed up). On the other hand, these objects necessitated the institutional upbringing of schools, professions, bureaucrats, experts, and central administrations. They became the engines of making reality. The work of these institutions conferred to such abstract objects the legitimacy and autonomy that they needed to circulate and unify scattered practices and territories under an established set of rules that was centrally enforced. Amateur statisticians became new state-appointed bureaucrats and conferred official status to such entities and themselves, together with the data they relied on and the broader cultural assumptions they carried (Hacking 1990). Having first become official, these objects "become increasingly real" (Porter 1995, 42).

The project of rationalization, brought about by modernity, was supported by the conviction that universal laws governed by statistical rules could be read equally into data across any scientific subject or life domain. To guarantee its success, the project developed a powerful institutional apparatus made of standards, measures, and bureaucratic prescriptions that changed the makeup of data and the practices of data making. Quantification and measurement acquired more formalized and standardized notation requirements to confer less ambiguity on data and narrow down their variety and possible interpretations. For instance, Prussia founded a central bureau dedicated to data gathering at the end of the eighteenth century. As Hacking (1990) noted, "such an institution presupposes that there is a special type of knowledge, and a new kind of skill, the ability to collect, organize and digest numerical information about any subject whatsoever" (29). The tight link between such knowledge and skills and these institutions glued together the rationalization project and made it all-encompassing.

This shift was successful in conjunction with the rising power of the central state, the invention of bureaucracy, and its use of data to forge social objects that could be controlled and managed. Without the avalanche of numbers created by enthusiastic amateurs and early statistical bureaus, there would have been no patterns to uncover and describe the laws of society or the work of nature. With the introduction of probabilistic thought, several disciplinary domains, such as mathematics, medicine, and psychology, entered a new era of values and methods (Foucault 1963/2012). Statistics became the science of the state, orienting public actions and giving the state the means of planning and control. Probability and the outputs of calculation were used to validate the very existence of the institutions that produced them and to legitimate their increasing influence.

This powerful epistemic shift promoted a vision of society governed by regularities and statistical laws. Yet such regularities could be discovered only by applying what was perceived as the correct scientific approach, measures, and tools made possible under the very close inspection of institutions and their powerful data-making apparatus (Hacking 1990). Apparently, data were used as the essential elements of the turn toward objectivity and the project of rationalization, de facto data and measures were instrumental devices for the rhetoric of the state and tools of its consensus building.[17] Social control via data and statistics did not come from knowledge of presumed social laws or regularities, but rather from the institution of an official social object, which, once made real, became the basis for social and individual discipline.[18] Measures gave stability to novel social objects such as crime rates, as they gave states and other powerful actors (such as insurance companies and actuaries) the knowledge and means to act (Bouk 2015). Data and the newly founded apparatus with which they have been an integral part became a social technology through which disparate areas of social life were rendered as impersonal thinglike qualities (e.g., citizens or patients), amenable to mastery, control, and intervention.

DATA, COORDINATION, AND CONTROL

The invention of new data and the advent of novel data-making technologies contributed to establishing the corporation as a diffuse legal and organizational form, and management as a field. New technologies such as the railway, the telegraph, and later the telephone furnished the means for the growth of organizations that became not just bigger but more complex, increasingly made of a dispersed number of semi-independent units that required a shift in their coordination and control. The change in the organization of economic production and the creation of mass markets have been closely associated with the sociocultural orientations of modernity and the formation of the modern social order. As shown in the preceding section, these ideals are relatively well established and recognized across the social sciences. Less obvious are the ways that data have been part and parcel of the diffusion of organizational forms that came to dominate the industrial order (for a rare instance of a study on such a topic, see Beniger 1986). To exist and be managed, corporations needed data that were substantially new and, at the same time, had to find new ways of storing, handling, and making sense of these data.

The rise of modern management is bound up with shifts in knowledge and data-making practices that sought to chart and document processes that occurred within organizations and across functions, including the movements of goods and people and the coordination of core production processes which, for the first time, took place across organizational units (Chandler & Cortada 2000). The newly constituted class of managers and business administrators created and used internal data as the primary language of business and "instruments of management" (Chandler 1977, 104). The Industrial Revolution and its shifting requirements of control brought the need to produce a different kind of data, which in turn helped establish a new breed of management practices and tools (Beniger 1986). Internally generated data and more complex accounting tools developed in tandem with modern corporations that used these tools to monitor, control, and coordinate workers and the production and distribution of goods across the vast geographies of national and international markets. By establishing specific ways of gathering, handling, analyzing, and transmitting data and, over time, providing further specialization of administrative roles and tools, modern corporations instituted themselves and modern management (Chandler 1977; Yates 1989). Placed in this context, data records emerged as essential preconditions for effective and efficient business administration and, simultaneously, they became the key media by which a good deal of management decisions was made and coordinated (Beniger 1986). As Yates aptly puts it, "administration without records is like music without notes" (1989, 13).

Modern accounting also appeared in this period. Administrative roles primarily included creating, keeping, and processing documents, records, and data (Hoskin & Macve 1986; Power 1997, 2007). The role of the manager or administrator was the most relevant new profile that arose from the shift. Several reforms were implemented to increase control and coordination within companies that were all explicitly related to the production, transmission, and handling of data. In the prevailing paradigm of efficiency, data became the instruments for controlling people and flows of goods, and their use started to be formalized as a principal tool of communication and coordination among several organizational units. In 1884, Frederic Taylor already employed timekeepers and other specialized clerks to control the pace of work and generate data to monitor production (Beniger 1986). In his first paper on scientific management in 1895, it is worth remembering that he called for the need to rely on data standards rather than experiences to scientifically determine work time and output targets. The workers who failed to live up to this "scientifically determined" standard time and output targets received a lower rate per piece assembled (Chandler 1977, 275).

Innovations in bureaucratic organization, programming, information processing, and communication have all been instrumental in shaping modern organizations and the structural arrangements that came to epitomize them. Formalized in methods such as the scientific management championed by Taylor, this infatuation with facts and numbers indicated a broader mindset that paid heed to a variety of indicators, ratios, and models as fundamental means for ensuring control over people and resources and achieving efficiency in the running of the enterprise. Placed against this backdrop, data exhibit constitutive links to the dominant Western idea of management. Preceding Taylor by some years, Andrew Carnegie famously implemented a voucher system for the collection and processing of quantitative data on the shop floor of the Edgar Thomson steel production plant. Robert Metcalfe invented novel calculating devices such as "tickets" and "slips" to follow the production line. Daniel MacCallum, the manager of the Erie railroad company, organized a hierarchical system of information gathering, processing, and communication that was designed to streamline channels of communication through data and converge control on the central administrative offices. For the first time, together with other pioneers, he saw the problem of coordination and control within organizations as a problem of communication that could be solved by implementing new methods of information production and processing. Thanks to technological innovations in the transmission and storing of information and document management, it was now possible to use data from the daily and monthly reports that were then submitted to McCallum's office. MacCallum was the first to control specific targets and operations with data generated for other purposes, basically inventing data reuse. He also pioneered continuing time series data to control rate structure and maintain maximum revenue despite uncertainty—an application of data collection to control, affirms Beniger, which would be adapted to industrial production only in the late nineteenth century (Beniger 1986, 231).

"No earlier American businessman," Chandler says of MacCallum, "had ever experienced the need to develop ways to use internally generated data as instruments of management. None had shown a comparable concern for the theory and principles of organization" (1977, 104). *Internal information*, information produced by the same organization, instead of external information on markets, goods, and prices, which was in use for years preceding the invention of the modern corporation, became the essential knowledge tool needed to control and coordinate production in more efficient ways. Thus, for the first time, competition became a matter of achieving efficiency in production by generating more accurate data, innovating information processing, and building feedback capabilities across units and levels. Organizations set up an internal apparatus of record making, storing, and processing to control and monitor their own internal operations with the aim of coordinating work across units and functions.

These changes in record keeping were carried out by several innovations in the practice of encoding and standardizing data, including changes in filing, indexing, and archiving together with new transmission and communication technologies (see Robertson 2021). Internal reports, minutes, memos, tabular weekly or monthly schedules, and several other standardized forms or new genres of data processing and visualization, quickly found their way into work practices and proliferated with the creation of new roles designed to increase data effectiveness for communication and coordination (Yates 1989).

Several interesting new methods and practices consolidated in creating and optimizing organizational archives, or the institution of communication offices dedicated to regulating the speed and accuracy of the flow of information. Letterpresses, typewriters, cabinet files, index cards, and document-handling techniques largely contributed to the revolution that increased the volume of records, documents, and files and thus raised new problems of data storing and sorting. As data genres and practices became more sophisticated and data abundant, they were gradually systematized into "more convenient tabular forms" (Chandler 1977, 103). These operations in turn required training a specialized workforce, institutionalizing new occupations or professions such as administrators, clerks, secretaries, and managers.

The establishment of novel social objects has accompanied the administrative reforms we outline here; that is, the objectification of areas of organizational life that were hardly perceived before these reforms. The fashioning of new objects out of internally produced data started early in the history of modern corporations. By the late 1850s, data about profit and loss were deemed insufficient to monitor business performance. They had to be coupled with newly created objects, such as operating ratios, which remain among the basic standards with which managers judge the performance of business enterprises (Chandler 1977, 110). The early attempt to establish management practices through objects made of data was relatively successful, and other examples quickly followed. At least, from clay envelopes onward, institutions and organizations have been bound up with objects made of data, working as representational entities and accounting devices, through which they have sought to understand and interpret their internal and external environment and act on it. Objectifying procedures that embed intentions into solid and durable social artifacts are essential to cognition and critical to institutionalization, as we have seen in the case of clay envelopes, one of the first objects to be fashioned out of data tokens (Hasselbladh & Kallinikos 2000; Kallinikos & Hasselbladh 2009; Kallinikos, Hasselbadh, & Márton 2013; Labatut, Aggeri, & Girard 2012).

Objects of this sort shape the way in which actors understand themselves and their roles. Social objects have always been relevant for the establishment and diffusion of specific social and organizational practices. They have been commonly perceived as social artifacts across a broad and cross-disciplinary body of literature and variously linked to the making of social practices, organizational configurations, and professional identities (see, e.g., Appadurai 1988; Barley 1986; Bowker & Star 1999; Knorr Cetina 1999, 2001). Across many different settings, the introduction of novel social objects made of data is associated with more significant changes in the structure of teamwork, the professional identity of workers, and coordination of collective action (see, e.g., Espeland & Sauder 2007; Espeland & Stevens 1998, 2008; Knorr Cetina 1999, 2001; Poon 2009; Power 1997; Star 2010; Star & Griesemer 1989; Star & Ruhleder 1996). However, the role of data and the cognitive functions, processing techniques, and technologies with which they are associated have yet to be studied in connection with social objects. Objects such as documents, memos, charts, and models are the bearers of a broader class of knowledge or epistemic objects (Ewenstein & Whyte 2009; Knorr Cetina 1999, 2001; Miettinen & Virkkunen 2005) that stand in close connection with data and data practices across organizations. These objects have been studied as targets and recognizable sites of interpretation and action (Beyes, Holt, & Pias 2020; Gitelman 2014) and have emerged as record-keeping tools connected to occupational groups and to the rise of certain professions such as managers, administrators, and clerks (Beniger 1986; Yates 1989). At the same time, knowledge objects have contributed to institutionalizing specific ways of doing and acting within organizations that later become the norm.

These innovations in data-gathering and -processing techniques, the making of new social objects, and the nascent logic and culture that consolidated behind them constituted the notion of administrative control that would later define management and business administration. Data, reports, documents, and statistics became the core of a newly formed administrative body, which specialized in production and processing capabilities. The "visible hand," to follow Chandler's famous title, was made visible by the data, objects, infrastructures, and practices that were established as a response to the changed need for coordination and control of modern organizations. As activities became internalized, internal data became necessary to run ever-expanding corporations. A new class of specialized workers, administrators, secretaries, clerks, and managers contributed to innovating data production and processing.

SUMMARY AND IMPLICATIONS

Data have existed for thousands of years. They have variously been at the center stage of social practices and the operations of the corporations and the modern state and have served as core elements for representing and knowing the world. The belief in the novelty and the pathbreaking role of digital data tends to gloss over the historical functions and practices with which data have been associated and virtually sets their constitutive links to society conveniently aside. In this chapter, we retraced the historical origins of data long before the digital revolution. The historical episodes that we have outlined attest to the essential role of data in establishing institutions and social practices. Protobureaucracies have been supported by clay tokens, whose use in turn facilitated the institution of shared cognition and gave rise to a general notion of exchange. Modern institutions, professions, and disciplines emerged from the institutionalization of novel social objects made real by their sophisticated measurement systems. Corporations were aided by management because "they were summed up somewhere," as Chandler (1977) put it, by the work of standards controlling objectified versions of workers and goods. None of these cognitive and epistemic functions are extraneous to the world of digital data.

The analysis of data offered in this chapter affirms the necessity of looking back before looking forward. It asserts the importance of studying digital data as the latest manifestation of a long history that stretches back to clay tokens and comprises records and tokens of different natures. To appreciate how digital technology transforms the constitutive links between data and society, we need to look back at the social role played by data before the digital revolution. Each of the three historical episodes (clay tokens and exchange, modernity and the state, and corporations and management) recounted here offers a fruitful path for pursuing the social study of digital data. All three bespeak the importance of individuating the functions that data play through their rules, significations, and logics. The primary function of data is objectifying. Whenever records are made, something contextual and situated, like an individual event, is transformed into something else. It is *thingified* and made able to overcome specific situations or contexts.

Objectifying opens a vast cognitive territory that allows communities, individuals, and groups to share concepts, knowledge, and plans for action (Kallinikos 1995, 2010). In the episode of clay tokens, a general concept such as that of exchange is teased out of situated barter. Together with it, complex social practices and institutions emerge. A further step along the cognitive possibilities that data offer is represented by the establishment of novel social objects whereby abstract notions of the social, such as unemployment or suicide rates, acquire an existence of their own and assume a specific political role that is centrally linked to the advent of statistics as the science of the modern state. The objectifying function of data is a double-edged sword that isolates novel areas of intervention (Hacking 1983) at the same time as it allows control and governance. Making new things and making them indisputable are the main aims of what we have called the "politics of data."

The term "politics" should not lead to misinterpretation. We use it to mark how data make things and make them real objects of intervention. Data not only allow signification, knowledge, or understanding, as this chapter describes, but they also enable social and political action. "It is because the moment of objectification can be made autonomous that the moment of action can be based on firmly established objects," Desrosières (1998, 9) reminds us. The complex cognitive and epistemic dimensions of data are seldom acknowledged in critical approaches to digital data, and yet they are fundamental to unravel the links between data and social changes. As we will see in the following two chapters, digital technology enters frontally in the making of a whole range of novel social objects, such as credit scores, profiles, and ratings, that mediate action and intervention across several spheres of society (see chapters 4 and 5).

The implications of bracketing and analyzing these vital functions of data unfold across several paths. First, such an approach calls for establishing links with the work of many scholars who have studied how data were defining elements of the modern social order long before the advent of digital data (see, e.g., Daston 2022; Desrosières 1998; Hacking 1990; Porter 1995; Power 1997). Also, an inquiry into these vital functions of data reconnects them with their epistemic history and necessitates acknowledging the primary role of culture and institutions in making social objects created by data "real." Clay tokens, unemployment rates, and medical records, as well as clicks and click-through rates, emerge with novel institutions and forms of organizing.

A critical contribution of this chapter is the reconstruction of the constitutive links of data to society, which requires juxtaposing their emergence with that of the institutions with which they are associated. As seen in the third historical episode in this discussion, internal data contributed to establishing corporations themselves by measuring and tracking their activities over sites and time. There are no data without institutions. Moreover, as it happens, there are increasingly no institutions without data. In part II of this volume, we weave this thread in the context of digital data and the novel institutions that they are associated with as we untangle the links among data, platforms, and ecosystems. In the next chapter, we tackle the issue of the changes that digital technology and computation have brought to the vital functions of data.

3   THE DIGITAL DATA REVOLUTION

MECHANIZING RECORDS

The rise of modern corporations and the invention of what has come to be known as "scientific management" contributed to preparing organizations and individuals for the profound changes brought about by the diffusion of machines and mechanization. The streamlining of organizational activities and processes that accompanied the birth of modern corporations grew in tandem with the proliferation of technologies and techniques invented to aid various nascent management practices and raise efficiency. Data and data management techniques were at the center of these far-reaching changes. Fashioned purposefully by organizations to monitor people, tasks, materials, and processes, improve internal communication, and achieve production efficiency, such large and regularly produced amounts of internal data needed to be supported by new data management systems. The management of organizations required constant innovation in data storage, information handling, and processing. Advancements in data making were effectively provided by hundreds of inventions, including the typewriter, desktop calculators, adding machines, punch card tabulators, and billing machines (Beniger 1986; Cortada 2011, 2019; Yates 1989). Innovation in technologies of data and document filing, storing, copying, manipulating, formatting, and transmitting contributed to the change and brought, for the first time, new kinds of data practices, such as the practice of reusing identical records for different purposes invented by McCallum (see chapter 2).

When mechanization came, organizations were already prepared. As Mumford pointed out, "Behind all the great material inventions of the last century and a half was not merely a long internal development of technic: there was also a change of mind" (1934, 3). Data mechanization took first the semblance of the punch-card tabulator of Herman Hollerith (Ceruzzi 2012; Cortada 2016).[1] He famously introduced his tabulating machine during the 1890 US census (Cortada 2016, 21), which, thanks to the machine's speed and efficiency, was established as a permanent solution. In 1911, Hollerith's Tabulating Machine Company merged with other companies in the Computing-Tabulating-Recording Company (C-T-R) and subsequently became IBM. Hollerith's enterprise contributed to the foundation and growth of the American computer industry, which, until the late 1970s, primarily dealt with tabulators, analog computers, and mainframe computers. The history of computer development between 1950 and 1980 was essentially concerned with incrementally applying new inventions, components, and methods to the encoding and processing of data, which were designed "to make machines operate faster and more reliably, be easier to operate and be able to perform a greater variety of functions" (Cortada 2016, 157).

Despite this history being told numerous times, it has rarely been linked to the changes that it brought to the cognitive, epistemic, and communicative functions of data. Such changes mark a significant turn with far-reaching technical, social, and economic implications that are the aim and focus of this chapter. Rather than taking digital data and their definition for granted, the chapter discusses how they came about, what they reveal, and what they gloss over, along with the variety of functions that they perform in organizations. When did data cease to be considered semiotic entities and knowledge artifacts and came to be framed predominantly as countable things? How were marking and representing facts transformed into a system of operations that used holes in stiff paper cards to capture and transmit these facts? How and when were information and communication separated from data? This chapter analyzes the sociocultural and technological elements that have brought digital data to the forefront of the current economy and society. More particularly, we look at how technological and epistemic shifts have transformed data and the discourses around data. The preceding chapter was about the cognitive and epistemic continuities of data and the ways that they are linked to broader knowledge

FIGURE 3.1
Hollerith 1890 tabulating machine with sorting box. *Source*: Wikipedia (https://en
.wikipedia.org/wiki/Tabulating_machine#/media/File:HollerithMachine.CHM.jpg);
photo by Adam Schuster licensed under CC-BY 2.0 (https://creativecommons.org
/licenses/by/2.0/deed.en).

paradigms and social infrastructures, while this chapter is about the discon-
tinuities introduced by digital technology in the makeup and functions of
data. The next chapter will take these ideas further, exploring the emerging
apparatus of big data production and how it revolutionizes most aspects of
contemporary living.

The introduction of the first tabulator machines and punch-card calculators set the foundations upon which successive uses and applications of
mainframe computers in organizations were developed. It is worth pointing out that from the invention of the punch card onward, the material
and cultural history of data was gradually dissociated from expert practices,
the rules and systems of data generation, indexing, and recording, along
with the knowledge domains in which expertise is usually grounded. Data
came to be just one element of complex technological machinery made of
physical devices, mathematical rules, and formal logic—all changes that

have left an indelible mark on our age and the ways that we understand life situations and social relations.

The early adoption of tabulators, calculators, and mainframe computers across governmental bodies and businesses alike paved the road for the diffusion of more comprehensive computational systems because it allowed the gradual mutual adjustment of business processes and data-handling machines to one another (Norberg 1990, 754). The success of the first mechanical devices in aiding the handling of data rapidly brought about the integration of tabulators, bookkeeping machines, and then calculators and computers into the flow of organized work activities. Mainframe computers assembled and commercialized by IBM from the late 1940s until the 1980s developed along with the standardization of administrative tasks and processes in organizations. Companies had to accommodate the work of machines and, at the same time, were active in adopting ways of working or in suggesting modifications and implementations to IBM to better suit their own needs.[2] The integration of mechanical devices into organizational operations contributed to loosening the links between types of data, devices, and expert practices, which previously had been closely tied to one another (Kittler 1985).

A new *culture of data* emerged from the nascent computer industry, its technological and commercial path dependencies, and its links with the military complex. Data as material and cultural artifacts rapidly evolved along specific directions that were dictated by the interdependencies between business convenience, technological efficiency, and commercial success. Some historians of technology have gone so far as to trace several technological legacies of modern computers to the functioning of specific components or methods in Hollerith's machines (see, e.g., Aspray 1990; Norberg 1990, 764). Yet again, what is often overlooked is that all these developments are bits and pieces of a broader cultural shift that had already put data (and, perhaps more correctly, a certain perception of data and data management operations) at the center of business conduct, government administration, and the economy more widely (von Oertzen 2017).

Data preprocessing, storing, and processing had already become the building blocks of many organizational operations and were integrated into the management of large corporations through complex hierarchies of communication flows and control structures (Beniger 1986). Because of these interdependencies, data and their histories, material, and cultural path dependencies influenced the making of computers in complex ways. As Arthur Norberg (1990) states, even if it may seem strange, the fact that in the first computers "sorting speed increased, but calculating speed improved only marginally, if all" (761) can be explained by looking at how computers' latest implementations at that time were more a matter of competitive strategy and adjustments to client feedback than the result of new applications or inventions. The observation bespeaks the essential role that data and emerging data practices had in the making of computers (see also Agar 2003, 2006). At the same time, it attests to the power that computers, as data processing machines, had in managing organizations and restructuring the various organizational operations connected to data.[3] Strange as it may seem, the role of data and their practices has never figured prominently in the history of digital technology, which is primarily a history of machines, programming, and engineering. The technological remediation of data operated by computers brought about profound organizational changes that rearranged most data-intensive practices, including the more critical activities of accounting, controlling, management, and planning, that had developed since the advent of modern corporations. On the other hand, those practices were key to introducing and implementing computer technologies in organizations (Agar 2006; Kling 1996).

The acceleration of technological evolution and computer sophistication first rewrote all the data-related practices that made organizations modern, in Chandler's terms (Chandler 1977). Communication flows and control channels were restructured because computers decoupled data from some of their existing cultural features and domain expertise and introduced new tasks and operations (Zuboff 1988), together with new expertise. The shift was visible already by the time of the punch-card tabulator and the changes that it initiated. Hollerith's machine standardized, broke down, and mechanized data processing in several distinct steps. In the punch-card tabulator, the basic device was constituted by the punch, the tabulator, and the sorter. As a result, the punch-card tabulator broke data processing down to different tasks and operative phases, which were physically allocated to different machine parts. By doing this, it also separated data from their outputs; that is, from their informative capacity (and the message they carried). This apparent decoupling introduced an artificial and clear-cut distinction between data and information. From that moment on, information was defined as something that was no longer an attribute of data and the work of data infrastructures (Kittler 1985), but rather was an output of a machine.[4] As Charles Babbage had before him, Hollerith built a device that produced information from mechanical operations (Gleick 2011; Kallinikos 2012).

The change has had far-reaching and ramifying technical and cultural repercussions. The partial decoupling of data from information was brought about with a view to implementing a mechanical process whereby a machine massively and regularly read data. Data had to function independent of the information and content that they could support. Interestingly, data in the punch-card tabulator became perforations. The fundamental element of the tabulator system was the punched card. The perforations on such cards stood for data. Even though the cards were the bearers of data and perforations, the medium was quickly perceived as the data rather than its bearer. At this point, the communicative or informative capacities of data perforations could be observed only in association with a preprocessed card and a card reader.

Perforations were informative because they were made at predetermined, numerically arranged positions in the card (see figure 3.2). As data processing was broken into chunks to be mechanized, data-as-perforations ceased to be human-readable tokens. The new standardized and mechanized preprocessing, the whole combination of card and punches, was devised and optimized to be decoded by machines. Without a preprocessed card, the punch, the tabulator, and the sorter, data were not any longer *visible* qua data. Punch-card tabulators introduced a mechanizable version of data-as-things that were agnostic by virtue of having to read different kinds of information-as-data. In essence, perforations and cards could process anything—crops, production prices, even social security data. "The most remarkable feature of this new system was its versatility" (Norberg 1990, 762). Data-as-things enabled mechanization and set the standards for an essential antecedent of the "all-purpose machine," which would later be perfected with computers (Agar 2017).

THE MATHEMATICS OF TRANSMISSION

A leap forward into decoupling data from information (cognition) and communication came from advancements in electrical engineering and solid-state electronics that profoundly transformed the data mechanization of punched cards and tabulators. Claude Shannon famously recognized the

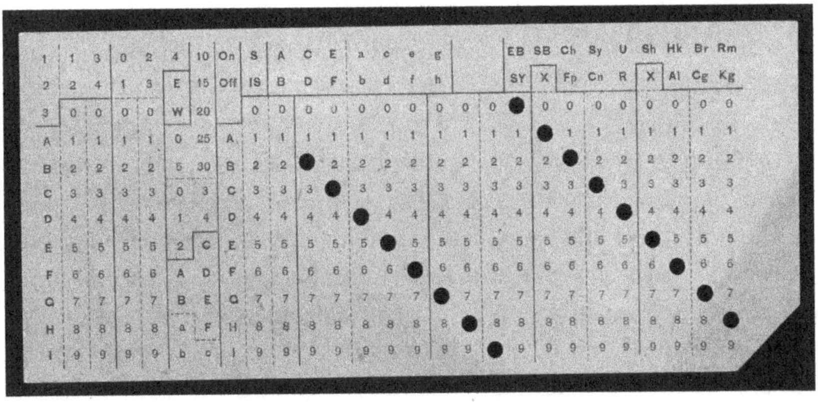

FIGURE 3.2
Hollerith punched card. *Source*: Wikipedia (https://en.wikipedia.org/wiki/Tabulating
_machine#/media/File:Hollerith_Punched_Card.jpg).

potentialities of using change of states or electrical signals to carry data
and elaborated a formal theory of data transmission (Shannon & Weaver
1949).[5] He integrated Boolean logic, electrical engineering, and cryptography to theorize information production as a process that could be understood, reproduced, and optimized within the logic and formal language of
mathematics and probability theory, and also executed by changes in states
or quantities of physical materials such as electrical signals, circuits, and
electrical switches. The mathematical and engineering approach of Shannon was undoubtedly innovative, and yet it was also very much the epit-
ome of a cultural trajectory in the perception and use of data that, coupling
data with objectification, quantification, and efficiency, had already transformed the business world, as well as the government and its military wing.

The consequences of Shannon's approach were vast and far-reaching. His
breakthrough idea of formalizing the correspondence between things and
data and manipulating their states through electronics, probability theory,
and formal logic paved the way for information theory. By formalizing and
theorizing the artificial separation between data and information, he fixed the
basis for computer science. To work, Shannon's mathematical theory of communication had to attenuate all the preexisting links between data, meaning,
communication, and information based on history, context, expertise, notation systems, material culture, and cultural functions and reduce those links
to a matter of probabilities that could be electrically coded, transmitted, and

eventually computed. Data became things, bits and bytes, and neutral syntactic tokens amenable to mechanical operations that optimized the production of information (Borgmann 1999; Boland & Hirschheim 1987; Buckland 1991; Eco 1976; Kittler, 1997).

Computers quickly developed thanks to the accruing agnosticism and immateriality of data and their capacity to work across several physical and logical layers and functions. Increasingly computers extended their ability to embed different streams of techniques, devices, and machines (each with its own history and path dependency) as part of their operations (Agar 2017; Ceruzzi 2012; Kittler 1985, 1996, 1997). Simply put, all the devices and machines already in use were gradually integrated into one "universal machine" that could execute all the data-intensive operations in organizations. The decoupling of data from information certainly contributed to a growing convergence of functions as digital data simultaneously became not only the stuff of machines but also, as John von Neumann foresaw, their own instructions. Into computers converged the previously separate operations of processing, calculation, storing and retrieval, programming and (crucially for our argument) the control and the expertise or discipline they belonged to, including information and archival science (Ceruzzi 2012, 157). Organizations were already prepared to accept the massive change: "When electronic computers finally proved sufficiently versatile for any sort of computations, business and government had been thoroughly primed for their use through fifty years' experience with mechanical tabulators" (Norberg 1990, 779). This priming, together with the convergence of technologies and functions into a universal machine, gave computers the potential to embed and optimize, basically in order to mechanize and later automate, most data-intensive processes and operations within organizations. Still, the consequences of the profound changes that computers brought to the workplace, the meaning of work, and the structuring of organizations would become visible only later and documented in several studies in the last two decades of the twentieth century (see, e.g., Boland and Hirschheim 1987; Kling, 1996; Zuboff 1988).

COMMUNICATION STRIKES BACK

Reducing data and information's informative and communicative potential to transmission, computation, and automation problems had significant structural repercussions. Within and across organizations, communication and interaction flows were broken down and streamlined into computer-based information systems and data flows to fit the logic and rules of machines (Beniger 1986). The introduction of computers as communication and information devices made it possible to translate and recast organizational and work activities as data and computer operations. It is characteristic of such shifts to redraw the patterns of cognition and the interaction of workers with machines and one another. Despite (or perhaps because of) these advancements, the problems of communication, interpretation, and meaning became more urgent, as "the proper interpretation of data as they appear on the screen is rarely self-evident" (Zuboff 1988, 197). In studies such as those performed by Zuboff, the context and meaning expelled by computerization return in the form of complex, comprehensive, and layered electronic text that puts the interpretive capacities of workers and clerks to a stern test (see also Kallinikos 1999, 2010).

The considerable disruption of the cultural and communicative trajectory of data, however, came from unexpected sources. Until the era of mainframe computers, data had remained the object of experts, businesses, governments, and research. Indeed, data's technological and digital makeup changed the relationships among work, expertise, and knowledge production. It triggered sweeping social changes that shifted the power toward a new class of engineers, mathematicians, and computer and information experts at the expense of those that helped manage data in predominantly manual and traditional settings (Agar 2003; Hicks 2017). Yet with the advent of personal computers and the beginning of online connectivity, the disrupting potential of data-based technologies entered the lives of households, persons, and society. This hugely impactful change in data makeup and epistemic function resulted from two different yet intrinsically connected innovations: the personal computer (PC) and the Internet. A turn away from the insulated spaces of mainframe computing and the involvement of digital devices and technologies in individual and social life changed, forever and irreversibly, the nature of data and the ways that they came to be generated and used.

The beginning of the PC era and the Internet is the subject of several historical accounts (Abbate 2000; Aspray & Ceruzzi 2008; Ceruzzi 2003; Chandler & Cortada 2000; Norberg, O'Neill, & Freedman 1996). It suffices here to say that the innovation in personal computing came from the tinkering of hobbyists, amateurs, and video gamers rather than from big conglomerates

(Zittrain 2008). The second distinctive trait of the PC revolution was that this cheap and easy-to-use device was made essentially for *communicating*. Alan Kay of the Xerox Park in Palo Alto affirmed that the "computer is a communication device first, second and third" (Ceruzzi 2003, 124). The PC could be used to make one or another computation and store and retrieve personal documents. Still, above all, and especially with the advent of the Internet, it became the preferred way of communicating and connecting with others.

Communication and interaction via dial-up systems prepared users for the upcoming Internet revolution. Despite the nominal attempts to separate data transmission from communication, and data as carriers of facts from their informative potential, the insertion of computing devices in the context of ordinary living reinforced data's communicative and media dimension. At the same time, these same developments came to punctuate, for the first time in history, the whereabouts of individuals and their interaction with others by the computational logic that undergirds the operations of these devices. The PC and the early Internet did not exactly reclaim the innocence of communication, nor did they reassert, as it is often believed, the prevalence of people vis-à-vis the impersonal world of institutions (Turkle 1984, 1995, 2011). Roughly, the same rules and logic previously tried in the context of organizations were carried over to structure and mediate personal communication via links, chat, shopping via dial-up systems, gaming, and online content consumption. The social and commercial sides of online communication developed hand in hand. Only technological constraints such as slow connectivity, lack of accessible interfaces, and low navigational capacity restrained the diffusion of pre-Internet online services.

The advent of the Internet, with its open and distributed character and its power of connectivity, laid the infrastructural (i.e., cultural and material) ground upon which a new design of communicating and interacting could be effectively built (Ryan 2010). This emerged hesitantly at first, and decisively after Tim Berners-Lee's invention of the web and its protocols. Yet these developments helped establish the rudiments of a new paradigm of computing-based communication and interaction that later became central in the programming of web-based applications. The sudden possibility of connecting via computing machines and transmitting texts, messages, emails, chats, and images via bits and bytes triggered a massive shift in how computers were designed and information science developed. The rapid diffusion of novel ways of communicating and interacting via hyperlinks and electronic text across most walks of life transformed data from administrative support tools into a pervasive medium of interaction (Turow & Tsui 2008; Turow & Couldry 2018).

This time, the shift was not restricted to a specific sector of the economy, an institutional setting, or a field; rather, it was all-encompassing. The power of Internet connectivity and the web brought data, their operations, and their devices at the forefront of public and institutional life and made them available to nearly everyone. What followed resembles the period of organizational adaptation between data-intensive processes and the mechanized version offered by machines that were observable during the era of mainframe computers. The same adaptation, although in different terms and with a much faster pace, was now required by unprepared households and individuals that (mostly unwarily) changed their everyday chores, communication and ritual habits, and related patterns of cognition to adjust to the possibilities offered by machines. A new and comprehensive digital infrastructure was thus established to cater to the quickly expanding digital capabilities. Those capabilities resulted from what was possible to achieve at the interface by establishing a vast data machinery in the back stage that served communities and individuals by black-boxing its complex operations (Hanseth & Lyytinen 2010; Tilson, Lyytinen & Sørensen 2010; Yoo, Henfridsson, & Lyytinen 2010).

If the history of computers has been mostly told from a machine, computational, and programming perspective, with no due attention to the role of data, the history of the Internet and the web is no different. Protocols, programming languages, platforms, modules, and architectures have taken most of the attention of scholars.[6] The role of data has been taken for granted, at least until economists such as Hal Varian (2010) understood their power in mediating and recording computer-mediated transactions at the same time. As data mediate transactions, Varian guesses, the records that they produce cease to be only records of transactions. They become *stuff*, the resources for novel economic pursuits and business organizations. He correctly perceives data and computers as the latest examples of accounting technologies that date back to clay tokens and their envelopes. In both cases, he contends, these artifacts have enabled the shift toward new forms of social exchange such as contracts (Varian 2010, 3). As expounded in the previous chapter, once data are produced, they rewrite (quite literally) the rules of cognition, knowledge, and social action. Having anticipated this, Varian proceeded to write some of the rules himself as the chief economist of Google.[7]

With the advent of digital and social media platforms, what was mostly a web of transactions became a web of interactions (Swanson 2020). Platforms have fundamentally rewritten the rules of how actors, both organizations and individuals, interact. Google, Amazon, Facebook (Meta), TripAdvisor, fintech apps, Netflix and Spotify, Uber, and Airbnb have all come up with unique ways of designing novel forms of interaction and using the data that those interactions produced to optimize their technologies and create and capture value. Users interact with digitized content, opinions of users, and other users (Alaimo & Kallinikos 2016, 2017, 2019). Data became the universal media of interaction. At the same time, they created something that was not there before, which, coupled with powerful technologies, facilitated new patterns of cognition, new forms of knowledge, and organizing. The connectivity and computation capabilities of the web afforded very different versions of many aspects of private life and everyday communication. They triggered a massive chain of social effects, which will be the focus of the following few chapters.

UNDERSTANDING DIGITAL DATA

Whether they are cast in clay, printed on paper, transmitted by electrical signals, or otherwise communicated, data are, first and foremost, semiotic tokens, carriers of content that form parts of larger systems of knowledge. As claimed several times in this book, data are artifacts of cognition and knowledge that are used to select, encode, and record events in particular formats that allow exchanges between social agents variously linked to social practices, institutional orders, and the knowledge systems that support them (Beniger 1986; Kallinikos 1999, 2007; Kling 1996; March 1999; Yates 1989; Zuboff 1988). Cognition and communication are always implied in selecting and encoding events and life situations and processing data even when each step of data making is outsourced to machines. Placed in such a broader context, data can hardly be divested of their cognitive and communicative nature and the practices and institutions in which they are embedded (Markus 1983; Markus, Majchrzak, & Gasser 2002; Schultze & Boland 2000).

The snippets of the history of data summarized in the preceding chapter and the brief history of data mechanization and computation presented here suggest that the technologies of data production and use inexorably interfere with modes of cognition and communication and the attendant social practices, knowledge, and institutions. It would hardly be a surprise that digital technologies' material and cultural history has profoundly changed how data are generated and linked to social practices and institutions. While this may sound evident, the story of exactly how digital data and technologies reframe the construction of facts, the ways that these facts are encoded into electrical signals and sign systems and redefine the practices of knowing remains largely untold. When transformed into digital bits and brought to bear on strings of 0 and 1, data become heavily mediated by and variously entangled with the language and materiality of machines. The logical and material foundations of digital technologies change the constitution of data, confer upon data several distinct attributes, and establish new conditions for producing, sharing, and making sense of them. Such conditions are, among other things, dictated by the fact that it is possible to create, access, manipulate, and interpret digital data only via technological systems and digital devices such as mobile phones or tablets, technical interfaces, application programs, and software more generally.

In what follows, we outline an alternative way to understanding digital data, which considers the role of technology against the sociocultural foundations of data and the cognitive (semiotic, epistemic) and communicative functions that they perform in this digital age. Digital data are still records, cognitive and communicative artifacts that encode events in an agreed-upon format on physical support of some kind. They codify things, events, or life situations in various formats bearing on strings of 0 and 1, digits encoded on electronic signals or magnetic fields (their physical carriers or material bearers) and processed by computers. As with most data, digital data feature a format and a physical embodiment that convey content or information (Borgmann 1999). Yet, as distinct from other types of data and records, digital data are constituted dynamically by the orchestration of their material, formal-logical and communication layers. Electrification and its ephemeral character imply that any digital stuff (code, software, or data) bearing on electric signals remains constantly malleable and editable

(Faulkner & Runde 2013, 2019; Kallinikos et al. 2010, 2013; Redström & Wiltse 2018). The middle computation layer is also executable and performative (Lyytinen 2022). The interaction of material, computational, and communication layers grants digital data specific attributes that frame the modalities of cognition, communication, and action that they enable (Yoo, Henfridsson, & Lyytinen 2010; Zittrain 2008). Figure 3.3 illustrates a schema of the layers whose attributes and dynamic interplay confer upon digital data their uniqueness and specific character.

In the digital world, the technological infrastructures supporting data making have been developed to be largely indifferent or agnostic to the content of what is recorded. As shown earlier in this chapter, one of the principles of computer science is to reduce the notion of information to something *agnostic*, a quantifiable resource (Shannon & Weaver 1949) whose transmission error could be expressed in probabilistic terms and whose production, storage,

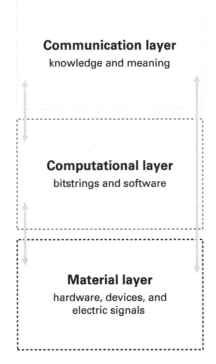

FIGURE 3.3
Schematic illustration of digital data as layered artifacts.

and potential value could constantly be optimized via increased computation and technological (or channel) capabilities (Buckland 2017). The notion of agnosticism has been vital to developing universal machines able to churn any kind of data and traverse the cultural regions that have historically been linked to literacy and numeracy, and later the handling of visual images and sounds (Kittler 1985; Manovich 2001). Data signify and communicate differently thanks to the fact that their logical layer (computation) remains loosely coupled to their communication layer and its external referents. However, by disregarding content and external references, the agnosticism of machines leaves communication and the transmission of information and meaning unbridled, a substantial issue that must be addressed sooner or later in the process. Despite the widespread assumption that underlies data mechanization from Babbage onward (Gleick 2011; Floridi 2010), machines or machine learning applications never operate alone in producing information (Weaver 1949). Information is still the result of complex social processes where cultural assumptions and practices remain decisive (Aaltonen, Alaimo, & Kallinikos 2021; Borgmann 1999; Buckland 1991; Eco 1976, 2000; Tuomi 1999).

The content-agnostic approach of machines and computation does not imply neutrality in the modality by which data are made, ordered, transmitted, or used (Dreyfus 2001; Markus 1983; Winner 1986) or, as the recent literature on critical big data or algorithms has pointed out, in the conditions and consequences of their production (Eubanks 2018; Iliadis & Russo 2016; Noble 2018; O'Neil 2016). Data are never neutral. Being agnostic and being neutral are not the same. Being agnostic means being indifferent or fencing off the content and the context of what is recorded. This is what machines do, even if they can never remain neutral, as the engineering and social conditions by which they achieve their signifying functions encode several predilections (the politics of data) that partly descend from the rich and intertwined history of culture, devices, and institutions (Mumford 1934).

Nonneutrality in data production can arise from any component in the vast material and symbolic infrastructure of data-based knowledge production. Predilections can be embodied in device design decisions, the path dependencies of existing technologies, established field beliefs, organizational aims, or physical constraints that severely limit the options of what can be displayed as digital records and further elaborated on as knowledge. The nonneutral character of data reweaves the politics of data via a thick infrastructure of rules and technologies.

As seen in the previous chapter, much of the cognitive functions of data derive from the format of the tokens and the logic and rules under which they are organized in larger collections which so far have been closely knitted to knowledge and institutions. Today, massive amounts of data are produced by various Internet-based systems, stored, and sorted by infrastructures and connected devices under varied conditions that are not readily inspectable. Therefore, the politics of data acquires blurred contours that are difficult to assess. Data are constantly repurposed, aggregated, and exchanged across different systems and organizational settings (Alaimo, Kallinikos, & Aaltonen 2020a; Ekbia et al. 2015; Floridi 2013; Jones 2019). As data production and handling become ubiquitous and sensor technologies more distributed, embedded in multiple devices, and interconnected, the balance between material and symbolic constraints will likely shift. The constraining conditions that material and computational layers impose on modalities of data production, storage, and structuration often grow more stringent with time and accumulated path dependencies (Bowker & Star 1999; Hanseth 2000, 2022).

The technological conditions of data and content management contain strong elements of a dynamic that is often at a remove even from domain knowledge and the contexts in which specific forms of expertise are exercised. Domain experts such as scientists, doctors, and engineers today are often extraneous to the complex and distributed devices and mechanics of data production and called to intervene only at later stages of data processing (see, e.g., Barrett et al. 2012; Bowker & Star 1999; Lebovitz et al. 2022; Leonelli 2019; Pachidi et al. 2021; Passi & Jackson 2018). These observations indicate that the agnostic character of data production, the built-in technological constraints, and the formal logic dominating the language of machines loosen the links of digital records with the specifics of content and practices and, therefore, domain knowledge. This is a process that started with data mechanization, and yet it is constantly expanding as data have become the media through which organizations and individuals operate.

Loosely linked to expert categories and guidelines, validation procedures, and checks, and supported by an ever-expanding technological apparatus, the language of machines and the conventions of online communication interfere with the contexts of working and living, which have hitherto remained at a remove from these developments (Alaimo & Kallinikos 2017,

2018, 2020). Doctors and medical researchers, for instance, have come to identify data produced by patients through online personal diaries, patient communities, and social media (Kallinikos & Tempini 2014). Prosecutors and police officers nowadays deal regularly with evidence produced for infotainment and information hunting via crowdsourcing platforms and other systems (Gray & Benning 2019; Waardenburg et al. 2022). Social media data are routinely used to make investment decisions in finance or to compute credit scores for insurance companies (Hansen & Borch 2022; O'Neil 2016). The ways that such data are produced represent a break with the traditions, principles, rules, and methodologies of generating medical, financial, or criminal records and remain either black-boxed or at a remove from experts, yet they are routinely embedded into knowledge, decision making, and action (see, e.g., Eubanks 2018; Kellogg et al. 2020; Levy 2015; Noble 2018; Smith 2020).

Much of this spin has been brought to digital data by their homogenizing capacity. The increasing datafication—that is, the translation of the diversity of cultural codes and conventions (e.g., image, sound, and text) and different information-processing systems (e.g., sales, accounting, bookkeeping, and archiving) into the language of machines—promotes the homogenization of knowledge and knowledge making (Yoo et al. 2010). When diverse things are rendered as digital data, they are bound to lose part of their distinct makeup. They can be stored, organized, transmitted, processed, and made sense of using the same methods and devices. These cardinal characteristics of digital data are briefly summarized in table 3.1.

Datafication operates under entirely new premises, which are partly derived from the convergence of several technological functions and new technological possibilities and partly from the commensuration of contexts previously held at arm's length from one another (Espeland & Sauder 2007). Digital methodologies and modalities of knowing traverse domains and contexts and make data portable and less context- and domain-dependent. Two effects are worth stating clearly. First, the agnostic character of data production and the formal language of machines contribute to loosening the links between procedures of data making and domain knowledge. Second, these same processes shrink the distance across different, sometimes remote knowledge, industry domains, and life situations.

Table 3.1

Characteristics of data production

Characteristics	Definition	Implications
Content-agnostic	The machinery of data production is indifferent to or disregards the content and the context of what is recorded.	Domain knowledge such as categories and rules, validation procedures, checks, and methods, as well as work profiles and experts, are often at a remove from data production.
Nonneutral	The engineering and social conditions of recording always entail predilections that are embodied in device design decisions and closely linked to the path dependence of technologies, beliefs, organizational aims, and physical constraints.	As systems and devices become ubiquitous and distributed, the technological path dependencies and predilections will likely acquire a greater leeway in shaping data production with their standards and rules.
Homogenizing	It entails the translation of cultural conventions (e.g., image making, sound making, and video making) and different information processing systems (e.g., sales, accounting, bookkeeping, and archiving) into the language of machines. When everything is digital data, then everything can be stored, transmitted, processed, and made sense of using the same methods and devices.	It shrinks the distance across different, sometimes remote knowledge and industry domains. Many types of data can be in principle related, exchanged, and clustered together.

SUMMARY AND IMPLICATIONS

This chapter focuses on the impact of mechanization and digitization on the makeup and functions of data. It considers the revolution brought about by digits. The main argument of this chapter is that even in the case of hole-punching machines and computers, data continue to work as artifacts of cognition and knowledge, although they do so in considerably different ways. Mechanization, followed by digitization, broke up the data-making process and outsourced it to machines. Computers developed by isolating key operations of data making from their organizational contexts and domain expertise (i.e., archiving, filing, and accounting) and gradually rose to all-purpose machines able to deal with most data-intensive practices. From this perspective, the formalization and specialization of data practices advanced by digitization continue the decoupling of data and data processing from the context and knowledge already introduced by mechanization.

The advent of the PC and the Internet brought another significant change in the patterns of data production, interpretation, and use. As the PC and the Internet were used mainly as communication devices and tools, data became the universal media of interaction. Many of the activities that until then had been either enclosed in the private sphere or left into the largely spontaneous order of social interaction (Alaimo & Kallinikos 2019) were brought into the orbit of large computational systems. Communication socialized computation at the same time as it itself became the object of computational rendition and mediation. On the one hand, these developments reinforced the cognitive grip of data upon organizations and institutions and substantially expanded the spectrum of economic operations that are structured and conducted through data. On the other hand, they made data a diffuse means of online sociality, mediated and performed through the scores and personalized recommendations of computational systems.

The fascinating character, complexity, and ambiguity of these developments get lost when data are solely perceived as just technical elements or economic resources. This chapter offers an alternative definition of digital data whereby the cognitive and communicative qualities inherent in all data making (encoding, representing, learning, sharing) are both exponentially expanded and punctuated by the operations of computational systems. Digital data are unique artifacts made of loosely coupled layers of computation and communication that coexist and interact. They are dynamically constituted in real time by the interactive functioning of their material (hardware), formal (software), and communications layers. A significant point that we make here is that the digital makeup of data recursively interacts with their cognitive and communicative functions, leading to the emergence of novel features. We spell out some of these emerging properties by showing how data operate by being agnostic to context, non-neutral, and homogenizing. These properties and the operations that they support do not happen in a vacuum, of course. Data are always part and parcel of complex sociotechnical processes and are embedded in broader institutional and cultural settings. We acknowledge the relational, multiple, and complex nature of data at the same time as we remain keenly aware that their social impact cannot be addressed if we treat them as just components of large technological infrastructures. The cognitive (semiotic, epistemic) and communicative nature of data confer upon them specific functions and roles in the mechanics of digital transformation. The understanding of data put forward in this chapter allows us to connect the mechanics of computation to the larger machinery of knowledge, in which data are not simply digital tokens of automated operations, but also artifacts of communication and cognition—media through which the world is perceived and performed.

These ideas indicate that there is a virtue in being specific about data and their sociotechnical dynamics (more on this in chapter 4). Being specific allows us to see how the role of data differs from that of other computational components (like algorithms or software) and to theorize the social nature of such differences. As we will see in chapter 6, the agnosticism, nonneutrality, and homogenizing of data imply that computationally embedded data practices increasingly disregard existing expert knowledge and domain procedures, crisscross life domains, and bypass the confines of institutional contexts. Living and working with digital data break through the boundaries that have separated personal from public life and kept specific domains at arm's length from each other with important social implications (more on this in chapter 5). Understanding the complexity of data, how they operate, and how they still make things "real" becomes even more crucial as data-driven technologies such as artificial intelligence (AI) advance and traverse domains and institutional borders.

4 THE DATA LIFE CYCLE

In this chapter, we delve further into the dynamics of digital data expounded in the preceding chapters and analyze the processes of data making, circulation, and use. A key point that we advance is that once social and economic events are captured as data, they tend to acquire a novel and considerably autonomous life. Unlike their paper-based antecedents, digital data are remade on a continuous, real-time basis and often on demand. As they enter the gears of a capillary infrastructure by which they are generated, data are continuously edited, rendered compatible with other data, standardized, ported across settings, and recontextualized. A piece of news on the web is constantly edited, and its delivery is personalized. So do most data-based services offered online. During this process of ongoing data production, editing, and processing, several data types emerge and constantly change. Data are cleaned and aggregated, are combined and repurposed, change formats as they travel across systems and software applications, lose some of their properties, and acquire new ones as they are brought to bear upon various contexts or markets. Far from being a simple and linear technological process, the life of data depends on a global and dispersed socioeconomic apparatus and is supported by complex technological infrastructures that cut across institutional divisions, industries, organizations, and forms of knowledge development and use (Jarvenpaa & Markus 2020).

Many organizations that dominate our age heavily rely on complex data production processes, whereby data serve as the building blocks of organizational operations and the bases for developing novel goods or services. The dynamics of data innovation and the role that these actors play in shaping the digital economy and society can be adequately framed only by unpacking the mechanics of data production and the journey that data undertake within and across organizations. What is it that remains unchanged in this constant digital flow? How do organizations across large ecosystems coordinate if data are never stabilized? While working with data is never a straightforward or linear process, it is increasingly the center stage on which much innovation and value creation unfold (Aaltonen et al. 2021; Alaimo & Kallinikos 2017, 2021; Alaimo, Kallinikos, & Aaltonen 2020; Beaulieu & Leonelli 2021; Flyverbom & Murray 2018; Jones 2019; Passi & Jackson 2018). The widespread assumption that organizations can gather data and extract value from them by just applying standard operations makes sense only if data are considered as technical elements devoid of those qualities analyzed in the foregoing chapters. Such an assumption is limited, if not straightforwardly flawed, and captures only a part of the processes through which data contribute to innovation and value creation (see, e.g., Alaimo & Aaltonen 2023). Likewise, defining data only as ready-made resources says little concerning the modalities by which these resources are produced or repurposed, made sense of, and aggregated. We complement these views by addressing the transformations that data as artifacts of cognition and knowledge undergo when they enter the machinery of data making and the institutional contexts characteristic of this machinery.

Our claim that data are *made* reflects the presupposition that data are sociocultural artifacts that acquire economic value under conditions that serve specific purposes. Chapter 3 suggested that data still maintain those attributes that make them artifacts of cognition, knowledge, and communication even when machine systems generate them. The argument of this chapter concerns the modalities by which this happens. An automatically recorded click, for instance, needs to be first defined, classified, and labeled as an online act, and often as an act of a particular kind (i.e., a purchase transaction, a click-through on a link, or a "like"). Classifying an event is a cultural operation that a machine is instructed to do either in advance or on the fly as the outcome of contingencies whose interpretation is embodied in data processing, such as the learning of algorithms. Classification, labeling, aggregation, and interpretation are not just technological operations, but part and parcel of marking and knowing the world (see, e.g., Paullada et al. 2021). By analyzing the process of data making, we observe how the mediating function of data coupled with the computational language of machines advance and establish novel modalities by which events are selected, encoded into data, and classified or processed as facts or evidence. Compiled against other facts, the making of data institutionalizes knowledge about the world, which serves as the basis for individual and collective action across several domains.

Despite the contingencies and idiosyncrasies of a process that varies quite consistently across industries, social contexts, and technologies, it is still possible to distill some essential and recurrent characteristics of the data life cycle (data making and use). Some of these characteristics are associated with the fact that data, as digitally based cognitive and cultural artifacts, are always the result of a long and often tortuous interactive design and implementation process. As indicated in the previous chapter, the agnostic, nonneutral, and homogenizing character of digital data imposes several constraints on the making of data and, at the same time, opens this process to novel possibilities of knowledge making. As distinct from previous forms of data, digital data can be constantly edited, ported, and recontextualized (Alaimo et al. 2020). In this respect, the process of data making and use is a nonlinear, recursive journey that remains open-ended, continuously generating new data (and therefore new data life cycles) and adjusting to various feedback and optimization mechanisms.[1] For analytical reasons, we have identified three main stages along which the social life of data can be studied: (1) the making of data, (2) the production of novel knowledge objects, and (3) the systematic use of data in various contexts, including the packaging of data-based commodities exchanged in the market. Figure 4.1 illustrates the three main stages of the process.

THE MAKING OF DATA

Data are made, and digital data are no exception. As repeatedly claimed in this book, they are sociocultural artifacts generated under specific conditions and constraints of a social and technological character. Even when data already exist in other formats (e.g., analog pictures or movies), there is always more than one way of making them digital. Rather than being a straightforward translation from one format to another (e.g., analog to digital), this passage should be better understood as reconstructing signals or analog data via digital rules. Such reconstruction brings about a significant

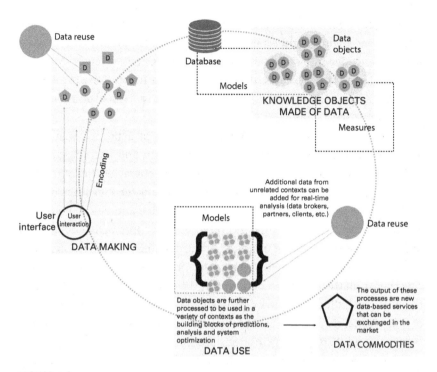

FIGURE 4.1
The data life cycle.

transformation in their making and the experience of use or consumption they afford (Dourish 2017; Redström & Wiltse 2015).[2] Yet most data used today by economic actors and organizations are data that did not exist in some other format and are native to the online or computational environments to which they belong. The conception, design, and implementation of such data often entail a complex and distributed human and technical effort that tends to remain in the background or, worse, is taken as an accurate (and thus unproblematic) rendering of some events or facts "out there." This is the case for sensor data, which are often mistakenly taken as some exact representation (a contradiction in terms) of events or natural signals (for a debunking, see, e.g., Monteiro 2022; Monteiro & Parmiggiani 2019).

Social data, the data that encode user engagement on social media platforms and other social online settings, are among the most conspicuous examples of digital native data that illustrate the institutional nature of the processes underlying their generation and use (boyd 2015; Lomborg 2013).

Continuous or bundled social activities and forms of interaction are made discrete, regrouped into clusters or classes of stylized actions, and encoded into data. The encoding of the social is made possible by the digital mediation of user platform participation, standardized, and formalized along specific activity types such as commenting, posting, sharing, tagging, liking, or following. These social data, which are usually assumed to represent the opinions and whereabouts of users, are, in fact, the by-products of user interactions that are designed mainly to accommodate the operations of social media platforms as business organizations, implemented under the constraints of technological infrastructures (Bechmann & Lomborg 2013). As a result, new digitally mediated forms of conviviality have been established by social media platforms that we have earlier referred to as "computed sociality" (Alaimo & Kallinikos 2016, 2017, 2019; Leonardi 2014; Lomborg 2013; Turow & Couldry 2018).

Despite some apparent resemblance to social forms of interaction, the notion of computed sociality suggests that social media participation and online conviviality are engineered and constantly optimized for technical efficiency and economic profit. This engineering provides the grid that orders platform participation into standardized activity types that, recorded as social data, become further involved in all subsequent operations by which user experience is computed and related to the experience of other users online and offline. These stylized interactions and the data that they generate partake in the infrastructuring of online social engagement. Users resocialize those data by reacting to the personalized suggestions that those data help construct. Furthermore, it is now a very diffuse practice to reuse data from social media in various settings, including financial investment (Hansen & Borch 2022) or software development through the training of several standard artificial intelligence (AI) applications (Paullada et al. 2021). Opinions, comments, recommendations, likes, follows, views, and other elements have rapidly become a set of universally formatted, easy-to-perform, and quick-to-repeat social interactions that, once rendered as data, are increasingly taken as the bases of social life and used to compute a variety of metrics on user behavior within but also beyond social media.

It is characteristic of digital data and their standardized formats to make data reuse and repurposing widely diffuse operations. Straightforward as they may initially seem, data reuse and repurposing are intricate (Aaltonen et al. 2021; Gebru et al. 2021). On the one hand, several technical issues result from different formats, missing records, data inconsistencies, duplications, cor-rupted fields, and the like (Markus 2001). Rather than being trivial or limited, these are recurrent issues reinforced by the frequent updates and changes in software systems applications that are endemic to digital technologies. The serious character of these issues notwithstanding, other crucial semantic prob-lems emerge that are linked to the reinterpretation of the original data and the new functions or purposes that they are called upon to serve (Lyytinen 2022). As data travel across contexts and are reused, the predilections, assumptions, and design choices on the basis of which they are initially produced become opaque and fade into the background. Reusing and repurposing data requires reimagining their roles and building the organizational capabilities to fuse such operations with established organizational and knowledge functions and practices. In this regard, data reuse and repurposing should be better seen as increasingly widespread instances of data making.

What repurposing conceals is that the making of data inescapably implies the liquefaction and transformation of the real (Flyverbom 2019; Monteiro & Parmiggiani 2019). All digital data entail encoding complex and interrelated social processes into discrete tokens and remapping these interrelations as data relations (Borgmann 1999; Bowker & Star 1999; Eco 1976). In this respect, the making of data is less concerned with the accu-racy of representation and more related to the computational and commu-nicative potential data acquire as discrete tokens that are essential to the functioning of complex technological infrastructures. On a variety of occa-sions, data do not represent reality because of their fidelity to external refer-ents (signs qua icons), but rather because of several other reasons, including their conformity to standard rules or the links that they form with other data (Bailey et al. 2012; Kallinikos 1999, 2010). Correspondingly, social data are not valuable for the accuracy of their representation (e.g., what does a Facebook like exactly represent?). Instead, they are valuable due to the functions that they perform in a complex data-based infrastructure tuned to modes of representing and knowing that emerge from the interplay of the material, logical, and communication layers of data. A Facebook like, for instance, acquires its value from how masses of likes can be related to profile data and location data and facilitate the discovery of patterns or rela-tions that may turn out useful or profitable for some actors. Many of these operations are the products of design choices, business objectives, emergent interaction patterns, and technological rules. They all have implications for data sharing, porting, and repurposing that must be better assessed and acknowledged.

A case could be made that some data are closer to reality than others or less ambiguous than others. An opinion on Twitter, for instance, has a different and admittedly more ambiguous representational value than the energy level of a pump. Although this is certainly true, it is worth reminding that the difference between the two is only a matter of degree. The mediation process remains largely similar even for signals that may be taken as less ambiguous than an opinion (Monteiro & Parmiggiani 2019; Østerlie & Monteiro 2020). The physical world of natural processes is very ambiguous, and the making of data in such instances is, in Knorr Cetina's words, "decision impregnated" (1981, 136; see also Edward 2010; Knorr Cetina 1999, 2001). The selection of what signal to encode and the decision of how to do it are just the initial steps of a very complex mediation process. As in any mediating process, the medium dictates a set of rules (Eco 1976, 1986, 2000; McLuhan 1964), on the basis of which the transcription or encoding of events occurs.

Consider how even apparently simple acts such as the tracking of user listening behavior in music streaming platforms are seldom the recording of events happening out there. To make music listening "social" Last.fm, one of the oldest music discovery platforms (see Alaimo & Kallinikos 2021), developed Audioscrobbler, a technology that detects a playback signal and creates a data token called "playcount" every time a listening event occurs. Detecting playback signals is tricky, given that each of the approximately 600 streaming platforms, personal computers (PCs), and devices connected produces them slightly differently and with different data and metadata standards. In addition, as with many other data-tracking technologies, there is no precise rule on how to track events. Often there are too many different or ambiguous signals (e.g., does skipping a track count as listening?). Here, a "playback" must then be defined with a set of requirements. Only as such can a signal become visible and be tracked by machines as the index of related events. In this case, the platform defines a playback signal as an indicator of a listening event if it is longer than thirty seconds.[3] Every signal that does not fit the formal definition is automatically excluded. This apparently simple decision caused quite a bit of discontent on the part of determined listener communities, as it ended up excluding genres of music with tracks of shorter duration.

All classification decisions have repercussions. Data are always the outcome of several contingent processes and organizational negotiations rather than the straightforward mapping of an area of reality out there. If they represent facts, data often do so in a relatively narrow sense. In the case of Last.fm, the system had to define what indicates a listening event (via playback signals) in online platform settings and negotiate data rules and parameters with users, developers, and other stakeholders (e.g., music labels). At the same time, these negotiations were heavily limited by several other constraints, such as the kind of technology employed, its functional prerequisites, and different technical and industrial standards prevailing in the industry. Very often, the specific formats of data and the formal language used to record them considerably determine the event that is recorded, stored, and sorted (Alaimo & Kallinikos 2019; Bowker & Star 1999; Flyverbom & Murray 2018; Gitelman 2013). An event is inscribed into data only because it fits the format of the digital token and possesses functional attributes, such as metadata, which are important for its interoperability and computability.

The case of Last.fm demonstrates that even tracking, which is usually taken for granted as a merely technological or automated function, results from a complex sociocultural and organizational process that requires several up-front decisions to work. Importantly, even if the specificities of data making vary considerably across organizational settings, technologies, and industries, the logic supporting the making of data is consistently the same across all the contexts that we have encountered in our empirical investigations. Playcounts represent user listening behavior only within the possibilities that new technologies establish and the limits of several technical and social constraints. These ideas suggest that data are made valuable thanks to the function that they perform in the broader system of marking and knowing set up by one or several organizations and the technologies that support it. Making data thus entails an act of selection, interpretation, and encoding that is, at the same time, also an essential organizational or infrastructural decision conditioning subsequent actor operations, decisions, or tasks.

Technical approaches to data would claim that technological standardization and formatting imply that once transcribed to data, events lose their links to social and cultural contexts. In their view, data are just a set of points in a vast geometry of formal relations made of the distributions, frequencies, and correlations of the occurrences that they encode.

The diametrically opposite view, that data emerge out of the particularities of contexts and are therefore local or meaningful to those that deal with them, is also widely diffuse (Loukissas 2019; Rawls & Mann 2015). Any form of representation from writing onward, we suggest, is always made to overcome the hard boundaries of context, even if it is bound to be produced locally. The formal rules, standardization, and computational logic of digital mediation are designed specifically to loosen those links. At the same time, the links of data with their referents (the event and its context), while certainly attenuated by the formal nature of digital representations, still work on the background as a potential pool of relevancies (meanings) that set the boundary conditions of what can and cannot be done with certain types of data.

It is important to recognize that the formal character of data, their granular makeup, and their unstable links with external references open a space of interpretive possibilities which lead to innovation, provided that they are properly managed (Aaltonen et al. 2021; Kallinikos 2010; Lyytinen 2022). This is the greatest opportunity offered by digital data at the same time, as it remains a steady source of risks, simplifications, and drifts. Their novel attributes provide many different, continuous, and nonrival modalities by which the same set of data (with the same referents) can produce several different outcomes, serve purposes that were not planned, and lead to additional data operations. With loose links to context and knowledge domains, the agnostic, nonneutral, and massive generation of new data can sustain the development of knowledge because it is supported by two interrelated and strongly ingrained expectations (Lyytinen, Nickerson, & King 2021):

- The expectation of constant technological progress, in this case intended as the refinement of technological processing capacity (including machine learning algorithms and AI applications).
- Its intrinsic promise that any problem or limitation arising from loss of reference and loss of contextual or domain knowledge during the stage of data production can always be addressed at later stages.

KNOWLEDGE OBJECTS MADE OF DATA

Data making and the practices with which it is associated are technology-driven, socially embedded processes that produce novel knowledge artifacts.

The modalities and different conditions that underpin the constant data manipulation, aggregation, and processing give rise to a whole new breed of entities that weren't there before, at least not in their current shape. In their simplest form, these entities are only aggregations of multiple instances of the same data; for example, all the playcounts related to an artist's name on music streaming platforms, all the clicks of an individual user on a given web page, or all the recorded instances of a given sensor embedded in a wearable device. In more complex forms, these objects are configured by putting together different data types under a given structure or shape. We call these entities "data objects." "Data" is used because, different from the broader class of digital (software) objects to which they belong (Ekbia 2009; Faulkner & Runde 2013, 2019; Kallinikos, Aaltonen, & Márton 2013), they are mostly made of data and metadata; and "objects" is used because they have a duration, relative stability, and a structure (Faulkner & Runde 2019; Hui 2016).

Data objects should be distinguished from software objects or digital artifacts (Hui 2016; Lyytinen 2022; Redström & Wiltse 2018). They are technologically and structurally simpler than software objects and are brought into being by a structure or schema whereby data items are put together in a pattern or form. Such data-structuring schemas differ from software programs and the detailed instructions that the latter embody. A typical example of a data object is a customer profile made of several attributes that are themselves clusters of data (i.e., transactions and login data) structured under a given format. In this sense, data objects differ from software objects and the functionalities underpinning such objects. In the homogenizing world of digital technologies described in the preceding chapter, in which everything is ultimately data, the difference is admittedly not always clear cut. Even the simplest arrangement of data requires some instructions as to how to identify, select, and assign tokens to it.

Rather than capturing an underlying essence, the conception of data objects that we put forward stems from the function that they fulfill in the process of knowledge making and use in which one or more organizations participate. Data objects and software objects perform different functions in the emerging knowledge infrastructure linked to the making and processing of digital records. While technical entities, data objects remain semantic artifacts or cultural constructs, recurring arrangements of the events data encode, ordered according to certain logics, and criteria that serve several aims. They are, in fact, the basic cognitive units, the elemental reality cuts—in the sense that Eleanor Rosch and her colleagues attributed to basic objects (Rosch 1975; Rosch et al. 1976)—of a complex infrastructure of knowing and acting, without which other more inclusive perceptions or knowledge management operations would be virtually impossible (Leonardi 2020). Credit scores, user profiles (see figure 4.2), ad impressions, click-through rates, viewability metrics, lookalike audiences, bid request and response objects in online auction infrastructures, customer profiles, worker profiles assembled from several data logs, assets (virtualized physical machinery), and their aspects (datafied attributes) in industry 4.0 are some conspicuous examples. They are all entities built by data aggregated under a schema or structure that makes the world legible and actionable in new ways, enabling new social interactions and new work practices within and across organizations (Alaimo 2022a; Alaimo & Kallinikos 2021, 2022).

Data objects inherit many of the functions of knowledge objects. The epistemic or cognitive functions that data objects perform are analogous to those of knowledge objects such as the operating ratio considered in chapter 2. At the same time, the digital makeup of data objects alters several of these functions. The attributes of data objects, for instance, are heavily mediated by the operative demands of the digital systems and technologies in which they are embedded (Bowker & Star 1999; Hanseth & Ciborra 2007). Their accessibility, both in terms of knowability and operability, is considerably shaped by digital interfaces, computational tools, and interconnected and layered devices (Lyytinen 2022). Unlike other instances of knowledge objects, the functions that data objects fulfill are heavily overlaid by the technical prerequisites that stem from the fact that they operate as technical components in a larger technological data management infrastructure. As shown here, data objects are always put together in standard ways to be machine readable and interoperable across systems and devices.

Consider the example of virtualized machinery in smart manufacturing (see figure 4.3). These digital representations of physical machinery (e.g., a pump or an engine) are data objects made of several lower-level data objects that encode facets or operations of a machine, such as energy consumption. Every aspect or attribute is in turn composed of several even lower-order data objects (e.g., power, current, and voltage), which are the aggregates of the numerous and continuous instances of the same data point (i.e., the bits recorded as power signals). Making these objects in manufacturing allows a good enough virtual representation (a digital twin, as it were) user   User object   The user who posted this Tweet. See user data dictionary for complete list of attributes.

Example highlighting select attributes:

```
{ "user": {
    "id": 6253282,
    "id_str": "6253282",
    "name": "Twitter API",
    "screen_name": "TwitterAPI",
    "location": "San Francisco, CA",
    "url": "https://developer.twitter.com",
    "description": "The Real Twitter API. Tweets ab
out API changes, service issues and our Developer P
latform. Don't get an answer? It's on my website.",
    "verified": true,
    "followers_count": 6129794,
    "friends_count": 12,
    "listed_count": 12899,
    "favourites_count": 31,
    "statuses_count": 3658,
    "created_at": "Wed May 23 06:01:13 +0000 2007",
    "utc_offset": null,
    "time_zone": null,
    "geo_enabled": false,
    "lang": "en",
    "contributors_enabled": false,
    "is_translator": false,
    "profile_background_color": "null",
    "profile_background_image_url": "null",
    "profile_background_image_url_https": "null",
    "profile_background_tile": null,
    "profile_link_color": "null",
    "profile_sidebar_border_color": "null",
    "profile_sidebar_fill_color": "null",
    "profile_text_color": "null",
    "profile_use_background_image": null,
    "profile_image_url": "null",
    "profile_image_url_https": "https://pbs.twimg.c
om/profile_images/942858479592554497/BbazLO9L_norma
l.jpg",
    "profile_banner_url": "https://pbs.twimg.com/pr
ofile_banners/6253282/1497491515",
    "default_profile": false,
    "default_profile_image": false,
    "following": null,
    "follow_request_sent": null,
    "notifications": null
  }
}
```

FIGURE 4.2

Example of a user object on Twitter. (a) An example of a user object with selected and unspecified attributes; (b) the description of attributes (data) composing the objects (partial selection). *Source* https://developer.twitter.com/en/docs/twitter-api/v1/data -dictionary/object-model/tweet and https://developer.twitter.com/en/docs/twitter -api/v1/data-dictionary/object-model/user.

Attribute	Type	Description
id	Int64	The integer representation of the unique identifier for this User. This number is greater than 53 bits and some programming lanugages may have difficulty/silent defects in interpreting it. Using a signed 64 bit integer for storing this identifier is safe. Use `id_str` to fetch the identifier to be safe. See Twitter IDs for more information. Example: `"id": 6253282`
id_str	String	The sting representation of the unique identifier for this User. Implementations should use this rather than the large, possibly unconsumable integer in `id`. Example: `"id_str": "6253282"`
name	String	The name of the user, as they've defined it. Not necessarily a person's name. Typically capped at 50 characters, but subject to change. Example: `"name": "Twitter API"`
screen_name	String	The screen name, handle, or alias that this user identifies themselves with. screen_names are unique but subject to change. Use `id_str` as a user identifier whenever possible. Typically a maximum of 15 characters long, but some historical accounts may exist with longer names. Example: `"screen_name": "twitterapi"`
location	String	*Nullable.* The user-defined location for this account's profile. Not necessarily a location, nor machine-parseable. This field will occasionally be fuzzily interpreted by the Search service. Example: `"location": "San Francisco, CA"`
derived	Array of enrichment objects	Enterprise APIs only Collection of Enrichment metadata derived for user. Provides the *Profile Geo* Enrichment metadata. See referenced documentation for more information, including JSON data dictionaries. Example:

FIGURE 4.2
(continued)

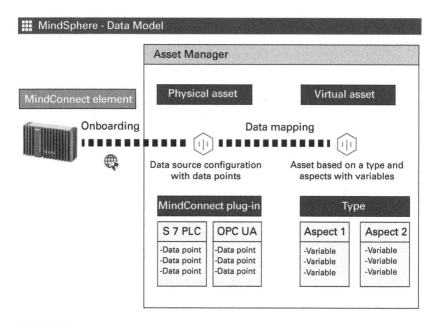

FIGURE 4.3

Example of a data object created by the virtualization of physical assets such as machines and engines in smart manufacturing. This is taken by the Siemens Mind-Sphere platform, which has open specifications. *Source* https://siemens.mindsphere .io/en/docs/tutorials/asset-manager.

of the operations of physical machines and furnishes a vital cognitive step toward new knowledge and organizational processes that develop around the monitoring of the performance of these machines. An instructive example of such methods is predictive maintenance, which is not just the prediction of when the maintenance should be made, but also a profound transformation of the process of maintenance itself (Jonsson, Holmström, & Lyytinen 2009).

The capacity to anticipate impending equipment dysfunctions or failures derives from the possibility of aggregating and combining equipment performance data with data from various systems held within and, crucially, outside the organization hosting the physical asset. These include historical records, enterprise resource planning systems, manufacturing execution systems, supervisory control and data acquisition systems, and distributed control systems. The introduction of data objects and related technologies such as sensors, Internet of Things (IoT) platforms, application programming interfaces (APIs), and data lakes radically transforms how organizational operations and resources are known and acted upon and changes the role of the actors involved in the process. Data objects are vital for allowing a new breed of data-based knowing practices and data management techniques as they structure data in more flexible and scalable ways, overcoming existing data storing techniques (e.g., relational, nonrelational, etc.), specific uses (e.g., analytics and predictive maintenance), or systems. As distinct from traditional maintenance, predictive maintenance is rarely the output of an individual team, or even of an individual organization, but is instead the result of collaborations and exchanges occurring in emerging complex ecosystems.

Two aspects of this illustrative example are worth restating: (1) data objects as placeholders of data that make visible and accessible organizational resources in novel ways, fostering several novel knowledge and organizational processes such as predictive maintenance; and (2) the consequent changes in organizations dealing with data objects instead of physical assets and the novel knowing practices that transcend the confines of existing domains of work and expertise and established organizational boundaries. In many contexts, objects made of data constitute a firm point of reference—the center stage, as it were—upon which organizational knowledge and practice unfold. They define units of knowledge, provide focus and orientation for action, and circumscribe the ground upon which other organizational and industry operations develop (Faraj, Jarvenpaa, & Majchrzak 2011; Faraj et al. 2016; Kallinikos & Mariátegui 2011).

To provide another illustration, the advertising industry has historically developed around the creation of audiences (i.e., access, measurement, and report of viewing, listening, or readership habits) (Napoli 2011). Advertising audiences today are compiled from the aggregation of several data types such as clicks, browseovers, likes, transactions, and others. Rendered as data objects, audiences become ubiquitous in the current digital world and one of the most telling examples of the new universe that data and their objects bring about, for an audience is an entity that has little tangible reality apart from the data that are gathered (often repurposed) and assembled to provide (indirect) evidence of it (Aaltonen et al. 2021). There is no entity such as an audience without the clustered data (clicks) that make the data object-audience in the first place (Alaimo & Kallinikos 2018; Turow 2011). At the same time, advertising audiences constitute the central reference point for the activities of marketers, publishers, social media platforms, and other media companies that usually assemble, model, and trade them, together with the range of industry actors concerned with the relevance, facticity, and commercial value of these entities. Data objects not only become central knowledge objects of the industry (i.e., repository of data on audience) but also the core operational units that can execute the main exchange in the advertising industry.

Nowadays, buying and selling advertising online coincide with the automated auctions of data objects in real time. In programmatic advertising, data objects, such as the so-called bid request and bid response objects, are both the goods being exchanged and the enablers of the practice of exchange, as they embed rules for the automated and real-time bidding that happens among thousands of disperse actors. Data objects carry all the information needed to complete a deal. What has previously been constituted as a complex process with several knowledge objects (i.e., creatives, contracts, audience metrics and reports) and several different practices and exchanges between marketers and publishers (and other actors) is increasingly carried out automatically by bidding requests and bidding response objects supported by a hypertechnological infrastructure of APIs, algorithms, protocols, and platforms. Such developments have radically reframed a good deal of the operations in which advertising is embedded and gave rise to new actors and organizational and industry practices, which are all mediated by learning and acting with and through data objects (Alaimo 2022a).

These observations attest to the central role of data objects and show that the making of data and data objects are closely associated with one another. Yet they also signal an essential difference between data objects and the conditions and modalities of data making. Data objects operate as mediating cognitive devices between the agnosticism of data production analyzed in the preceding chapter and the broader context within which these data need to work. In contrast to data procurement or generation that may remain agnostic to their final use, data objects maintain various links to domain knowledge and field practices via their attributes (fields or metadata). For instance, in the example given here, bid request objects contain several attributes (i.e., audience metrics, prices, modalities of ad delivery, and formats of creatives) through which data objects dynamically interact with their data environment (i.e., acquiring data related to the attribute, responding to other objects' attributes). This makes the function that these objects perform particularly relevant.

By structuring the often unstructured, dispersed, fragmented, and continuous data flows of several data types, data objects reestablish a connection between data records and the novel infrastructure of knowing that they help construct. The utility and instrumental involvement of data are centrally linked to their capacity to monitor things and activity patterns in real time and summarize and respond to the perpetually shifting contingencies characteristic of the current world. Data objects thus help address the cognitive hurdle arising from constant change (objects made of data aggregates are never the same) and the continuity needed to coordinate action (a schema of an object made of data has some durability). In this sense, they operate very much like basic objects in categorization schemes, which are middle-range constructs that reduce the variability of the world and yet deliver entities concrete enough to aid perception, knowledge sharing, and action (Rosch 1975; Rosch et al. 1976). Data objects work as the building blocks of more abstract categories (Hui 2016). At the same time, data objects are essential coordinative devices across many industry settings in platforms and platform ecosystems, as we will see in chapter 8. These ideas are summarized in table 4.1.

In online music streaming platforms, to refer to the case of Last.fm from earlier in this chapter, data objects are artist names composed as aggregations of user playcount data. The making of artist names qua data objects does not draw from cultural music conventions, and it is only loosely linked to real artist names, even though this may seem strange. In the technical systems of relations in which it is embedded, the data object "artist name" is put together as the result of the formal computational rendering of the idiosyncratic listening of users. The system automatically creates an object once it detects artist names as metadata of a music track file associated with a listening event. Still, it cannot avoid creating objects for misspelled or incorrect names, as it does not know which version of an artist name is real or correct. Online and in the formal world of digital data management systems, there may be as many data objects as are incorrect metadata associated with any Louis Armstrong track. "L. Armstrong," "Armstrong," and "Louis Armstrong" each can be metadata serving as inputs to create its own artist name–data object. The objects so created then structure the

Table 4.1
Data objects

Definition	Structured entities with a lifespan (duration) composed by aggregated data which are organized according to a logic or schema
Digital Materiality (Form)	Belong to the broader class of digital objects as they are based on digital technologies and composed of digital data
	Present the same characteristics of digital objects such as malleability, openness, editability, generativity etc. (as in Ekbia 2009; Faulkner and Runde 2013, 2019; Kallinikos, Aaltonen et al. 2013).
	They structure and standardize data to make them machine readable.
	Differ from digital (software) objects as they are made mostly of data and metadata (rather than programming functions) and because they serve different functions.
Knowledge Functions	Belong to the broader class of knowledge objects sharing the characteristics of being abstract, question generating, incomplete (as in Knorr Cetina 1999; Miettinen and Virkkunen 2005).
	Function as basic objects, the intermediate cognitive entities that link singular events (i.e., data) with more complex categories (i.e., data outputs such as predictions).
	Constitute central elements around which knowledge practices and organizational and industry operation develops (i.e., credit scores or advertising audiences).
	Work as mediating cognitive devices between the agnosticism of data production and domain or contextual knowledge.
	Constitute mediating devices between ideas or schemas and their realization or instantiations.
	Work as boundary objects mediating between different knowledge communities or expertise.
	Differ from epistemic objects as their digital materiality considerably alters their knowledge function and the role they play in the whole architecture of knowledge.

Table 4.1 Continued
Data objects

Examples	Assets of virtual machinery in smart manufacturing (digital twins or digital doubles).
	Profiles (users, customers, workers, such as drivers in Uber, clients, patients in online medical communities, stores, etc.).
	Products or exchange entities in various settings such as tweets in social media, ad impressions in advertising, audiences in advertising, artist names or tracks or playlists in social music platforms.
	Composite objects (made by data and metrics) such as credit scores, popularity indexes, click-through rates, viewability metrics, etc.
Knowledge and organizational processes	In all these cases data objects are not the final output but an intermediate step on to which other more complex organizational processes develop.
	Examples can include prediction, forecasting, monitoring, nudging, exchange.

categorization activities and organizational operations of the music discovery platform. Artist names operate both as basic objects, from which more complex categories, such as similar artists or popular artists, are derived, and as boundary objects allowing massive collaboration through the platform and its community of developers, partners, and users (Alaimo & Kallinikos 2021). By the same token, artist names are the central entities in the recommender systems used to personalize music discovery. The making of such data objects shapes music knowledge genres and categories together with the possibilities of browsing and playing music given to users. Users online can see and listen to artists only if they have been correctly *datafied* into objects by the system. On music streaming platforms, this happens because of the transformation of users' listening behavior into data. By these means, a self-reinforcing cycle of knowledge production about music is established, which appears very distant from the socialized and culturally embedded traditional process of music listening (see figure 4.4. for an illustration).[4]

The creation of data objects establishes new machine-driven and system-tuned categories that take the place of traditional ones and, despite their computational makeup, are resocialized into novel music consumption

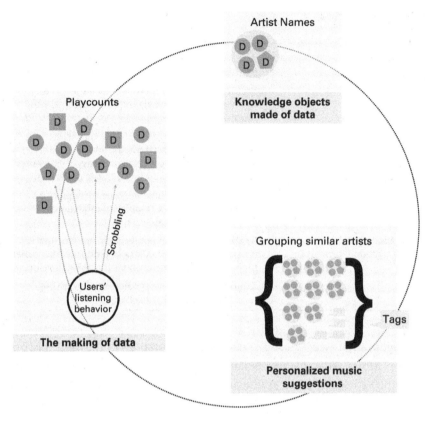

FIGURE 4.4
The data life cycle on Last.fm.

patterns, novel objects constructed of data aggregation and structuration
such as playlists, and novel genres (Lyytinen 2022). These shifting knowing
processes have conspicuous and ramified economic and organizational consequences. Music producers, for instance, are adjusting the length specifica-
tion of music tracks to better fit online requirements.[5] Data objects become
the entities through which different actors and communities collaborate in
a newly defined space of collective action (Kallinikos & Mariátegui 2011).
Knowledge objects have been studied in their functioning as boundary
objects that allow collaboration among different experts and communities
(i.e., Barley 2015; Barley, Leonardi, & Bailey 2012; Ewenstein & Whyte 2009;
Jonsson, Holmström, & Lyytinen 2009, Star 2010; Star & Griesemer 1989). Yet
data objects express this boundary function differently, as the formal nature

and standardization of digital technologies alter considerably the knowledge processes that they enable, the actors that can participate in these processes, and the patterns of their collaborations (see, e.g., Aaltonen et al. 2021; Alaimo & Kallinikos 2021; Monteiro & Parmiggiani 2019; Pachidi et al. 2021; Passi & Jackson 2018). While they enable massive collaboration across dispersed organizational and field boundaries, they simultaneously lack the plasticity that would allow them to adapt and speak to different communities of practice. In the case of Last.fm, the use of computationally arranged artist names qua boundary objects led to the proliferation of rules and parameters that govern their production and use and ended up excluding data sources and membership categories (i.e., specific genres of music that do not fit the parameters of data ingestion and external developer practices), triggering along the way protests from users and developers.

DATA COMMODITIES

Data objects such as user profiles on commercial platforms, artist names on music streaming platforms, and records of machine functions in manufacturing work as coordinative devices that structure the operations of organizations and shape the relationships between economic actors and their environments. In this discussion, we have analyzed the type of knowledge, reality interventions, and collaborations that digital objects enable. There is, though, a distinct and growing class of data objects that enter the dealings of economic actors in the form of commodities; that is, items of exchange traded on the market for a price. Advertising audiences, reputation scores, popularity indexes, and credit records are some typical examples. Data commodities present a few distinctive attributes worth considering in some detail, granted their diffusion and increasing social and economic importance.

Unlike traditional production, distribution, and consumption processes, a data life cycle is rarely planned and executed to end with a ready-to-market product. Data and data objects are never "finished" and data commodities present a stark contrast to traditional commodities in this regard. Essentially a data commodity is a data object that acquires value because of specific market conventions. Unlike other commodities, however, even when data are stabilized into specific structures, such as in the examples reviewed here, data objects obtain only a temporarily bounded stability that is valid along specific dimensions (i.e., number and content of fields or metadata and functions that they execute in a system). Data objects are constantly updated with new data while continuously executing themselves by performing specific functions. As we saw, their utility and strength derive from the communicating and coordinating role that they assume within a system of organized action (e.g., bidding in programmatic advertising). Much like data, data objects are cognitive and communicative artifacts that are relational in nature; they are always linked to something else (e.g., a real event, data, other data objects, technologies, or functions). These characteristics make data objects commodities of a particular kind. They do not respond well to traditional market mechanisms or business models.

In addition, like the fictitious commodities of Polanyi (1944/2001) such as labor, land, and money, data and data objects are not originally produced to be sold in a market, even if they sometimes are. Data are relational in nature because, as we saw earlier in this chapter, they are the by-products of human activities, organizational operations, and machine-to-machine signals. What does this mean for the mechanisms upon which such markets are based? Despite the allure of Polanyi's idea that a market works only insofar as it embeds an economic order as a function of a broader social order, when confronting the fictionality of data and data objects, we are left with the puzzling question of what kind of social order such a market does embed. If anything, this will be an economic order that is based on the characteristics of production, circulation, and consumption of data and data objects, which, as we have seen, bears very little resemblance to the organization and coordination principles of the standard economic order. Even the broader social order that embeds data production is hardly comparable to the well-fenced and well-organized order that Polanyi would have thought of as social order, infiltrated as it is by *data rules*. Consider the data produced by social interaction on social media. What happens online is already a "computed sociality"; that is, a social order assembled ex nihilo by data and data objects and the computational rules that construct the similarities and differences of users (Alaimo & Kallinikos 2017, 2019). When data objects are made commodities and sold to marketers, as in the case of lookalike audiences on social media, their prevailing characteristics still derive from the computational rules and cultural predilections of data and the online environment, rather than from the observations of real-life patterns of consumption.

Given the complex, ambiguous, and mutable characteristics of data and data objects, what kind of principles would such a market follow? How would its actors agree on a measure of value for its commodities? How can a market price something so changeable as a data commodity with no fixed boundaries? Critically, how does a market work when prices are no longer the principal mechanism of coordination?

In general, commodification is implemented by repurposing data and data objects for a given commercial context (i.e., a market opportunity, a client need, or a user behavior). In many settings and industries, the making of data commodities entails automatically recontextualizing and tailor-packaging data objects in real time (Aaltonen et al. 2021; Alaimo & Kallinikos 2021; Lyytinen 2022). However, even in this largely automated universe, where traditional market practices leave space for data rules, commodification remains an ambiguous process.

Emblematic in this respect is the case of programmatic advertising (Alaimo 2022a; Alaimo & Kallinikos 2018). In a data-replete environment where data objects automatically coordinate exchanges, assigning a price to a good is a mechanism that must obey existing conventions, as well as formal logic and data rules. The traditional way to set a price for ads was to count "ad impressions," or ads sent to an individual (Turow 2011). Such an ambiguous definition has been the battleground of contestation and contributed to digital advertising's rush to measurability (does an individual effectively see the ad?) and its price structure. The Cost per Mille (CPM) system counts impressions (e.g., Cluley 2018),[6] but how to count an impression remains a controversial practice. An ad impression does not represent an entity whose existence can be referred to an event outside, tracked, or counted. It needs to be defined with data, parameters, and various other criteria. Programmatic advertising, somewhat reminiscent of the financial instruments of futures (Esposito 2011), constitutes ad impressions as probable events and sells them ahead of being effectively produced (i.e., before ads are even displayed, let alone seen, which is still not possible to track). This means that marketers automatically bid money on the likelihood of an individual user seeing ads, not on the actual viewing of an ad (Alaimo & Kallinikos 2018).

It is important to stress that the possibility of defining an ad impression as such stems from the fact that masses of data are available in real time and to a degree of granularity that captures details at the individual browser level (e.g., time exposure, pixels, and position on the screen). All these data minutiae make sense because they are produced and then assembled, aggregated, and structured to form some-*thing* (a data object) which, even if it does not refer to anything existing out there, acquires a semantic meaning and an essential function for a given field and can be exchanged eventually as a data commodity. In our case, a data object such as an ad impression becomes valuable because it makes a bid request object biddable (i.e., worthy of being bid for). The object's structure encodes attributes such as viewability that give sense and purpose not only to the ad object but also to its exchange value, which is eventually legitimated by the action of the exchange itself (the effective transaction taking place). The case well illustrates the logic at play in digitized and highly automated exchanges, whereby more data and more sophisticated metrics are employed to lend facticity and legitimacy to commodities that, even if they do not exist outside the exchange to which they belong and are not made to be exchanged, nonetheless constitute the basis of the exchange.

What kind of commodities are data objects? The main characteristic of data commodities is their digital relationality. For these fictitious commodities, economic value is linked to hypercomplex operations that often remain hardly accessible to most of the actors involved in the exchange. Data commodities are only loosely coupled with the infrastructures of relations and interaction that generate them and are more dependent on data, metrics, procedures, and rules. These days, commodities can be packaged from repurposed data, from rates, or from the likelihood of future events. They are commodities because they rely on the apparatus of data production, a thick infrastructure of technologies and organizational practices that sustain novel forms of exchange and, as we will see in chapter 8, establish markets that are structured and function differently from what we have known so far.

SUMMARY AND IMPLICATIONS

The ideas outlined in this chapter indicate that a new breed of practices centering on the management, processing, use, and commodification of data have been installed at the core of economic activities and the dealings of organizations. Such practices are increasingly crossing institutional confines. They are performed recurrently across industries in which many actors are engaged in producing, maintaining, and reusing data; negotiating routines, metrics, and standards; exchanging data and data-based objects; and agreeing on the market value of new data commodities. As a result, data that have previously been strictly confined within the specific domains or sectors in which they were initially produced and made sense (e.g., health data, hard science data, social media data, and traffic data), via established practices and professions, are traveling across domain boundaries and become repurposed, repackaged, and frequently combined with other types of data.

It should not come as a surprise that along this journey, data tend to lose their proximity to the facts that they originally signified or represented and the epistemic procedures that constructed those facts. Partly, this is the reason why data work as tokens of signification. As they travel along the gears of production, data become targets of formal and increasingly abstract operations that signify and refer to aggregate and less tangible entities that we call "data objects." Examples include audiences, consumer preferences, traffic patterns, and the like. Data and the objects that they help construct are increasingly detached from existing industries and professions and undergo heavy manipulation by new organizational actors such as data management platforms or data brokers (Martin 2015). Most of the data and data objects are not produced to be sold on a market, Yet when they are, their rendition into data commodities remains ambiguous. Entities such as the attention of users are exchanged in markets that function differently from traditional ones. Massive exchanges happen in real time and are automatically coordinated by opaque technologies and novel intermediaries which, as in the case of Google in the programmatic advertising ecosystem, do not own only the marketplace but also its main demand- and supply-side platforms (Alaimo 2022a). Within these marketplaces, the value of commodities, their prices, and the modalities of their exchange obey data rules rather than traditional market rules and are linked by various feedback loops that are still overlooked and rarely investigated by academics and regulators alike.

Beyond commodification and exchange, unpacking the various entities and operations partaking in the making of data and composing the various operations of data life cycles across contexts becomes essential. By "data life cycles," we do not mean a linear value chain that progresses from a given resource to produce an output. Rather, we point to the complex and interlinked set of cognitive, communicative, and organizational operations that bracket areas of social life and crystallize them into novel social objects. The implications of such a complex undertaking are numerous and not yet well understood. Making data may produce innovation or economic value, but it also creates novel ways to see the world and novel institutions such as automated exchanges that reorganize entire sectors of the economy. Empirical works on these backstage processes of data creation and use are unfortunately scarce (for an exception see, Parmiggiani, Østerlie, & Almklov 2022). The same holds true as far as theorizing of sociocognitive dynamics that emerge from the interplay between data life cycles, technological infrastructures, and novel practices of work and exchange of commodities is concerned.

Investigating the data life cycle also implies understanding how data live, prosper and decay (Brown & Duguid 2000; Swanson 2021). Data are not ready-made or fixed; they are fabricated, constantly edited, and often erased and reborn in other contexts and relations. Data are both corruptible and fallible. Learning about the complexity of data life cycles has implications for assessing when data fail and why, or why some typologies of data make sense only if constantly updated or reused. As data travel, issues linked to their technological corruptibility and cognitive fallibility are likely to multiply. Knowing more about data life cycles becomes crucial to draw distinctions among production processes as they become less bounded to knowledge specialization and rely more on data. Some of these issues bear significant consequences for data governance, the regulation of data and data production, and will be discussed in chapters 5 and 8.

Data life cycles do not exist in a vacuum. Communities of data provision and use (Swanson 2021) are constantly forming novel alliances which, in some cases, position themselves as alternatives to the current status quo of institutions and industries. The example of music production and distribution exemplifies the transformations that a sector undergoes when such alternatives mature. As data and data objects become the principal objects of work and organizing across industries, novel data practices infiltrate the very fabric of organizing and the relations that organizations maintain with one another. This shift is becoming more diffuse today because the objectification of procedures and scripts embedded in the makeup and functioning of data and data objects are no longer the result of internal coordination and administrative work (Chandler 1977), nor do they derive from market mechanisms. Rather, they are linked to more comprehensive, often ecosystem-level processes and infrastructural constraints (e.g., protocols, standards, national regulations, and industry negotiations) that feed back to organizations and markets alike. We will return to these fundamental changes in chapters 6 and 8.

The last implication of this chapter is that the value of data and data objects is not a given. Commodification is the process through which the value of data and data objects is negotiated, legitimized, and embedded into specific sociotechnical mechanisms of exchange that overwrite existing market rules. It is important to avoid wholesale attributions of value to any kind of data at any stage of their production process and rather question how such value attributions often reify markets. A critical perspective on data commodification would help sidestep gross simplifications (e.g., "more data, more value") and point toward a more sustainable approach for regulating the contemporary data-driven economy and society. We turn to these central issues over the next few chapters.

5 TECHNOLOGIES OF DIFFERENCE: EXCURSUS ON SURVEILLANCE

Along with the positive prospects that they might open, data and the technologies that support data generation, circulation, and use have frequently been recognized as user-tracking and behavior-monitoring instruments, raising several knotty problems of data governance. How data from people's whereabouts and interactions on the Internet, social media, and commercial platforms are generated, accessed, shared, and used poses significant social and political challenges in most contemporary societies (Couldry & Mejias 2019; Obendiek 2023; Schwartz 2019). The scale of these operations and their intrusive and often opaque nature make them uneasy companions to vital democratic ideals and freedoms (Nissenbaum 2004, 2010; Zuboff 2015, 2019).

The troubling prospects of tracking and surveillance have been around for quite a while (see, e.g., Clarke 1988; Hildebrandt & Gutwirth 2008; Hildebrandt & Rouvroy 2011; Lyon 2001; Mayer-Schönberger, 2009; Nissenbaum 2004, 2010; Turow 2011), but they broke forcefully into the public awareness in connection with the 2018 Cambridge Analytica scandal.[1] Far from being an isolated incident, this case made widely evident the uneasy institutional repercussions of the regular use of data about individuals for political and economic purposes. Shortly before the incident, in 2016, the European Union (EU) introduced the General Data Protection Regulation (GDPR),[2] a comprehensive legal framework that established user consent and a host of other restrictions as prerequisites for the use of personal data by businesses and other institutional actors. Threats to individual freedoms obviously emerge from the exercise of power across the spectrum of political and economic institutions. Yet user tracking and monitoring have routinely been associated with the functional anatomy of the digital economy and the regular intertwinement of the operations of economic organizations with the ordinary pursuits of people and their domestic affairs. In this regard, data governance and privacy link to matters of economic power and the degree to which control over the generation and use of data may confer disproportionate economic benefits and be conducive to economic concentration and empire building (e.g., Brynjolfsson & McAfee 2014; Cennamo 2021; Saura, Ribeiro-Soriano, & Palacios-Marqués 2021). It thus comes hardly as a surprise that several other EU economic policy initiatives, such as the Digital Markets Act (DMA) and the Digital Services Act (DSA),[3] have followed suit in recent years.

Whether and how these regulatory measures can be enforced to alleviate the social, economic, and political concerns that evolve around both privacy and economic performance are issues that fall outside the remit of this book (see, e.g., Hildebrandt 2019; Saura et al. 2021; Schwartz 2019). The ideas that we put forward in this chapter instead discuss the quest for data regulation against the widespread concerns of an emerging society of surveillance. Intervening upon the terms by which data are produced, circulated, and used, we claim, requires a persistent meditation on the type of artifacts that data are and how they partake of and condition innovation, value creation, and welfare. Short of understanding the variety of cognitive and communicative functions that data perform in economy and society, data regulation may produce meager or even undesirable effects. The chapter is therefore more concerned with how regulation should be framed and approached when data are the objects of legislation than making specific propositions regarding how the production and use of data should be regulated. Here, we explore how the quest for intervening in the institutional system of relations underlying data generation and use can be understood from the perspective put forward in the preceding chapters. Can the claims that we have advanced concerning the nature of data and the functions that they perform in economy and society be drawn upon to reframe and enrich this debate, and if so, how? Conversely, can the ways by which institutional risks, individual rights, and the anatomy of the digital economy have been hitherto discussed be drawn upon to qualify our claims?

We begin our exposition by addressing the difficulties of separating data tracking and monitoring from the background of technological, social, and economic relations in which they occur. These difficulties, we suggest, are aggravated by the subtle nature of the cognitive and communicative functions that data assume in the lives of people and the operations of organizations and institutions, making intervention upon the process of data production, exchange, and use a tricky undertaking. This is followed by the discussion of surveillance in terms that go beyond the "Big Brother" deadlock of watching and being watched. Drawing from Foucault and other eminent scholars (e.g., Desrosières 1998; Hacking 1999), we contrast the Big Brother approach to the concept of surveillance that emerged during modernity, which we claim make up a complex relational or interactive game whereby those subjected to it are required to be active and, critically, capable participants. Approaching surveillance in these terms allows us to be critical, and yet at the same time, it allows us to account for the risks and opportunities associated with the irrevocable diffusion of digital technologies and the generation and use of digital data. Most important, it enables us to move the discussion forward by reconsidering some of the motives that insert data into everyday life. We do so in the next section, where we examine how the technological and institutional matrix in which the diffusion of data is embedded challenges the modern separation of society into distinct spheres (e.g., economy, politics, and personal and domestic life) and blurs the difference between economic transactions and social interactions. We finish with a few reflections on these pathbreaking developments and the need to ground regulation in an adequate understanding of what data are and how they work as agents of social and economic change.

THE INSTITUTIONAL MATRIX OF DATA

A good deal of the data used for user tracking and monitoring is generated through online purchases, Internet browsing, social media participation, Internet of Things (IoT)–based service consumption, use of smart phones, intelligent devices, and wearables, among others (Greenfield 2017; Lyytinen & Yoo 2002; Turow 2011). The generation of data by these means extends the range of data about individuals far beyond the traditional confines of personal information (e.g., employment, gender, income, and health records) and contributes to establishing a historically unique context in which people are essentially profiled through data automatically produced by their devices, their clicks, browseovers, and social networks. The quest for regulating the conditions under which personal data (in this broad sense) are generated, traded, and used has emerged against this backdrop.[4]

Straightforward as the objective of this quest may seem, achieving it is a far more complex undertaking. To begin with, user tracking and monitoring are hard to dissociate from the background of relations in which personal data are routinely generated. More generally, these difficulties stem from the sociocultural context in which the use of digital devices and online media and participation are embedded and the diffuse habits, cultural schemes, and modes of conduct with which the provision of commercial services and the operations of economic organizations are intertwined. In many cases, the diffusion of data and data tracking and monitoring are the by-product of the same infrastructural arrangements that allow Internet browsing, online purchases, IoT-based service provision and consumption, and social media participation. While these arrangements and practices are variously shaped by the business objectives that they serve, they have not emerged all of a sudden. They are themselves sustained by the wider technological and sociocultural developments that have made the Internet the communication and interaction backbone of current societies and contributed to the formation of several of the habits and predispositions that characterize our time.

Looked at closely, it would seem a complex (surgical, as it were) operation to pull apart individual tracking and monitoring from the technological infrastructures, diffuse modes of conduct, and the institutional and business practices in which these illicit activities occur. The subtlety of this surgical operation is further aggravated by the fact that the technological developments that made the Internet the communication and interaction backbone of current societies, and data the ever-present companion of social practices, have themselves grown out of and are strongly reinforced by the long-standing social demands to mark, represent, remember, know, and communicate in ways that transcend the bounds of situated encounters (Gleick 2011; Kallinikos 1995, 2010; Searle 1995), as discussed in chapters 1–3. In this regard, the diffusion of data in modern times reflects a variety of strategies of cognition that establish the conditions for modes of knowing and acting that otherwise would have been hard, if not impossible, to pursue (Beniger 1986; Latour 1986, 1987). Placed in this larger time frame, the intervention on the premises of data generation and use runs the risk of interfering not simply with specific economic and institutionally embedded practices of monitoring and targeting but the entire span of conditions with which these practices are associated. Addressing these issues, therefore, requires not simply adequate understanding of the most recent technology-driven developments but also an appreciation of the long-standing trends that have rendered data a systemic component of economy and society and a diffuse element of cultural, social, and economic activities.

These observations indicate that data regulation must be built on the recognition of data as pervasive artifacts that perform significant cognitive and communicative functions that are refracted throughout the sociocultural and economic fabric. The use of data for economic purposes cuts across the ordinary divide of economy and society and links social interactions to the operations of economic institutions. As most signs, data are relational elements. Their cognitive and communicative value grows (or declines) in connection with the cognitive and communicative relations that they enter and the flows in which they are embedded. Separating data tracking and monitoring from the multitude of flows that sustain personal and institutional patterns of living is far more difficult and complex undertaking than it may initially seem. Wholesale designations such as those of surveillance capitalism seldom help navigate these perplexing questions constructively. Often, addressing these issues calls for the collaboration of many experts and the awareness that any intervention may have significant trade-offs between competing practices and value orders such as freedom and the right to self-determination, security, efficiency, innovation, health, and justice (Obendiek 2023). These matters can hardly be coped with by legislating the premises by which data are generated and shared alone.

How can these claims be drawn upon to reframe and enrich the debate on data regulation? To start with, the variety of functions that data perform as diffuse sociocultural and economic elements need to be adequately represented in the discourses on data regulation (e.g., Nissenbaum 2004; Schwartz 2019; Voigt & Von dem Bussche 2017). Regulation needs to operate between Scylla and Charybdis; that is, it should be effective against illicit data practices and yet cautious about the possible wider and often unintended consequences of such interventions. The acute problems of tracking and surveillance besieging current societies cannot be addressed on the assumption that data are just pervasive tools for surveilling and monitoring. Urgency does not justify simplification. It is an unfortunate fact that current public discourses frame data simplistically, as hardwired technical elements with relatively unambiguous signifying and representing qualities. The alternative offered by economists is to define data as fixed, ready-made resources that can be extracted, accumulated, traded on a market (commodities), and automatically associated with value. None of these approaches does justice to the gamut of functions that data perform for organizations and individuals and the relations out of which their cognitive and communicative functions are reinforced and performed. None of the assumptions underlying these approaches adequately reflect the diversity of economic and institutional relations and processes to which data contribute, both by being a central component of innovation and a pervasive element of the production of wealth (Beniger 1986; Kallinikos, Hasselbladh, & Márton 2013; Swanson 2021).

We elaborate on these ideas in significant detail over the next chapters, particularly in chapter 8. It suffices here to say that the narrow perception of data as technical, unambiguous signs or resources that can be owned, packaged, and traded as is any other resource not only simplifies the web of relations in which data are embedded but also misconstrues the interactive complexity that makes data indispensable and pervasive elements of social life and the processes of value creation. Data are part and parcel of an ecology of diversified operations in which data pass through several stages of development, distributed across various business operations and actors. This distributed ecology of data joins hands with their cognitive and communicative performances to establish a context in which data production and use become highly complex achievements that entail the active encoding (what data should represent and how) of facts in standardized formats, and various roles and operations whereby standardized data are aggregated, shared between different stakeholders, combined, subtracted, and computed on a nearly permanent basis (Alaimo et al. 2020). This complex, often backstage, and distributed data work is unduly oversimplified whenever data are treated, wittingly or unwittingly, as *technical elements*, *unambiguous carriers of facts*, or ready-made *resources*. What runs the risk of being compromised is the functioning of data as variable filters of perception, epistemic tools of institutional knowing processes, and communication media. Before being discrete entities used to track and monitor, data are complex artifacts through which tracking and monitoring tasks are perceived and organized and relationships and interactions are carried out.

As it is often the case, all these operations happen in a stratified topology of relations in which economic actors occupy distinct positions. Those with a central position in these flows can use that position to build up market power, restrict access to the common pool of interactions that generate data, and eventually use or share whatever data are generated in ways that promote their own objectives. A glance at the economic landscape of our time confirms these ill-fated prospects (Power 2022). The risk of empire building is pervasive and speaks to the need to establish a regulative order that impedes the self-reinforcing processes whereby economic power begets more power and extinguishes competition. At the same time, it is of utmost importance to uphold the variable nature of the operations in which the production and use of data are embedded. Designing meaningful interventions confronts the delicate issue of maintaining the variety of functions that data perform, along with the interactive complexity and operational interdependencies from which they emerge. Attributing the complex, backstage data work and the delicate interactions that it entails to a reified notion of control over data unduly misrepresents the complexity of economic life and the machinery of technological and cognitive operations through which data partake in innovation and the production of wealth. To put it bluntly, platform ecosystems that rely on data to innovate and create value cannot be regulated as traditional organizations (see more on this in chapter 8).

We recognize that simplifications in the perception of data are often inevitable in the pragmatic context of regulation and policymaking and the compromises that they entail. We are also keenly aware that legal scholars, policymakers, economists, and other experts approach the relevant matters from the concepts and perspectives of their fields that provide them focus, disciplined conversation, and cumulative outcomes. Yet understanding data and the functions that they perform in the lives of individuals, the economy, and society requires thinking outside the box. Misrepresentation of the cognitive, interactive, and economic complexity by which data are linked to the production of wealth and innovation is harmful to all and should be avoided. It may be worth adding here that the quest for regulation cannot be advanced from a point outside the economy and society. Such a neutral, Archimedean point (Arendt 1959) does not exist. Addressing who has the license to speak for, represent, and act for others in these contexts is a delicate matter in democratic and nonpaternalistic societies. The quest for regulation rarely represents society. It usually reechoes compromises between diverse sectional interests and pursuits, as anyone familiar with the realities of GDPR and other EU regulatory initiatives knows.

We analyze in considerable detail the restructuring of the process of value creation within and across organizations over the next three chapters. It is worthwhile nonetheless to reiterate here that the ways by which data are involved in knowledge discovery, value creation, and innovation defy the perception of data as bounded entities—things, as it were—that can be put in siloes, preserved, or ported. While data making requires cognitive categories, proper formats, and technical standards that allow easy registration and retrieval, both the innovative uses of data and the creation of wealth out of data are much more complex and adventurous undertakings. As in most creative contexts, discovery and innovation call for quickly available data turnarounds that allow the exploration of different versions of the world. These conditions enable rehearsing, exchanging, and combining data to develop new goods, establish new processes, and, generally, find modes for piercing the ordinary unfolding of standardized economic operations (Weick 1979; Zittrain 2008) that favor exploitation at the expense of exploration, short-term thinking, and local adaptation instead of confronting the wider forces that shape the course of events in the long term (March 1991, 2006).

These observations suggest that innovation requires widespread access, exchange, and use of data within and between organizations, but also across the private-public divide, as the ideal and practice of open data make evident. Regulative restrictions that do not reflect the varied performances of data in social and economic contexts and inhibit rather than facilitate the interactive relations, and data flows out of which such performances emerge may endanger mechanisms of data innovation and wealth creation and turn out to be as harmful as exclusive control over the generation and use of data would be (Peukert et al. 2022; Swanson 2021). Regulation undoubtedly represents an opportunity for correcting whatever distorts the course of events generates, including how competition erodes and, ultimately, extinguishes competition. However, without an adequate understanding of the nature of data and the processes by which data are implicated in innovation and the production of wealth, regulation may end up imposing artificial and cumbersome restrictions that complicate people's lives, impede rather than promote innovation, and hamper the production of wealth, welfare and, ultimately, justice.

SURVEILLANCE AND AFTER

Much of the debate on data regulation and governance is animated by concerns about surveillance in which data are assumed to play a central role. Despite its relatively recent revival associated with digital tracking, monitoring, and targeting, the notion of surveillance has been around for quite a while. In popular imagery and across much of the social sciences, the diffuse perception of surveillance is that it is a rather sinister practice that must be resisted. Those that seek to exercise it should therefore be exposed, critiqued, and ultimately rendered accountable to social values and institutions (Lyon 2001, 2007). In this view of the world, the forces of democracy must resist the ominous practices of surveillance. The standard recipe has accordingly been to work toward limiting its exercise by law, policy regulations, and institutional reforms.

Placed in the broader context of modernity, however, surveillance acquires additional and somewhat perplexing connotations that move it away from the perception of a zero-sum game with transparency and democracy. From such a historical purview, surveillance is centrally linked to the construction of the modern institutional order, as well as the establishment and diffusion of formal and hierarchically structured institutions like industrial firms, hospitals, and schools. The adequate functioning of such institutions requires knowledge and capabilities at the top, but also throughout the system of jobs and roles that underlies their operative fabric. The practices of control and surveillance that are characteristic of these institutions work in tandem with diffuse capability building and the empowerment of those over which they are exercised. As expounded in earlier chapters, knowledge development and expertise in industrial firms, hospitals, and educational organizations have been historically associated with the advent of numeracy and the spread of quantitative methodologies and other tracking techniques. These developments facilitated description, cumulative observations, and comparisons across time and settings and enabled courses of action that otherwise would have been difficult, if not impossible, to realize (Chandler 1977; Cline-Cohen 1982; Desrosières 1998; Foucault 1977, 1980; Hacking 1990; Porter 1995; Rose 1991). Industrial firms, schools, and hospitals are good illustrations of the double-edged nature of surveillance and the tensions, multidimensional nature, and far-reaching social and institutional implications that surveilling practices bring about. Thus understood, surveillance is a pervasive principle that constructs abilities as much as it invents controlling practices.

Framing surveillance in these terms tells the history of ruling practices in modern times and recounts the logic and broader processes by which modern society and its institutions, including forms of being human, have been built and operated. Often associated with the work of Michel Foucault (1977, 1980, 1988, 1990), such an understanding of surveillance has been widely used across the social sciences as a framework (or sometimes as just a root metaphor) for investigating a good deal of power relations, governance practices, and the formation and reproduction of institutions, both in the broader social sciences (e.g., Burchell, Gordon, & Miller 1991; Dean 1999; Desrosières 1998; Donzelot 2008; Dreyfus & Rabinow 1982; Hacking 1986; Lemke 2015) and within management and organization studies (Hoskin & Macve 1986; Hasselblad & Kallinikos 2000; Kallinikos 1996; Miller & O'Leary 1987; Power 1997, 2000; Zuboff 1988). The relevant research is now vast, and the body of literature that it has produced is hardly surveyable. A few quick observations, however, could be made that help unravel the ambiguous nature of surveillance and the ways that it works as both a principle of control and a generative force of social relations and institutional patterns.

The mutually reinforcing links between power and knowledge, control and empowerment that have been at the core of Foucault's (1980) work have been taken further by Ian Hacking and his study of the dynamic character of the interactive loops that tie together power holders and those that they seek to monitor and rule (Hacking 1986, 1999). In a way roughly like what we have described as knowledge and capability building, the unfolding of institutional practices (in health care, education, immigration, and unemployment policies) requires institutions to provide the resources, systems of knowledge, and opportunities that enable people to enact the roles that these practices seek to promote. This provision is an act of building rather than an act of depriving, conducive to subjugation and control. The enactment of the roles and their rights and obligations is thus seldom a passive or mechanical performance. It often gives rise to a dynamic whereby institutional practices are brought to bear on people's behavior, constantly calibrated and changed to reflect lessons from experience. Rather than remaining external to one another, the bonds that tie institutions and power holders with those they seek to monitor introduce interactive loops and dynamics that make their relationship relatively open, recursive, and, crucially, generative and evolving.

The dynamics of the interactive loops to which surveillance practices give rise have often been obscured by the negative framing of surveillance and the flatter perception of the term that recounts George Orwell's Big Brother imagery, or at least the ways that imagery has been broadly interpreted. While resistance, superficial conformance, or even gaming of institutional practices and the monitoring objectives that they instantiate are frequent, the corresponding processes tend to acquire over time attributes of a far more complex, substantial, and ambiguous dynamic that entail mutually reinforcing loops. As surveillance practices unfold, those that exercise it and those subject to it substantially alter their behavior, learn and develop their capabilities, and reshape their goals and practices. In this sense, surveillance helps expose a dynamic beyond the deadlock of observer and observed, while providing the means for investigating how social roles are fashioned and institutions established and maintained (Espeland & Stevens 1998, 2008; Espeland & Sauder 2007; Hacking 1986, 1999). The performance metrics of current academia and the ways that it has shaped the institutions of higher education and academic life over the last few decades represent a good example of this process and the complex dynamics that it entails.

Placed against this backdrop, the widespread view of surveillance (á la Big Brother) spawned around the technological conditions of tracking, monitoring, and targeting tells only a small portion of the overall innovation, knowledge, behavioral dynamics, and institutional change with which the generation and use of data are associated. Much in the spirit of ideas outlined in the preceding chapters of this book (e.g., Desrosières 1998; Hacking 1986, 1990; Foucault 1977, 1980, 1988), we consider data production and use as generative forces of personal and institutional (social and economic) relations rather than simply the outcome of an external and powerful machinery of economic and political exploitation. This is not to say that such practices of exploitation do not exist. Neither does this view of ours deny empire building and the power that key economic actors of our time have accumulated, processes that must be rendered democratically accountable. All it claims is that such a conservative and ideologically driven view of surveillance can hardly contribute to illuminating the functional anatomy of the digital economy and the epistemic and communicative constitution of current capitalism. Such an intellectual undertaking calls for the detailed deconstruction and assessment of the fabric of relations that involve data in the production of wealth (the production and trading of goods), but also the making of habits, modes of conduct, and, ultimately, identities (see, e.g., Levy 2023; Power 2022).

The ways by which economic institutions make themselves relevant to their environments and, ultimately, profitable these days require the steady detection of differences that map how people move and choose and relate to things and to one another. Such an objective can hardly be achieved apart from a complex and potent machinery that generates data on nearly everything, compares and computes these data to construct relations, and infer possible courses of action on a real-time basis (Kallinikos 2007, 2009a, 2009b). How this machinery works is not well tuned with the classic image of an omniscient center that observes, retains, and controls it all. Search engines are typical examples of how this system operates and makes itself relevant and, eventually, profitable. Each query adds to previous queries, and each result page qualifies further queries and its results in a global game that is revised and extended minute by minute. Recommender systems are another case in point. A user choice is added to its past choices and qualifies them, a recommendation is calculated through comparisons with past decisions and other users' decisions, and on and on. Predictive maintenance, learning analytics, audience making, traffic-monitoring systems, programmatic advertising, and dynamic pricing provide other examples of this machinery and help expose the operative logic and functional anatomy of the digital economy.

None of these technologies and systems can work without this ever-present game of comparisons of data items out of which differences are made and further propagated. User tracking, monitoring, and targeting are intrinsic to that game. People are given the chance, the facilities, the knowledge, and the incentives to participate in the process, but it would be a misperception to consider user tracking, monitoring, and targeting the ultimate goal of the game. In some interesting ways, these practices and the technologies of data and computing that sustain them generate *machineries of difference* whose relevance and power derive from their ability to spot, encode, and compute many of the proliferating contingencies characteristic of the current world and turn them into opportunities for action, and further for the production and consumption of goods (Kallinikos 2009b). At the same time, people draw massively from these data to carry out their daily duties and interact and shape relations with others in a global and quickly shifting world. Viewed in these terms, data make themselves an inescapable companion of people's lives; diffuse means for interacting, communicating, and learning; and ultimately means for generating differences and constructing identities.

Short of examining the distinct patterns through which data and digital technologies restructure the production machinery of current societies, the functions of its institutions, and the patterns of daily living, the concepts of surveillance and control remain dubious allies to the critical analysis of the emerging socioeconomic order. The generation and use of data in the current world are anything but accidental. Tracking, as exposed in chapter 4, always partially constructs the events that it records. The entire game is predicated upon the massive introduction of *contingencies* (circumstantial details) into economic, institutional, and personal relations, as well as the consequent move away from stable orders and grand narratives. Such a cultural orientation recounts a deeply ingrained belief that the comprehensive mapping of billions of events encoded to data contributes to better tuning people, organizations, and society to the diversity that they confront. One may remain ambiguous vis-à-vis the relevance and worth of such a cultural orientation. At the same time, it is crucial to understand the complex historical origins from which data and information, probability rather than certainty, have emerged as the stuff upon which economic, societal, and personal critical decisions are made (Hacking 1990). Regulation and data governance must reflect these inexorable realities and combat the quick and unreflective use of terms such as power, control, and surveillance.

PERSONAL AND INSTITUTIONAL WORLDS

The developments outlined in the preceding two sections suggest that the boundaries that separated domestic and communal life from the broader world of politics, economy, and society are no longer as effective as they might have been in the past (Alaimo & Kallinikos 2017; Greenfield 2017). It has been an essential ideal of the modern social order to safeguard the integrity of individual and family life and protect it from unsolicited external intrusions. Since early modernity, such an ideal has been systematically pursued through institutional reforms, law making, and the building of social conventions (Hildebrandt 2015). Much of the current debate on privacy is built on the assumption that such an ideal can still be maintained. It is a widespread belief that the diffusion of data and the tracking and targeting of individual pursuits can be kept within largely determinable confines and, ultimately, regulated in ways that avoid the violation of key modern values linked to the integrity of individual and family life (see, e.g., Nissenbaum 2004, 2010, 2011; Schwartz 2019).

The notion that law and policy conventions can erect protective walls around individuals and their homes makes sense to the extent that personal and domestic life remains adequately separate from the broader economy and society. As already suggested, such an assumption is no longer warranted, if it ever was (Zelizer 2005). It does not take much to see that homes are currently transformed into data and information "centers" as various digital systems, technologies, and devices remake daily and domestic living patterns in ways that data and television (Wu 2016) would hardly have ever imagined. Streaming media and technologies, along with IoT-based services and artificial intelligence (AI) solutions, join hands with the pervasive use of smart phones, tablets, and wearables to establish a context in which the space of domestic living and of the human body is traversed massively, daily, by a variety of data and information flows. It is legitimate to wonder how far such forces can be contained and the diversity of practices that they bring about regulated. Much in the spirit of the ideas advanced in the preceding two sections, we view the ongoing transformation of contemporary homes to data and information sites as the unequivocal signals of far-reaching shifts in cultural understandings, habits, and the practices of conducting one's life. Individuals and families are not just the passive targets of the powerful technological and economic forces that drive the relevant developments, but also essential actors through which such forces operate.

These developments could be viewed as an instance of the colonization of individual, domestic, and even communal life by the economic and institutional forces that drive the production and use of data (Couldry & Mejias 2019; Ekbia & Nardi 2017; Greenfield 2017). To use good old Habermas's jargon, one could claim that the system world of data and the technological and economic interests that it embodies take precedence over the lifeworld (Habermas 1985). Such a framing, however, bears the indelible mark of nostalgia that obscures the mutated dynamics that tie together individual life patterns and social interactions with the structural world of economy, technology, and society. The imprint of the technological and economic forces upon the social and cultural context of data-impregnated societies ought to be given sharper analytic outlines than the idea of life-world colonization suggests. The recursive loops that link the structural world of economy, technology, and society with personal and communal life call for a closer examination of the making of daily life patterns; that is, an examination that does justice to the sweeping changes that have occurred since the Internet has become the commercial but also the inter-actional and communication backbone of current societies and ubiquitous technologies (smart phones, tablets, wearables) turned into inescapable companions of ordinary living.

We do not deny that our times are marked by the deeply seated infil-tration of social and personal relations by the broader forces of technology, economy, and society. This is too evident to forgo. We maintain, however, that it is misleading to view these changes as the straightforward imposi-tion of the external imperative of profit upon the lives of people and their priorities. Rather than being passive targets of power or dopes of a society and economy that are made by others, individuals and families draw upon the data and the world that data help put in place to fashion their lives, conduct their duties, and understand themselves and others (Alaimo & Kallinikos 2017, 2019b; Greenfield 2017). Whatever elements of economic exploitation and subjugation these processes entail, they never suffice to explain the character of the interactive loops through which broader forces unfold across the variable frontiers of ordinary life. If the ideas of alien-ation, false consciousness, and consumer society have lost their grip on the social imaginary, it is also because they remain too remote from the battles of ordinary living and the patterns that tie together economic and institu-tional worlds and people's whereabouts.

A case could therefore be made that the changes that mark our time are not running in only one direction, from the economy to the social world. These changes attest that the economy itself is cast in an entirely new opera-tive context, pervaded by cultural and social concerns that take economic operations out of their traditional confines. One of the most conspicuous manifestations of these developments is the preeminence of social media in current societies and their economic (and political) power. Social media are not just technology-based sites of self-presentation, networking, and relation-ship building (boyd 2015 boyd & Ellison 2008). Neither are they just sites of personal data exploitation. They are central socioeconomic arrangements through which social interaction becomes a major force for creating economic value (Alaimo & Kallinikos 2017; Gerlitz & Helmond 2013; Helmond 2015). Viewed in these terms, the advent of social media to power is anything but accidental. Through social media, the economy extends itself to operations and settings that it could hardly have imagined in the age of mass media (Napoli 2011; Wu 2016). In doing so, it is itself subjected to other forces and rationalities. If social media shape the private sphere, the private sphere shapes the economy through social media by infiltrating the rationality of economic operations with concerns that pivot around the management of people's interactions on social media and the data that they generate. The same holds true for the entire Internet (Turow 2011) and the intertwinement of economic transactions with computation and communication occasioned by its diffusion (see chapter 3).

The notion that the economy cannot stand on its own, apart from the social and cultural forces that shape it, is widespread in social science scholarship. In varying formats and along different lines of argumentation, such an idea has been proposed by celebrated social science scholars such as Polanyi (1944/2001) and Hirschman (1977, 1982) and later Granovetter (1985, 2017), Granovetter and Swedberg (2018), and Tilly (1984, 2001), among others. The underlying commonality of these great scholars' reflections concerns the social roots of the economy and the variety of ways in which social and cultural preoccupations form the background of economic relations.

What is currently at stake instead is the blurring of whatever differences economic action and exchange maintained vis-à-vis social interaction and communal life more generally. The pervasive economic use of data derived from social media, the Internet, and other online social settings could be interpreted as a signal of the fact that social interaction does not simply condition economic action and exchange but becomes the frontier, as it were, in which innovation and the production of wealth take place. It can always be disputed whether these changes make any difference to the steamroller that is economic rationality and the imperatives of profit and market power at the heart of economic action and exchange. However, something new seems to be at stake here, even though the precise outlines of what is going on may be hard to foresee. Economic operations are not simply instances of resource transformations (even intangible resources such as knowledge) and remain no longer distinct and separate from those of the interactive order (Knorr Cetina & Bruegger 2002). They are pervaded by concerns that increasingly blur the differences between the economy and other social spheres (e.g., Heller 1999; Luhmann 1982; Walzer 1983) and renegotiate the rationalities that have underlain each of these social functions or spheres.

It is certainly possible to argue that the differences that have been supposed to separate the economy from the social world and the conduct of ordinary life have never had the sharp status ascribed to them at the apex of the modern social order (e.g., Luhmann 1982; Walzer 1983). Social boundaries never exactly obtain the tight proof separations of physical things. The construction of social roles and divisions is both a fragile and revocable achievement. In her critique of the "hostile worlds" argument, Zelizer (2005) shows that the view of the economy and personal living as irreconcilable orders is a social science simplification. Such a view tends to overlook the actual social patterns and practices through which people have always sought to bridge the demands of intimacy with those of the economy (e.g., life insurance policies, dowry arrangements, and inheritance law). Zelizer's observations are reminiscent of the need to be more circumspect when abstracting and theorizing social relations. Her account also asks us to study the web of practices and relations out of which daily orders are sustained and intermingle with the broader systems by which they are encircled.

These insightful observations certainly moderate but hardly undo the tensions existing between the world of intimate relations and the structural forces that condition them. Neither do they account for their variable manifestations across different compartments of life, societies, and historical periods. The conflation of technological, economic, and personal worlds outlined in this chapter requires thinking about privacy and the integrity of personal life in terms that do justice to the ambiguous status of the developments underway. While part of the process of self making may remain incalculable, and thus beyond the shaping power of the technological-economic complex (see, e.g., Hildebrandt 2019), a good deal of it has increasingly been made visible and insertable into the operations of that complex (Power 2022).

SUMMARY AND IMPLICATIONS

The arguments put forward in this chapter interrogate some of the assumptions upon which the quest for data regulation is predicated. The most flawed of these assumptions concerns the perception of data as technical elements or resources that can be regulated along well-established lines. Such a narrow perception of data overlooks both the broader sociocultural shifts that made data a ubiquitous accompaniment of people's lives and the institutional matrix of relations in which data perform various cognitive and epistemic operations that are critical to innovation and the production of wealth. Equally unsatisfactory is the prosaic perception of surveillance as primarily a force of control, selective targeting, and personal diminution that usually drives the quest for data regulation. Drawing upon the work of many of the scholars that have inspired our understanding of the role of data in shaping the modern social order, we have briefly retraced in this chapter the intrinsic dynamics that govern the relations of those over whom surveillance is exercised with those that wield it. Surveillance, we have claimed, controls but also builds up the institutions and relations that empower those over which it is exercised. From this point of view, data tracking and behavior monitoring constitute only one aspect of a much richer sociocultural and technological paradigm shift that constructs novel forms of living and organizing. Understanding the morphology and diversity of those forms and asking whether they are sustainable, fair, and for whom may offer a more constructive way forward. The need to extend our understanding of data is further reinforced by the transformations of the patterns by which personal and institutional worlds, domestic life versus economic operations, bear upon one another. The conditions under which data are currently generated and used traverse the boundaries that once seemed to separate social interactions and the conduct of daily living from the broader societal and economic contexts. Under these conditions, the feasibility of raising protective walls around individuals and their homes becomes questionable.

Taken together, these ideas justify the claim that data regulation as a policy and legal project rests on rather inadequate foundations that underestimate the polyvalent involvement of data in people's lives and simplify the matrix of relations in which data perform functions critical to innovation and the production of wealth. Resting on such inadequate foundations, the quest and practice of data regulation do not exactly forebode constructive outcomes. Let it be clear in these concluding remarks that we do not advocate a neoliberal stance of light regulation. Neither do we underestimate the formative and forward-looking effects of law and policymaking (Lessig 2001). All we claim is that such effects have no chance of producing constructive social and economic outcomes if the complexity of the relationships that they aspire to shape is misconstrued. Whatever data regulation is put in place must, in some way or another, reflect the cognitive, epistemic, and communication performances of data and how data, after a long-standing evolution, came to be deeply wired into the lives of people and the operations of economic organizations.

There are many reasons why such analytic insights tend to be set aside. Some of them reflect the pragmatic circumstances surrounding regulation and policymaking and others are linked to the privileged institutional position and occasional arrogance of law. Still others recount the institutional and disciplinary fragmentation of regulation and the prescriptive horizons of legal and economic perspectives that quickly reify and black-box the technological forces and the institutional processes by which data are made pervasive accompaniments of current ways of living.

We are aware that these ideas of ours have a slim chance of being heard by practitioners and policymakers. Our analysis is mostly meant to appeal to social scientists to study the perplexing issues that the deep involvement of data in social and economic affairs raises beyond the fashionable, the apparent, or the feasible. Social developments are slow and torturous. Exposing some of the limitations of the prevailing discourses on regulation might, in the long run, bring positive outcomes concerning how we understand data and, thanks to such an understanding, how we might wish to interfere with the terms by which they are generated, circulated, accessed, and used.

II SOCIAL AND ECONOMIC TRANSFORMATIONS

6 DECENTERING ORGANIZATIONS: DATA, KNOWLEDGE, AND INSTITUTIONAL CHANGE

In the preceding chapters, we outlined the social, economic, and managerial origins of data and analyzed the technological and organizational innovations that have made digital data into diffuse sociocultural elements and critical media by which economic facts are encoded, structured, communicated, and exchanged (Borgmann 1999; Swanson 2022). It is evident from these chapters that the functions that data currently perform in organizations and the broader economy extend far beyond the traditional confines of administration and performance control. In a large and growing variety of occasions, data furnish the semiotic and epistemic means through which organizational facts are filtered and registered, relationships are articulated and analyzed, and actions become instrumented and carried out (Alaimo & Kallinikos 2021; Power 2022). In yet other situations, data enter the dealings of social and economic actors as items of market exchange (e.g., media attention metrics, credit or reputation scores, ratings, and rankings) and, in this regard, essentially become commodities (Aaltonen, Alaimo, & Kallinikos 2021; Napoli 2011; Turow 2011). The line that separates the former from the latter is thin and often traversed.

The environment in which a good deal of organizations operate is irreversibly marked by the growing economic and functional importance of a bewildering array of data relayed into the economy by diverse actors such as social media sites, commercial and industrial platforms, Internet of Things (IoT) systems and applications, data aggregators and rating institutions, starts-ups of various kinds, online communities, and analytics companies, among others. This disperse, heterogenous, and frequently shifting reality in which data are key elements cannot be accommodated by the organizational arrangements that have historically been associated with the standardization of the production process and the pursuit of cost reduction through scale economies of predesigned product items and mass customization strategies (Lyytinen 2022). Taken together, these developments bring about significant transformations in the modes of producing and delivering goods, along with shifts in the perception of value itself.

The more thorough appreciation of this epochal change calls for revisiting the central position that the modern business enterprise has occupied in the production machinery of the industrial and early information economy. In this chapter, we undertake this task by first reappraising the foundations upon which the modern business enterprise has been constructed as a bounded and concentrated system, and subsequently exposing the challenges that it presently confronts due to the developments outlined in this volume. Building on the preceding chapters, we analyze the mechanisms by which data of large variety and fluctuating relevance reweave the fabric of the production of wealth and redefine the conditions under which organizational knowledge and capabilities are built. These developments, we claim, challenge the constitution of organizations as relatively self-contained units built around a well-fenced-off operational core (Mintzberg 1979; Thompson 1967; Winter & Szulanski 2001) and promote organizational arrangements in which the relations between external and internal events are radically refigured. We consider platforms and ecosystems indicative of these broader transformations and analyze some of the conditions and processes supporting their diffusion and growing economic importance.

ORGANIZATIONS AS CENTERED SYSTEMS

The business enterprise is a key institution of the modern economy, the primary unit in which largely standardized goods and services are produced under conditions sufficiently separate from the market, other business enterprises, and the wider society. It is and will most probably remain a contested issue, to which degree the vital functional and formal attributes of the modern business enterprise can be traced to the social dynamics of ownership and surplus appropriation versus the functional exigencies that govern the production of wealth, the coordination of people and resources, and the eventual achievement of economies of scale (Chandler 1977; Holmstrom &

Tirole 1989; Piore & Sabel 1984; Polanyi 1944/2001; Zuboff 1988). One of the main aims of this chapter is to unpack the functional imperatives that have made the modern business enterprise a key economic institution. We are keenly aware that these issues are often linked with matters of power and surplus appropriation. We bring these links to light whenever we can or find it necessary, and in alignment with the broader purposes of this volume.

The modern business enterprise has acquired diverse guises across industries, regions, and nations and throughout the industrial and early information economies (Chandler 1977; Fligstein 1990; Nelson & Winter 1982; Perrow 2002; Winter & Taylor 1996; Zuboff 1988). Rather than confronting this remarkable variety, we aim to reconstruct the technical and behavioral (i.e., forms of interaction and communication) foundations upon which the business enterprise has been made a diffuse and recognizable institution of the economy in modern times. The analytic intention is to distill a few defining attributes of the modern business enterprise and investigate in subsequent sections the degree to which these attributes are being challenged by the ongoing technological and economic developments associated with the diffusion of data and the functions that data perform in the economy and society.

A persistent and elegant conception of the modern business enterprise along these foundational lines is reencountered in the theory of the firm in economics. The theory presents a series of interrelated arguments that seek to explain the economic rationale behind the establishment of the firm and its central position in the modern economy. In what is perhaps the most compelling contemporary version of the theory, the firm emerges as an independent and pervasive economic institution thanks to the economic benefits that it provides under conditions of imperfect competition that distort the coordinative role of markets and raise the transaction costs of economic exchanges disproportionally (Arrow 1974; Coase 1937; Williamson 1975). In other words, the firm is a buffer from market uncertainty. Its functional relevance and, in certain respects, superiority derive from the institution of a system of relations whereby the resource conversion process and the decisions that it requires can be pursued without immediate disturbance from external forces.

There is little doubt that the conceptual elegance of the theory of the firm is offset by the forceful behavioral and social simplifications upon which it has been built. Over the years, some of the tighter behavioral assumptions of the theory (e.g., rational models of agency, profit, or interest maximation) have been instilled with more significant portions of realism in conjunction with the idea of bounded rationality (Levinthal & March 1993; March 1994, 2006; Simon 1997) becoming a canonical version of economic agency (e.g., Demsetz 1988; Holmstrom & Tirole 1989). While more complex behavioral versions of the theory have grown out of these developments, the centrality of the institution of the firm itself and the role that it is assumed to play in the market economy have never been questioned. The same holds largely true for elaborations of the theory of the firm that moved further beyond the orthodox economic core of the theory, such as the resource-based view of the firm (Barney, Wright, & Ketchen 2001; Wernerfelt 1984) and, to a certain degree, the conception of the firm as the locus of routines and dynamic capabilities (Dosi, Nelson, & Winter 2000; Eisenhardt & Martin 2000; Nelson & Winter 1982; Teece 2006; Winter 2003).

Theoretical developments of this sort have widened the scope of considerations that have been overlooked by canonical versions of the theory of the firm, and disclosed the behavioral and managerial complexity of firms, along with the circuitous paths that make them efficient, innovative, and economically competitive systems (see, e.g., Argyres & Zenger 2012). In Nelson and Winter's thoughtful treatise, the firm is as much an economic as a social interaction unit. Economic considerations blend with behavioral dynamics and their interaction context to shape the development of skills, specialization, and the formation of routines that encode tacit knowledge and learning from experience. Together, these conditions enable resource transformation to unfold in economically viable terms and essentially provide the behavioral foundations of the modern business enterprise as a discrete entity, sufficiently separate from its surroundings (see also Penrose 1959/2009). Written ahead of the information and data revolution of our time, none of these developments question the importance of the firm and the central position that it holds in the market economy.

There is much to critique in the concept of the firm in the theory of the firm that goes beyond the behavioral and functional complexity of firms and includes forceful simplifications concerning the social and cultural conditions in which the operations of business enterprises are embedded (Granovetter 1985, 2017; Kallinikos 2004, 2007; Perrow 1986, 2002; Power 2007). The social and cultural embedment of firms has historically become an object of analysis in other fields, such as organizational behavior and the theory of organizations, cybernetics, systems theory and organizational and economic sociology, often in parallel to the theory of the firm but mostly without explicit reference to it. An essential insight of this large and variegated literature is the critical role of firms and organizations as distinct institutional entities marked by the dynamics of the social, economic, and technological relations into which they are embedded (Perrow 1986, 2002). The recurrent picture emerging from these criticisms is the conception of the activities that make up the compound of production and value creation as economic, social, and cultural phenomena at the same time (DiMaggio 2001; Granovetter 1985, 2017).

What is often lost in the conception of organizations across that significant, often insightful, and miscellaneous body of literature is the contemplation of the forces and mechanisms that reproduce the establishment of organizations (of which the modern business enterprise is a pervasive specimen) as entities sufficiently separate from the background of relations and institutions that underlie economy and society. This separation of the resource transformation process from its environment is foundational for the modern business enterprise. As briefly touched on in chapter 5, it is indicative of the differentiation of economy from society (Luhmann 1982, 1995). The social and cultural embedment of the modern business enterprise does not annul the formal and functional attributes that have made it a primary economic unit and a widespread institution whose operations are fenced off from the surrounding conditions. For all its social simplicity, the theory of the firm maintains the conception of firms as production machines set apart from markets and the rest of the economy thanks to the benefits conferred on them by the concentration of resources and the building of product economies of scale that such concentration often affords. In this regard, the theory of the firm spells out the functional requirements that constitute and reproduce the firm as widespread economic institution, conditions that are often lost from sight in the broader cross-disciplinary literature on organizations.

Even so, the juxtaposition of the firm (the business enterprise) to markets and its treatment in exclusively economic terms tends to obscure the operations and principles through which the modern business enterprise is constituted as a separate institutional entity not simply from the market, but also from other business enterprises across the broader economy and, critically, from society as well (Kallinikos 2004; Luhmann 1995). Viewed from this perspective, the modern business enterprise is established as a structural unit, institutional entity, and a locus of learning and knowledge building by abstracting from the complexity of the broader environment into which it is embedded a simpler set of operations and fencing it off (Santos & Eisenhardt 2005). By these means, the modern business enterprise can provide the functional focus, the conditions conducive to knowledge building, and the conventions and facilities that help amass the resources and consolidate the practices required for its success or survival (Argyres & Zenger 2012; Brusoni, Prencipe, & Pavitt 2001).

Put differently, the modern business enterprise is a *bounded* and *concentrated* system.[1] It is the center stage, in which resources and functional abilities are pooled together and transformed under conditions sufficiently separate from the fluctuations of the market, the immediate competition of other similar enterprises, and the heterogeneity or turbulence of the wider economic, social, and political environments (Santos & Eisenhardt 2005). Knowledge and capability building accrue as the outcomes of specialization and learning from experience that such a functional focus enables. Organizational knowledge development is closely associated with the mastery of internal conditions that such a functional focus provides, as well as the establishment of a well-demarcated space in which causal connections can be inferred with a reasonable degree of certainty to allow periodic adaptation to internal and external circumstances (Brusoni et al. 2001; March 1994; Nelson & Winter 1982). These relationships have historically been given a formal, jurisdictional status and reinforced through the development of property rights and, in due course, labor law (Kallinikos 2004; North 1984; Perrow 2002). The firm is a site of production, a complex system of operations, and a locus of knowledge and capability building as well as a jurisdictional unit.[2]

The relevance of the functional framework epitomized by these principles is attested to by its reach beyond the economy and its adoption by widely diffuse types of organizations such as state agencies, schools, and hospitals. Each organization type is established as a unit through a functional focus (and jurisdiction) that sets it apart from the broader environment. Within these units, interaction and communication are heavily conditioned by the functional areas and subdivisions of their operations and a relatively well defined hierarchy of jobs, roles, and positions (Chandler 1977; Mintzberg

1979; Perrow 2002; Thompson 1967/2003). Along with the modern business enterprise, most organizations are constituted as independent entities of centralized command through a clear demarcation vis-à-vis other adjacent areas and the broader environment. These conditions are essential to the objectives of resource accumulation and specialization, cost efficiency, and capability and knowledge development. Whether the functional superiority of this model is real or culturally fabricated (it is undoubtedly both) has less significance here.

The theoretical treatment of the foundations of organizations as centered (bounded and concentrated) systems are widespread in the organizational literature of the second half of the twentieth century. They probably find their most emblematic exposition in James Thompson's *Organizations in Action* (1967/2003), essentially a sociological rendition of systems theory that was in vogue during this time, and of organizations as entities whose actions and decisions are underlain by bounded rationality. True, the portrait of organizations that Thompson's book succinctly outlines has, over the last quarter of the twentieth century, been questioned by the narratives of the decline of mass production (economics of scale) and the advent of various strategies of customization, the purported end of Fordism, and the emergence of new production logics such as those signified by flexible specialization and the diffusion of value networks (Castells 1996, 2001; Chandler 1990; Piore & Sabel 1984; Perrow 2002; Pine 1991; Tilly 2001; Uzzi 1997).

Viewed from the present standpoint and the advent of platforms as diffuse organizational arrangements, none of these remarkable narratives have ever provided a coherent alternative to the foundational principles of the modern business enterprise and the modern organization more widely.[3] Greater responsiveness to markets (or clients), attention to the sociopolitical environment of such units, and flatter hierarchies do not suffice to define a new structural archetype for producing goods and services (Kallinikos 2004). Modified as it may be by the demands for more open and frequent forms of interaction with its environment, in these accounts the modern business enterprise remains the center stage of capability and knowledge building and the institutional locus in which the resource conversion and value creation processes occur.[4]

No matter how variably, unevenly, or imperfectly (March 1994, 2006) done, the conditions outlined here have shaped the patterns of organizations (the business enterprise and organizations more generally) and the management practices that have prevailed over the twentieth century. The empirical variety (many different types of organizations) through which these fundamental principles have been manifested throughout history and its stochastic and incomplete nature should not dissuade from the fact that the bounded and concentrated model, along with specialization (a precondition for knowledge and capability building) and division of labor, have been essential to the establishment of the modern business enterprise and the formation of management as a practice.[5] The variable manifestations of the modern business enterprise by no means imply that firms and organizations are linguistic fabrications, nominal entities existing solely in the minds of observers (Clegg, Pitsis, & Mount 2021). This nominalism that denies the existence of collective entities is both deeply ideological and realistically untenable (Abdelnour, Hasselbladh, & Kallinikos 2017; Kempton 2022).

The principles outlined in this section and the broader time perspective that they introduce are a helpful reminder of the limitations of both theoretical agnosticism and the pretentious omnipotence of managerialism, which views reality as readily bending to the strategic initiatives of managers and leaders. But it also provides a measure of the broader forces at work that suggest that reality and its deeply ingrained social divisions cannot just be wished away by the interpretive inclinations of situated agents (Sismondo 1993).

THE COMPOUND OF KNOWLEDGE

The functions that data fulfill in the value creation and resource conversion process in bounded and concentrated organizations have not been at the forefront of attention in the theory of the firm, nor across the various fields that have made contributions to the science of organizations. There is undeniably a widespread assumption in the literature concerning the role that data and information assume in the planning and control of organizational operations and considerable scholarship across a variety of fields, including accounting (e.g., Macintosh & Quattrone 2010; Simons 1994) and information systems (e.g., Burton-Jones 2014; Markus 2001; Weber 1998). However, the prevailing perception of data across this body of literature is that they are mostly supporting elements of the models and practices used to monitor and control organizational operations.[6] For reasons that require explanation, this widely diffuse understanding of data as just supporting elements has been left untouched by the profound changes brought about by computerization and the introduction of computing machines, first in the office and subsequently on the shop floor during the second half of the twentieth century. Data have been perceived as tools in the computational tasks that digital technologies have been called upon to execute. Their status on the ladder of action and knowledge has been related to the function that they are assumed to serve in the traditional epistemic models or techniques used to achieve a variety of organizational objectives (Beniger 1986; Burton-Jones 2014; Kling 1996).

Two fundamental conditions underlie the functions that data perform in bounded and concentrated systems. First, data predominantly stem from exigencies *internal* to organizations. That is, they are closely linked to organizational operations and the data that the tracking, conduct, and assessment of these operations generate in the bounded space of organizations. Externally generated data (e.g., market research and official statistics) may serve one purpose or another, and yet the major functions of data are inextricably associated with the steering and assessment of organizational operations and are, thus, predominantly of internal origin. Second, data records work largely as input to the specialized knowledge areas by means of which these operations are planned, instrumented, and carried out. Under this regime, as already noted, data commonly perform an auxiliary epistemic role as supportive elements of models and practices that are dictated by well-defined functional divisions and the knowledge specializations that pertain to these divisions. These ideas require further exposition.

By the end of chapter 2, we outlined the critical role of knowledge objects in the materialization of knowledge and its instrumentation. Knowledge objects usually develop within specific areas of expertise and help provide them with the tools, models, and techniques that are essential to support their functional focus, as well as the ways that they are implemented and carried out (Bailey, Leonardi, & Chong 2010; Bowker & Starr 1999; Henderson 1991; Ewenstein & Whyte 2009; Knorr Cetina 1999; Monteiro & Parmiggiani 2019). Operating ratios pertain to accounting, credit scores to finance, and patient records to medical practice and health care, to mention just a few widespread examples of knowledge objects. Thus, knowledge objects provide the epistemic means by which the process of organizational knowing is instrumentalized and materialized. They are the tools and action scripts by which the various types of domain knowledge that infuse the functional areas and the value creation process in organizations are concretized, ordered, and consistently applied across a large spectrum of situations (Alaimo & Kallinikos 2021, 2022; Barley 2015; March 2006; Nelson & Winter 1982; Winter & Szulanski 2001).

Granted these observations, it would come as no surprise that knowledge objects trigger their own data and information needs. The evidence that serves knowledge objects must be domain relevant, resonant, and broadly compatible with the operational specifications of the models and techniques that knowledge objects embody. Operating ratios call for accounting data of certain types, credit scores are based on data about repayment histories and a host of personal and occupational details, and patient records include data of patient histories, treatments, and examination results as these are filtered by medical practice (Alaimo & Kallinikos 2022). In other words, the relevance of data required to accommodate the demands of the expert areas in which they are embedded is largely dictated by the knowledge objects that serve these areas. Evidence in the form of data and the knowledge objects that such evidence serves are commonly tied up in mutually reinforcing loops that strengthen their links with one another and, by extension, with the firms and organizations in which these objects are usually embedded. These are the knowledge foundations of the bounded and concentrated form of organization.

The spread of digital data and the functions that they assume as diffuse media of resource orchestration are symptomatic of radical changes in the epistemic position (Faulkner & Runde 2013) that knowledge objects have assumed in the process of knowing in organizations and the functions that they have accordingly performed as instruments of value creation and control. Data as generalized semiotic and epistemic media, and data objects as diffuse instruments of data structuring and knowing, contribute to unbundling the tight compound that domain knowledge, knowledge objects, and data have traditionally formed. The diffusion of data and data objects introduces an impressive variety of data sources that are potentially relevant and yet extend far beyond the epistemic confines of established knowledge objects and their functions.

The ways that such varied conditions are managed, and data accessed and filtered can hardly be accommodated by the models or techniques of management and use of knowledge objects underlying the bounded and concentrated organization. Data derived from social media, blogs, and the

Internet more broadly are ordinarily employed in contexts as diverse as manufacturing, health care, law enforcement, finance, and advertising. Their diffusion calls for data management techniques, role systems, and practices that stretch far beyond those that have regularly been linked to knowledge objects and the well-defined areas of expertise that are characteristic of bounded and concentrated systems.

These developments by necessity reframe the instrumental significance of internally generated sources of information and reinscribe their use in a context marked by the ubiquity of external and miscellaneous data types (Alaimo & Kallinikos 2021, 2022; Weinberger 2007). They ultimately contribute to *unbundling* organizational data collection, procurement, and acquisition from the prescriptive specifications derived in advance from expertise areas and knowledge objects that are largely tuned to internal organizational operations. The variable and heterogeneous epistemic relevance of data and their dispersed or distant origins establish a nexus of conditions that challenge the tight compound of practices and organizational knowledge making that have underlain the management of data in bounded and concentrated systems. These are changes of far-reaching importance whose organizational implications remain poorly understood.

We obviously do not suggest a simple and linear model of succession from a neat and tidy world dominated by the routine nature of knowledge objects to the miscellaneous and shifting universe within which digital data are pervasive elements. We claim that the formation of a novel nexus of conditions for knowledge, action, and control within and across organizations challenges the foundations of organizations as bounded and concentrated systems (Alaimo & Kallinikos 2022; Bechmann & Bowker 2019; O'Neil 2016; Smith 2020). In many situations characteristic of the developments outlined here, data and information reach social actors and organizations from events or sources upon which they have little involvement, insight, or control. Data produced by sensors and IoT-based solutions across a large variety of occasions, Internet site clicks and browseovers, records of orchestrated transactions in retail platforms, stylized forms of user interaction on social media (e.g., reviews, ratings, tweets, and likes), and equipment utilization and performance records in industrial platforms are increasingly laid upon internally generated data sources in organizations and used in a variety of occasions. As they gain momentum, these developments by necessity relax the tight grip that established types of expertise have traditionally maintained over internally generated data in organizations and reorder the significance that they have had. Along the way, they redefine the process of organizational knowing and its involvement in value creation, management, and control (Bowker & Starr 1999; Monteiro & Parmiggiani 2019; Kallinikos & Tempini 2014).

It is against the background of these conditions that digital data objects emerge as pervasive tools of knowledge management that afford bridging the gap between the massive, agnostic, and heterogeneous nature of digital data and the knowledge purposes that such data can be made to serve in and across organizational settings. As claimed earlier, data objects inherit important functional, social, and knowing attributes of both digital and knowledge objects. After all, data objects (e.g., users, audiences, credit scores, and consumption items) are social and cognitive entities deployed to bracket smaller or larger areas of reality that enable consistent attention, monitoring, control, comparison, and intervention. At the same time, the technological makeup of data objects by necessity carries much of the granular, agnostic, homogenizing, and standardized attributes of digital data at the heart of the knowing process in expert settings and organizations. In this regard, data objects are both the outcome and the cause of the unbundling of the traditional compound of domain knowledge, knowledge objects, and data mentioned previously.

It is of utmost importance to point out here that the realization of this new architecture of knowledge and action would have remained an unattainable ideal without the data-structuring functionality of data objects. The technological specifications on the basis of which data objects operate as sensing and structuring devices are generic enough to allow the automated harvesting of data and their packaging along lines that enable a large variety of posterior uses (Lyytinen 2022; Yoo et al. 2010). As a rule, data are recorded and assembled into data objects with some broad objectives in mind. But they are also put in place with the clear expectation of a standardized use that can serve a range of circumstances that is different enough from those that motivated their original generation (Alaimo & Kallinikos 2021, 2022; Zittrain 2008).

As expounded in chapter 4, data repurposing is a widely diffuse practice these days, made possible by the structural minimalism of data objects and the functions that such minimalism enables. This is a condition of immense significance that can hardly be overstated. Data objects are by design functionally and cognitively underdetermined. Rather than strictly defining in advance the relevance and type of data with which they are associated (as happens with traditional knowledge objects), the schemas of data objects are generic enough to perform an elemental ordering of the prevailing variety of data that is a vital requirement for whatever posterior uses data objects will come to serve through further data operations of aggregation and calculation (Kallinikos 2012; Lèvi-Strauss 1962). In this regard, data objects work as intermediate entities that afford bridging the agnostic, homogenizing, and standardizing qualities of digital data with the organizational and economic uses that such data serve, and still other uses that they may well be called upon to serve in the future.

The unbundling of the knowing process and the new architecture of knowledge that takes shape are closely associated with the understanding of any recorded incident, social exchange, or communication as potentially relevant to the pursuit of economic objectives. Nothing is too trivial to be recorded and stored (Zuboff 2015). The mediating capacity and reach of data in turn reinscribe the significance of economic transactions whose specialized nature has marked the divide between markets versus organizations and blurs the functional, cognitive, and epistemic difference between data that stem from transactions and data that result from mostly social interaction and online communication patterns (Swanson 2022). These conditions establish a new logic of action across organizations and industries and drive the emergence of new forms for producing goods and services that cannot be accommodated by traditional social, economic, and institutional divisions. The advent of digital platforms and digital business ecosystems is indicative of the transformations that we have pointed out. We dedicate the next two chapters to these questions. To better appreciate these far-reaching changes, however, we find it necessary to take a closer look at the structural repercussions that are associated with the decentering of organizations and the unbundling of the knowing process described here.

ISOTROPISM AND STRUCTURAL CHANGE

Bounded and concentrated organizations are essentially set up to monitor and conduct a bundle of internal operations. External facts make sense to the degree that they link to and impinge upon these operations. These fundamental structural prerequisites are nowadays challenged as firms and organizations increasingly confront an expanding variety of external data sources that are, or may become, potentially relevant to them. Such a situation contributes to redirecting attention from the exigencies of an internal and relatively well bounded space and its immediate environment (e.g., suppliers, customers, competitors, and funding institutions) to a large variety of events that occur way beyond it and over which firms and organizations often have little immediate involvement and control. Across a growing range of occasions, events relevant to an organization are derived from a much broader set of relations marked by dispersed actors such as commercial or industrial platforms, data brokers and intermediaries, online communities, social media, and blog sites, among others, with whom an organization may have only loose connections or, as is often the case, no connection at all.

These observations suggest that the range of organizationally relevant events that are generated externally are no longer limited to surrounding circumstances that occur around a well-defined unit (Gavetti, Greve, & Levinthal 2012; Gavetti, Levinthal, & Ocasio 2007; March 1991, 2006). Figuratively, such events do not make a circle around a dot, a contiguous field that envelops or rings a relatively well bounded and concentrated set of operations (Winter et al. 2014). The set of relations and forces that drive these developments should not be understood in terms of an environment to an organization, as environments have been commonly conceived in systems theory, traditional or autopoietic (Luhmann 1995, 2002, 2006; Von Krogh, Roos, & Slocum 1994), and adaptation-based models of action (Adner & Levinthal 2001; Aldrich & Pfeffer 1976; Gavetti et al. 2012; March 1994, 2006; Nelson & Winter 1982; Thompson 1967; Weick 1979), whereby organizations respond to and manage their relations with other actors and circumstances in their environments. Nor can these heterogeneous and constantly shifting relations be understood in terms of a resource environment in which natural selection rather than adaptation is the rule (Hannan & Freeman 1977, 1986; Hawley 1986; March 2006), nor in terms of an institutional environment of beliefs, cultural models, and predispositions (DiMaggio & Powell 1983; Scott & Meyer 1994).

The heterogeneous and shifting matrix of events that we claim no longer has the shape of an environment calls for imagery that traverses older and widely drawn distinctions between internal versus external relations, economic facts (transactions) versus social relationships (interaction and communication), distant versus close events, and past versus future. What is emerging out of these developments is a messy world, tuned around the management of eventualities—a world that gives, as it were, the stampeding of events (encoded and mediated by data) an ontic and epistemic primacy over more stable forms of sensemaking (i.e., beliefs, grand narratives, or power). This infatuation with events, which we briefly touched upon in the preceding chapter in connection with our critique of the traditional notion of surveillance, reflects a major sociocultural orientation of the age, expressed, among other things, in the ways digital technologies and data mark or mediate the bonds between people and things, market transactions, and intimate relationships. These conditions, we suggest, redefine the ground upon which firms and organizations have been built and intermesh their operations with hardly familiar and miscellaneous range of activities, far beyond their proximate environments (Rammert et al. 2018; Winter et al. 2014). Addressing these conditions requires responses that can no longer be based on copying with, containing, or absorbing uncertainty (Cyert & March 1963; Adner & Levinthal 2001; Cohen & Levinthal 1990), but rather on living with it and, it often happens, riding and capitalizing on it through the short-lived and opportunistic orchestration of events that data and data objects afford.

A characteristic illustration of these abstract propositions is the frequent migration of many organizations across markets, industries, or fields previously separated from considerable knowledge gaps, different operational and technological prerequisites, and widely divergent managerial capabilities, as cases such as Google, Amazon, Tesla, and Apple indicate. The possibility of quickly crossing diverse knowledge, technological, and institutional boundaries that is characteristic of our time derives from the ways that data and data objects can be used to overcome the distinct makeup of different regions of reality; that is, to construct a commensurable world in which previously unrelated things such as opinions on social media and credit behavior, health-care data and digitally enabled body monitoring, and traffic data and insurance policies can be brought to bear upon one another.

These developments redefine the very foundations upon which firms and organizations have been built as bounded and concentrated institutions and, by extension, the boundaries of products and industries (Henderson & Clark 1990; Kallinikos 2007; Lyytinen 2022; Yoo et al. 2010). They bring about the decentering of organizations manifested in the relapse of a stable and well-identified operational-technological core and the ubiquity of a shifting matrix of economic, social, and technological relations outlined in detail in this chapter and throughout this volume. Such a matrix, we contend, cannot be mapped, partitioned, or assembled by traditional instruments of industry analysis (e.g., an activity core made of a product or service, competition, and market share capabilities). It is not, as claimed here, an environment that drives organizational adaptation.

These developments converge to a change of paradigmatic import that was sensed by Manuel Castells some time ago but, precisely because it predated the advent of data and the associated transformations, it has been limited to the conception of networks as alternative business arrangements to traditional organizations (Castells 1996, 2000, 2001). Over the recent years, the issues that we seek to describe by the decentering of organizations have been associated with the establishment and diffusion of commercial, often multisided platforms whose model of organization epitomizes distribution rather than concentration and openness rather than boundedness. We analyze that literature and its variants in a considerable degree of detail in chapter 7. It may suffice here to recount a few arguments that link rather directly to the claims that we advance (see Parker, Van Alstyne, & Choudary 2016; Parker, Van Alstyne, & Jiang 2017). According to these authors, the diffusion of commercial multisided platforms reflects the relative decline of supply economies of scale and the rise instead of demand economies of scale as the central reference point for the organization and production of wealth. In place of the internal relations, traditionally set up to deal with the management of supply economies of scale, what drives demand economies of scale are the external dynamics of network effects and the patterns by which such effects build up, are established, and dissolve (Arthur 1994; Shapiro & Varian 1998).

Parker, Van Alstyne, and Jiang (2017), in particular, have gone to some length to show how these developments turn firms upside down, invert, or reorder the relevance and significance of internal (supply) versus external (demand) conditions. By their account, commercial multisided platforms are inverted forms of traditional firms (i.e., markets qua firms), geared to accommodate the dispersion of demand and several frequently shifting stakeholders that use the platform to pursue their own interests against the background of the evolving demand dynamics. These economically derived arguments are no doubt insightful and indicative of what we associate with the radical reordering of internally versus externally generated sources of reference, knowledge, and capability building. At the same time, the economic developments that Parker et al. (2017) pinpoint are only specific instances of wider transformations, whereby organizations, beyond the private service firms on which they focus, are constituted and managed.

Such transformations, we suggest, can hardly be understood apart from the encoding qualities of digital data and the making of data objects to pervasive instruments of knowledge, action, and control that we have been outlining in this and earlier chapters. The rendition of real-life events into data helps, as noted, transcend the intrinsic (material or semiotic) constitution of these events, while the use of data objects as the standardized and technology-driven methods through which data are arranged and managed further amplifies this process. This is how such diverse elements as equipment dysfunction, health status, cultural taste, and reputation are rendered semiotically equivalent and can all be read through data and the comparison that data objects afford. While deriving from different regions of the real (e.g., manufacturing, health care, and consumption), and thus varying with regard to the facts that they encode, the data practices by which they are made sense of and managed across these regions are largely similar and make data often relatable across a broad spectrum of occasions. Viewed in this light, data and data objects are vehicles of boundary crossing, the coding, representational, and performing instruments through which the intrinsic constitution of material and institutional worlds can be transcended.

These ideas bear upon the sociocultural roots of demand economies of scale that Parker and his colleagues suggest invert the firm. Demand economies of scale are just instances of an *isotropic* space in which data and the ways that they are computationally managed traverse the distance between remote and proximate events, one set of things and social relations and another (Borgmann 2010). Demand aggregation is a prerequisite for demand economics of scale. Demand can be aggregated only so far as differences between the preferences of large human populations are traversed and rendered as instances that are possible to capture and arrange in a standardized metric scale.

There are, of course, limitations to that process, linked to both cultural perceptions and habits and the variety of data formats and standards that impede cross-syndication and interoperability (Bowker 2005; Bowker & Starr 1999; Hanseth & Lyytinen 2010; Hanseth, Monteiro, & Hatling 1996). History nonetheless suggests that these limitations are possible to overcome or, at least, moderate and deal with. Like money and quantification that traverse the intrinsic value of things (Porter 1995), data and data objects allow for traversing the differences that separate the various regions of reality. In this regard, they contribute to the making of a commensurable space in which radically different instances (activities and goods) become potentially relatable and possible to bring to bear upon one another (Espeland & Sauder 2007; Kallinikos 2007). These are the essential foundations of the process of organizational decentering, of which commercial multisided platforms are widespread manifestations.

SUMMARY AND IMPLICATIONS

In this chapter, we have put forward several interrelated arguments that seek to explain the far-reaching transformations that the organizational forms and institutions that govern the production of goods and services in modern times are undergoing. Many of these transformations find their most conspicuous expression in the construction of an isotropic space in which a good deal of the differences that constitute the varying regions of the real can be overcome or traversed by data. The distinct character of the production machinery that marks this age and its organizations is the invention of an epistemic, technologically mediated conversion matrix in which equivalences between the diversity of economic facts can be arranged, related, and ultimately computed (Alaimo & Kallinikos 2022). The assessment of the economic significance of digital technologies, beyond its unquestionable engineering ingenuity, should take place against the essential contribution that these technologies make to this large project of reimagining the similarities and differences that mark the world. The cultural, epistemic, and technical foundations of this conversion matrix of equivalences and the isotropic space that it constructs are diverse and long-standing (clay tokens, notation, quantification, and money). Yet in its current form, this matrix would have never appeared apart from the coding conventions and methods of data management that the digital rendition of reality affords (recall chapter 3; see also Kallinikos 2009a).

As these developments become widely diffuse throughout the social and economic fabric, they render increasingly irrelevant the fundamental divisions that have underlain the making of bounded and concentrated systems. The boundaries separating internal from external space, an organization from its environment, one market or product area from another, proximate from distant events, lose any functional primacy that they have had. They accordingly give way to new modes of organizing the production of wealth that are no longer constrained by these divisions. Digital platforms and ecosystems increasingly emerge side by side and occasionally supersede the importance of older product-based industries (Lyytinen 2022; Yoo et al. 2010) and the central position that bounded and concentrated organizations have had in the management of such industries. An important frontier on which these transformations are manifested is the substantial reconfiguration of the knowing process in organizations in the direction of giving data a much more pronounced epistemic role. Digital data are not simply cognitive inputs to established knowledge objects or models. As they are packed and arranged in several data objects, data increasingly acquire knowledge discovery functions and emerge as indispensable components of the process by which knowledge supports the value-creation process and the production of wealth.

These transformations obviously transcend the sphere of the economy and link to important institutional changes that we have considered in some length in the preceding chapter and, in fact, the entire book. Perhaps it is worth making clear in these concluding remarks that none of these transformations should be interpreted as an unambiguous transition to a social and economic order of openness, greater participation, and polyarchy. The decentering of organizations should not be conflated with decentralization. All that the idea of decentering suggests is that the bounded and concentrated model of structuring and managing organizations is not well tuned to dealing with the fragmented, miscellaneous, and shifting character of contemporary social and economic life and the primary role that digital data play in it. The economic and social implications of these developments still require confrontation and a critical assessment of the institutional background of the modern social order and the socioeconomic relations that characterized that order. We deal with some of these issues over the next two chapters.

7 PLATFORMS AND ECOSYSTEMS

Research on digital platforms and digital business ecosystems has expanded quickly over the last couple of decades. Much of this research tends to be predominantly business oriented and is quite different from the brief ideas of platforms that we have intermittently advanced in the preceding chapters. Save for a few exceptions (e.g., Márton 2022; Power 2022; Stark & Pais 2020), there is little interest in this management literature in the wider social, economic, and technological transformations with which the diffusion of digital platforms and digital ecosystems are associated. We consider the quick growth of that body of literature as indicative of a diffuse awareness of the transformations that we earlier linked with the reorientation away from the management of internal operations to organizational arrangements (i.e., the platform) that allow the economic exploitation of external events of large variety and scope.

Having said this, available research on platforms and ecosystems is diverse and presents a rather miscellaneous assortment of claims. Even a cursory look at this literature (see e.g., de Reuver, Sørensen, & Basole 2018) shows that platforms and ecosystems have been conceived differently and approached from widely varying angles and theoretical perspectives (Adner 2017; Alaimo, Kallinikos, & Valderrama 2020; Iansiti & Levien 2004; Gawer 2009, 2014; Jacobides et al. 2018; Moore 1993, 2006; Parker et al. 2016; Phillips & Ritala 2019; Tiwana 2014, 2015). Although a few important blocks of ideas would seem to recur across the various contributions to the subject, it is still hard to identify a core set of propositions that converge to an emerging theory of digital platforms and digital business ecosystems.

In what follows, we review several strands of research on platforms and ecosystems. Rather than being exhaustive, our aim is to distill a few prevailing propositions and critically assess and reinterpret them using the framework of ideas that we have put forward in the preceding chapters. We first start by reviewing the management and innovation literature that construes platforms as product configurations of a stable core and variable peripheral components that are combined to extend core functionalities and promote flexibility and adaptation to external events with cost-efficient strategies. To the degree that peripheral components transcend the boundaries of firms and are distributed across the supply chain, product platforms essentially turn to interfirm collaborative arrangements (Baldwin & Clark 2000; Schilling 2000) that evolve around the core product and its producers. We then move on to consider a more recent and populous strand of research that approaches platforms as fundamentally exchange systems made of several types of participants (multisided platforms), whose platform relationships and transactional patterns are shaped by the dynamics of network effects (Rochet & Tirole 2003; Parker et al. 2016). Exchange systems of this sort are usually proprietary systems designed, set up, and governed by platform owners. This is followed by the literature on digital business ecosystems. We briefly review it and discuss the relationship of platforms with ecosystems outlining how they implicate but also differ from one another. We conclude the chapter by reappraising these strands of literature and placing their main takeaways within a broader system of relations in which data, digital technologies, institutional forms, and socioeconomic transformations implicate one another.

THE ARCHITECTURE-BASED VIEW OF PLATFORMS

It is quite common in management and innovation literature to use the term "platform" to refer to products that furnish the base upon which further developments extend the original product attributes and functionalities. Even though the idea of a platform on these terms has become popular over the last two or three decades (e.g., Baldwin & Clark 2000; Schilling 2000; Tiwana 2014, 2015), the practices that the term refers to have been common for a very long time in industrial contexts. Firms have often used core products as models and central reference points for the development of product lines and product families or as the springboard for successive innovations; for instance, this has been the case with the automotive, aviation, appliance, and electronic industries (Baldwin & Clark 2000; Lyytinen 2022; Teece 2018). Historically, the use of management practices of this kind in industry has provided the conditions whereby firms have been able to combine a stable product core whose production is subject to strong economies of scale with a variety of components that have enabled mass customization and organizational adaptation to markets and shifting consumer tastes (Chandler 1990; Gilmore & Pine 1997; Lampel & Mintzberg 1996; Langlois & Robertson 1995).

Such practices have taken on a new life as the result of the profound digital transformation of firms and organizations over several decades. The creation of digital items and the rendition of social and physical operations as digital help make them amenable to continuous developments and enable component recombination across a wide spectrum of situations, as the case of operating systems and apps makes evident. In this regard, digitization enlarges the scope along which component functions can be brought to bear upon one another and become part of new product configurations (Carr 2008; Lyytinen 2022; Yoo 2013; Varian 2010). To be realized, such possibilities obviously require the development of suitable technical architectures built on the principle of modularity (Langlois 2003; Schilling 2000; Ulrich 1995) and underlain by technical agreements and the adoption of standards that facilitate the use, exchange, substitution, and recombination of components (Baldwin & Woodard 2009; Garud & Kumaraswamy 1995; Hanseth & Lyytinen 2010; Lyytinen 2022).

The idea of an extendible product base, componentization, and component recombination considerably extends the old strategies of customization, scale, and scope characteristic of industrial capitalism, as analyzed by Chandler (1990), Langlois (2003), and others (Lyytinen 2022). Yet these principles acquire substantially different and far more radical attributes in the context of software-based technologies such as operating systems that furnish the product base, variously extended by the continuous development and quick proliferation of apps (de Reuver et al. 2018; Tiwana, Konsynski, & Bush 2010; Tiwana 2014). Software systems are certainly products, but frequently they are also the facilities or means through which innovation and constant product and process development are achieved. As digitization expands, however, the differences become blurred and the distinction between physical and software-based products loses some of its original connotations. Embedded computing is a case in point.

Under such conditions, it remains quite unclear at what level or unit of analysis (product, firm, or industry) the concept of "platform" applies (Brusoni, Prencipe, & Pavitt 2001). As digitization lays the groundwork for the interactions of different stakeholders, the notion of "platform" extends to include the patterns and methods of collaboration within and across firm and organizational boundaries. In this sense, the platform and its architecture provide the blueprint for interfirm collaboration and the emergence of value chain networks that are clustered around a product/system and its components (e.g., vehicles, electronics, and computer operating systems) (Baldwin & Clark 2000; Brusoni & Prencipe 2001, 2006; Chesbrough 2003; Chesbrough, Vanhaverbeke, & West 2006; Garud & Kumaraswamy 1995; Gawer 2009, 2014; Langlois 1995; Schilling 2000, 2007) and increasingly, as we shall see later in this chapter in the case of ecosystems, they include firm collaboration beyond product and industry boundaries (Alaimo, Kallinikos, & Valderrama 2020).

These observations take us to the core of a few extremely interesting ideas put forward by Yoo and his colleagues (Yoo 2013; Yoo et al. 2010) and, later, by Lyytinen (2022). Drawing upon and extending an idea that Henderson and Clark (1990) first developed on the relationship between product architecture and firm innovativeness, these authors unpack the ways by which digitization and digital technologies help transgress the boundaries of industries, structured around a core product and the components by which it is made. Product components in particular industries tend to be product specific; that is, they encode specifications linked to an original product design, as is the case with, say, automotive or computer industries. A component that is part of such a solution serves the original product; accordingly, it can seldom cross the boundaries of that product and its value chain, and almost never crosses the boundaries of the industry defined by the product. In other words, the product and its components are part of a single design hierarchy whereby the original product provides the overarching design specifications for the development and production of components down the line, distributed along the value chain. These conditions are drastically redefined as digital technologies provide ample possibilities for the design of components (physical components or software-based) that no longer need to remain product specific. Rather, as the case of apps demonstrates, such components are agnostic to posterior uses and can thus become part of multiple design hierarchies that extend across the boundaries of specific products and industries (Yoo et al. 2010).

The fuller understanding of these developments requires confronting the homogenizing force of digital technologies and the ways that software-based systems encode the diversity of the world in bitstrings that are in principle (if not always in practice) relatable across a range of circumstances that we analyzed in the preceding chapters (see also Borgmann 1999; Faulkner & Runde 2019; Kallinikos, Aaltonen, & Márton 2013; Lyytinen 2022). The agnostic nature by which, say, apps can fit several computer devices and often different operating systems (e.g., Apple iOS accommodating the Microsoft office suite) ultimately derives from the ways that software is able to transgress the diversity of the world and overcome the intrinsic constitution of things (Kallinikos 2010). Over the years, cumulative technological breakthroughs in software standards and digital functionalities have converged to establishing digital architectures whose modules increasingly encode agnostic interfaces. Such conditions enable these modules to be a posteriori combinable with other modules along a large spectrum of options that cross familiar products, organizational and industry boundaries, local enclaves of knowledge, and engineering traditions. Referred to as "modular and multilayered architectures" (Yoo et al. 2010), arrangements of this sort are expanding considerably the range of component configurations that often cut across different layers of the digital infrastructure from the content and applications layer down to the hardwired elements that make up these infrastructures.

Under these conditions, innovation emerges out of variable component configurations of products and product bundles that do not need to obey the prescriptions of an original design and the relatively fixed distribution of production tasks (e.g., division of labor in supply chain networks) among different organizations that a single design hierarchy brings about. Although certainly still constrained by established product architectures, engineering traditions, organizational arrangements, economic practices, and market power, modular and multilayered architectures in principle relax several underlying constraints and unlock economic action, innovation, and organizational change in ways that were barely possible to conceive of a little while ago (Chesbrough 2003; Chesbrough et al. 2006; Yoo 2013). The bottom line of these thoughtful propositions is that architectures of this sort give rise to platforms that can move beyond the stable core/variable periphery configurations. A product can be itself a platform and a component of other platforms at the same time. Modular and multilayered architectures, therefore, open up a far larger range of possible courses of action that can respond to contingent demands through recombinant innovation, expansion of component functions, the invention of new complements, and shifting connections to other platforms (see also Lyytinen 2022).

Fascinating as these ideas are, they mostly center on the software-based technological landscape and the business and organizational relations that modular and layered architectures enable. There is no or only a little regard for data and the institutional and organizational tensions that the diffusion of data and data objects brings about. Much of the crisscrossing of product and industry boundaries that Yoo and his colleagues analyze transcends the homogenizing effects of software and occurs at the level of data and content that drives technological innovation through the links of data and content to meaning and knowledge (Alaimo et al. 2020). Data or content is not an epiphenomenon of digital architectures, but rather a distinct layer that, sui generis, captures essential aspects of how the world is currently perceived, organized, and performed (recall chapter 3). To grasp such transformations accordingly requires confronting the ways that data encode the facts of the world and data objects remake knowledge and action as analyzed in the preceding chapters. Useful and innovative as it undeniably has been, the notion of "product and platform architecture" conjures up a world made of units and blocks, components, and their relations. This Lego-based view of reality, as it were, is not well tuned to analyze the process of data value creation and the semiotic, epistemic, and communicative conditions of knowledge, meaning making, and commodification with which the machineries of data are closely connected (Alaimo & Kallinikos 2022; Borgmann 1999, 2010).

Much of this literature on architectures and platforms explores, in several variants, the fundamental idea of recombinant innovation (Arthur 2009; Varian 2010, 2014) by looking at the patterns by which component configurations unfold as technological developments lift the constraints imposed by the material and contextual makeup of products, as well as the separate engineering and organizational traditions to which they belong. These propositions resonate well with our ideas of unbundling. At the same time, we recognize that this insightful literature on architectures and platforms does not have at its disposal the conceptual apparatus for dealing with the technological and organizational breakthroughs linked with the diffusion of data. The disjunction of data from specific strands of domain knowledge and the restructuring of the knowing process through the systematic use of data objects require another take on these matters. The root metaphor, as we have argued elsewhere (Alaimo, Kallinikos, & Aaltonen 2020), should be the *reading* of data rather than the *building* of systems, and the extraction of meaning out of data rather than the assembly of components to products. The focus on data represents the only viable analytical strategy to address the ongoing revolution and unpacking the cognitive and knowledge-based transformations that reweave the current socioeconomic fabric and remake the operations of firms and organizations.

PLATFORMS AS ADMINISTERED EXCHANGE SYSTEMS

A substantially different take on platforms than the versions outlined so far has emerged from the economic theory of two-sided markets, originally developed by Rochet and Tirole (2003, 2006). From this perspective, platforms are essentially market-resembling arrangements in which two or more types of participants engage and transact with one another. In contrast to traditional markets, platforms are deliberately set up by platform owners who (1) structure the roles of platform participants (e.g., buyers, sellers, advertisers, app developers, and other third parties); (2) provide the infrastructural arrangements[1] and facilities through which participants can engage with the platform and with one another; and (3) lay out the system of rules that govern platform participation, participant conduct, and benefit distribution (Boudreau & Hagiu 2009; Evans & Schmalensee 2005; Gawer 2014; Hagiu & Wright 2015; Parker et al. 2016).

It is a key platform attribute to admit participation on broad and often self-selecting premises (participants decide for themselves to join the platform) that differ from the patterns of recruiting and filtering participation, characteristic of membership rules in firms and organizations. Such a condition gives platforms an outbound orientation and confers platform operations specific, unique, and recognizable features that are absent from most known types of organizations. The success of platforms and the benefits that they procure for themselves and their participants are closely associated with the dynamics of platform participation. As distinct from the architectural, core-periphery view of platforms built around a product-component configuration, multisided platforms are portrayed as transaction or exchange systems that are marked by the dynamics of participation (i.e., network effects) and their capacity to sustain and manage large participant or user populations.

The understanding of multisided platforms as exchange mechanisms that resemble those of markets raises a few tricky issues that require clarification. Although often linked to markets through the emulation of market attributes and the transactions that they enable, platforms are markets in a very limited sense. Save a few exceptions, markets are not entities; they cannot and do not belong to anyone. They are just mechanisms of economic coordination (Arrow 1974; Coase 1937). By contrast, platforms, as we know them, are mostly independent organizations (e.g., Uber, Alibaba, Amazon, Facebook, LinkedIn). They are legally constituted as organizations on the basis of property rights, including commons-based ownership regimes (e.g., Wikipedia, Open-Source Software Development), and can accordingly be managed as any other kind of discrete economic entity is. While emulating market exchanges, multisided platforms maintain ownership and control of the management of their operations and largely shape the distribution of the benefits that they get from these operations. In this regard, platforms are more akin to firms than markets.

We interpret the hybrid status of multisided platforms as markets-firms as closely associated with the technological and socioeconomic transformations described in the foregoing chapters. The setup of business organizations as markets is indicative of the limits of bounded and concentrated systems to respond productively to the challenges of an external world that no longer can be held at arm's length from internal operations. While still units of profit accumulation, multisided platforms use or emulate market mechanisms to ensure large social participation, deal with the dispersion and fluid nature of participant populations (their resources and skills), and manage the swarm of events that digital data carry at their doorstep. Put differently, multisided platforms tell the story that the production and delivery of a growing amount of goods and services in this age no longer can be accommodated by the market-organization divide (Arrow 1974; Coase 1937; Williamson 1975), nor by the differences that once separated social relations from economic transactions. While we have analyzed some of these ideas earlier in this volume, it may be worth rehearsing a few core arguments here.

The establishment and growth of multisided platforms are contingent on the ways that network effects build up, and subsequently are maintained and managed. Network effects emerge from the dynamics of platform participation. Whether on the same side (direct) or across sides (indirect), participants confer benefits on other participants that are proportional to their magnitude and level of participation. Platforms are claimed to take off to the extent that they manage to attract a critical number of participants that make them attractive to the eyes of others and grow beyond that takeoff point as they build on and expand their participant base (Evans & Schmalensee 2005; Hagiu & Wright 2015; Parker et al. 2016). In essence, the economics of network effects describe the interaction and communication dynamics that govern many of the goods that characterize our age and the mechanism out of which demand economies of scale accrue.[2] The operative layout of platforms that emulates that of markets and their outbound orientation is a response to some of the organizational challenges emerging from the habits and communication-based patterns that rule the dynamics of user populations, build up network effects, and ultimately generate demand economies of scale (Parker et al. 2016; Van Alstyne et al. 2016).

As we have shown throughout this volume, such dynamics are intertwined with the ways that digital technologies weave the interaction and communication fabric of our time. The diffusion of information and communication goods (data and content) that indelibly mark the consumption landscape of current societies is essentially an interaction process. From this point of view, network effects are inextricably bound up with the technological foundations (devices and systems) that make interactions possible in the larger coordinates of a global, dispersed, and quickly changing world (Shapiro & Varian 1998). The rules of that world are such that the mediated forms of social interaction that it enables presuppose a well-tuned technological infrastructure that makes systems and devices functional and useful. Less obvious might be the fact that these same rules extend to and include the diffusion of new communication and interaction habits and the making up of online conduct models and, frequently, types of people (i.e., types of users) (Alaimo & Kallinikos 2016, 2017, 2019; Bratton 2016). No substantial demand can ever be built up in the absence of such sociocultural habits and the technological patterns and conventions that support but also stimulate them.

From this point, it is only a tiny distance to acknowledging the functions that data perform as filters of perception, instruments of knowledge creation, and media of exchange and communication. It is through data that the variable and hugely dispersed conditions under which users participate can be represented, tracked, managed, and inserted into the communication-based circuits of the current digital economy. Without such semiotic conventions and the technological solutions that support them, it would be nearly impossible to pull demand out of their local contexts and overcome the differences between individuals and the dispersed contingencies that they confront. This, as it were, digital infrastructuring of sociality constitutes the prerequisite for the aggregation of demand, the emergence of demand economies of scale, and ultimately the spread of platforms qua administered multisided exchange systems. Put differently, for many goods, demand economies of scale are an indirect measure of the digitization of social interaction. Digitized sociality is represented, measured, and assessed by its data footprint and computed by the variety of metrics and the scores derived from platform participation (Alaimo & Kallinikos 2017, 2019, 2021; Couldry & Mejias 2019).

These conditions apply across the board but are more forcefully shown in the diffusion and growing economic significance of social media platforms. As seen in chapter 4, the processes, products, and services that social media platforms rely upon (e.g., recommendations, user-generated content, and reviews) are mainly data-based. The positive and massive network effects (direct and cross-side) that sustain these organizations rely on the far-reaching stylization of the user interface and the considerable standardization of the interaction and communication options that they offer, conditions that Gerlitz and Helmond (2013) poignantly referred to, in the case of Facebook and its ecosystem, as "the like economy." In different ways, the structuring of roles and the stylization of interaction extend beyond social media and apply to commercial platforms and the pervasive standardization of transactions and behavior patterns upon which they rely (Swanson 2022; Varian 2010). The hugely distributed and often global operations of multisided platforms require social habits, actions, and predispositions to be represented as discrete and standardized options that are commensurable, interoperable, and ultimately manageable.

These ideas combine with those advanced in the preceding two chapters to extend the notion of multisided platforms far beyond their widespread perception as business models or simply as one of many enterprise forms encountered in management and economics. Platforms certainly are a new enterprise form, but one that stands as a coherent and diffuse system of producing and consuming goods that develops alongside established forms of organization that have been built on the distinction between an internal space of control and an external market and social environment. In this regard, platforms represent key organizational arrangements of the age— the outcome of the technological and sociocultural breakthroughs that make it possible to represent, remodel, and manage the exigencies of production and the facts of economic and social life qua data.

As with all key organizational arrangements (Power 2007, 2022), platforms are one of the frontiers in which social relationships are retried. The forms of membership that platforms feature reframe the pivotal role that the labor contract has played in bounded and concentrated systems (see, e.g., Kallinikos 2003, 2004, 2007) and establish a miscellaneous landscape of engagement in which patterns of work, civic engagement, hedonism, and frivolous behavior mix indiscriminately with one another. These developments increasingly interlace the pursuit of economic goals with the variegated nature of daily interactions and domestic life patterns and make platforms widespread agents of social change. A critical analysis of platforms, therefore, requires attending to the variable and heterogeneous conditions under which platforms operate, the types of issues and problems they confront in managing variability and diversity, and the social and economic consequences that their growth brings about. Without such premises, demand economies of scale and demand aggregation are concepts that are too coarse to be able to address the processes through which platforms reinvent the foundations of long-standing management principles and practices (i.e., the bounded and concentrated organization) and become agents of far-reaching societal change (Stark & Pais 2020).

PLATFORMS VERSUS ECOSYSTEMS

The body of literature on platforms versus ecosystems is closely related with one another and overlap in significant ways (Adner 2017; Autio & Thomas 2014; Clarysse et al. 2014; Corallo, Passiante, & Prencipe 2007; Henfridsson et al. 2018; Jacobides et al. 2018; Parker et al. 2016). Especially in their multisided incarnation, platforms have been considered as the center stage upon which diverse types of actors, including platform owners, producers, consumers, technology providers, and software developers, collaborate and compete (Alaimo, Kallinikos, & Valderrama 2020; Cennamo 2021; Iansiti & Levien 2004; Tiwana 2014, 2015; Van Alstyne et al. 2016). Against this background, it is reasonable to wonder what the notion of "ecosystem" exactly confers on our understanding on these matters that is not captured by the interfirm networks that develop around product platforms or the dynamics of network effects that rule the establishment and takeoff of multisided platforms (Shipilov & Gawer 2020). How do digital platforms and digital business ecosystems relate with one another? Does the corresponding literature on these quickly growing research areas really differ, and if so, how?

An obvious difference between the two bodies of literature and the corresponding concepts can certainly be traced to the ecological imagery that the term "ecosystem" conjures up. The original formulation of business ecosystems by Moore (1993, 2006) described them as mechanisms of aligning a diverse population of organizations together and organizing the development and production of goods in ways that differ from markets and organizations, much in the same spirit as research on business networks that preceded and to some degree ran parallel to the original literature on business ecosystems (Castells 1996, 2000, 2001; Nohria, Eccles, & Press 1992; Uzzi 1997; Uzzi & Gillespie 2002). Moore's original formulation did stress the importance of ecological processes of coevolution under various resource constraints. Very little of this admittedly vague ecological imagery is alive today in research on business ecosystems, save perhaps the acknowledgment of simultaneous patterns of cooperation and competition that are supposed to underlie the relationships of ecosystem participants. As managerial economics and strategy came to dominate research into these matters, the promise of a genuine analysis of ecosystems in terms compatible with ecological thinking was forgotten. Save a few exceptions (e.g., Iansiti & Levien 2004; Ritala & Almpanopoulou 2017), this legacy is nowadays largely lost from sight (Márton 2022).

If the sparse links to the ecological analysis no longer provide the ground for distinguishing ecosystems from platforms, then the varied scope of the two concepts probably does instead. Whether as product platforms or multisided platforms, the term "platform" predominantly refers to individual firms (platform firms) or organizations and their strategies for building up and maintaining business relations and managing network effects with a view toward ensuring competitiveness and revenue generation. By contrast, the term "ecosystem" applies to the formation of a variety of business ties (direct or indirect) on the resource, activity or output side that establish a structure of relations that makes sense designated as an ecosystem. In this regard, "ecosystem" is a designation of collective processes and outcomes and should entail an analysis at a different level than that of a platform.

The underlying assumption is that the structure of relations that coincides with the formation of an ecosystem shapes ecosystem performance and governs ecosystem participation and the distribution of benefits across the participant population. From this point of view, ecosystems are clearly not unitary entities (Kretschmer et al. 2022). They have no legal existence or jurisdiction other than those of the individual business participants by which they are made. In other words, ecosystems are relational networks that feature recurrent connections among ecosystem participants above and beyond the sum of their bilateral business relations (Adner 2017; Iansiti & Levien 2004). Ecosystems emerge as distinct interorganizational formations thanks to the structure of relations that engulf ecosystem participants, suggesting that ecosystems are unlikely to emerge in the absence of such a structure (Adner 2017).

Short of such an account, the concept of a "business ecosystem" appears redundant. Using the term to refer to collective business arrangements such as supply chain networks, interfirm collaboration, and business alliances in general does not get us very far. It is characteristic of the structure of relations underlying ecosystem formation to entail participants from multiple business areas with diverse production experiences, resources, and capabilities that thus cut across familiar aggregate designations such as "industry" or "sector" (Lyytinen 2022; Yoo et al. 2010).[3] It is worth pointing out that the structure of relations that coincides with the formation of an ecosystem does not require the development of direct ties, in the sense of deliberate mutual tuning between ecosystem participants. Perhaps similar to nature ecosystems, a structure of relations may feature dependencies of indirect character, expressed in the availability of resources, their competitive or cooperative nature, and/or complementarity of output (Iansiti & Levien 2004). Unlike nature ecosystems, business ecosystems feature normative orders, diffuse business practices, and technological standards and functions that tie participants together without requiring immediate acknowledgment of one another, and deliberate strategies of mutual adaptation and tuning.

From this point of view, ecosystems are established as the outcome of resource, technological, or normative conditions that transcend the pursuits of individual actors, entailing attributes driven as much by intention as by structural conditions, emergent relations, chance, or serendipity (March 2006). These attributes of ecosystems are worth stressing. Much of the literature on ecosystems derives from the field of business strategy that, intentionally or unintentionally, is informed by a rather simplistic view of how business worlds are established and dissolve. Even a sophisticated account, such as that of an ecosystem as a structure of relations (Adner 2017), ends up linking that structure to the realization of a value proposition that is supposed to drive ecosystem participation and the calculated extraction of benefits from ecosystem participation. While this may often be the case, it represents an unproductive restriction of the scope of the concept and the phenomena that it can be drawn upon to explain. We would like to reserve the formation of ecosystems for much more ambiguous processes that entail unexpected links, ad hoc ecosystem participation or exit, technological breakthroughs and standards, emergent properties, and unsuccessful results along with illusory projects. Critically, as we show in chapter 8, it is vital to acknowledge that the construction of actors and the roles that they perform in ecosystems does not often precede ecosystem formation, as is mostly assumed in the strategy literature, but rather is the outcome of it. The formation of ecosystems is accordingly far from premeditated and features dynamics that grant ecosystems complex and emerging properties. It is only against this background that the concept of "ecosystem" obtains its usefulness and avoids being reduced to the calculated outcomes of the pursuits of individual actors.

The complexity of these processes, along with the variety of direct and indirect links of competitive and collaborative kinds, can be drawn upon to distinguish ecosystems from other interorganizational formations and markets. Business ecosystems entail multilateral interdependencies of ecosystem participants of diverse operational profiles, backgrounds, and capabilities that are shaped by mechanisms that feature both direct (i.e., deliberate tuning) and indirect ties. Such ties are rooted in shared expectations and norms but also are embedded, as explained earlier in this chapter, in technological standards that enable impersonal and emergent exchanges of resources and indirect patterns of relations among loosely connected elements. Taken together, these conditions confer on ecosystems their distinct nature as interorganizational formations and justify their historical novelty. Acknowledging them helps to distinguish ecosystems from other aggregate formations such as industries, supply chain networks, and strategic alliances, but also from market-based coordination that, at least ideally, requires arm's-length relations.

It may be tempting to attribute the different scopes of the concepts of platforms and ecosystems to the emphasis that they place on consumer versus industrial markets and, in this regard, distinguish the study of ecosystems from that of multisided platforms. In this view, the study of ecosystems would entail the analysis of the forces that govern the structure of relations that coincides with ecosystem formation (Adner 2017; Autio & Thomas 2014). As distinct from network effects and their close association with the product/service perception of users or buyers (consumer markets), the structure of relations that underlies ecosystems is supposed to give rise to value-reinforcing complementarities[4] that augment, rather considerably if not exponentially, the value of resource and activity combinations of the ecosystem participants, including the value of the final ecosystem output addressed to consumer markets (Jacobides et al. 2018). In this regard, value-reinforcing complementarities—whether deliberate, emergent, or accidental—are essential for the establishment and diffusion of ecosystems and might be thought to perform on the supply side an analogous function to the one that network effects perform on the demand side. The focus on the supply side and value-reinforcing complementarities, therefore, may be drawn upon to conjure up an image of ecosystems that may seem distinct from that of platforms (Alaimo, Kallinikos, & Valderrama 2020).

While reflecting the diverse conceptual origins of the research literature on digital platforms versus digital business ecosystems, these differences are increasingly traversed by the growing awareness that these research areas obtain for each other, but also by continuing technological innovations that blur the line between demand versus supply side, consumption versus production, or commercial versus industrial platforms. Developments such as those linked to industrial Internet of Things (IoT) and the rise of industrial platforms (Greenfield 2017; Jovanovich, Sjödin, & Parida 2021; Visnjic, Jovanovich, & Raisch 2022) are a good reminder that these distinctions hold no more than indicative value. In the current digitally mediated world, the line that separates production from consumption and resource synergies from product value perceptions often does not provide a solid enough ground for distinguishing value-reinforcing synergies and complementarities from network effects. Things are getting even more complicated in the case of the major platforms that pervade our age and whose operations complexly traverse the differences that were once thought to separate production from consumption, product development from product commercialization, and network effects from value-reinforcing complementarities.

SUMMARY AND IMPLICATIONS

The strands of research that we have reviewed in this chapter are symptomatic of the efforts of an interdisciplinary and growing community of scholars worldwide to grapple with the changing patterns of socioeconomic transformation and the institutions that mark the production and distribution of goods in current economies and societies. We have identified three broad strands of research and outlined the logics and perspectives with which each of them is associated. We are aware that there are several ways of making sense of the literature on platforms and ecosystems. Our own review follows the perspective that we advocate in this book. That is, it is motivated by our effort to understand the scope of digital platforms and digital ecosystems, the problems that they seek to address, along with the ways that they work rather than map their empirical variety (Autio & Thomas 2014; Gawer 2014; Srnicek 2017). Our predominant objective has been the identification of the logics that drive the diffusion of platforms and ecosystems from a larger time perspective, as well as the appreciation of the structural and organizational innovations they bring about. Table 7.1 presents our brief dissection of that literature.

The predominance of platforms as organizational forms and ecosystems as coordinative frameworks for the production and sharing of goods betrays a socioeconomic change of great proportions in which the structural patterns, organizational forms, and modes of collaboration that have prevailed over a long period of time are radically reframed. Their contributions notwithstanding, the literature on platforms and ecosystems has been limited in their respective outlooks by the inexorable selectivity of the disciplinary fields to which they belong: predominantly strategy, innovation, and managerial economics. The simplification of the technological, social, and

Table 7.1

Literature overview

	Architectural View of Platforms	Platforms as Exchange Systems	Ecosystems
Definition	Modular configurations of a stable core and variable peripheral components	Multisided setups of economic transactions run by a platform owner	Cross-industry networks of loosely coupled organizations
Operative logic	Economies of scale and economies of scope	One-side and/or cross-side network effects	Value-reinforcing complementarities beyond bilateral links
Examples of major economic areas	Production of discrete physical products and software components	Online marketplaces; social media platforms	Industrial platform ecosystems; service platform ecosystems; operating systems/apps
Literature examples	Baldwin and Clark (2000), Brusoni and Prencipe (2001), Garud and Kumaraswamy (1995), Gawer (2009, 2014), Langlois (2003), Schilling (2000), Yoo et al. (2010)	Gawer (2014), Gerlitz and Helmond (2013), McIntyre and Srinivasan (2017), Parker et al. (2016), Tiwana (2014), Van Alstyne et al. (2016)	Adner (2017), Alaimo, Kallinikos, & Valderrama (2020), Jacobides et al. (2018), Jovanovich et al. (2021), Kretschmer et al. (2022), Tiwana (2014), Yoo et al. (2010)

economic forces that shape economic organizations and current societies more widely has yielded a body of literature that seldom reflects on the wider assumptions upon which it is itself predicated. It is more than remarkable that the patterns by which the apparatus of data and digital technologies reweaves the fabric of economic operations analyzed in this volume are either absent or only cursorily mentioned and almost never theorized about in research on platforms and ecosystems. Economics and management strategy as fields have predominantly been discourses about ends (the rationale and incentives for choosing one course of action over others) at the expense of theorizing the technological and institutional means that frame these ends and shape organizations and their actions (Holmstrom & Tirole 1989). The infrastructuring of economic action achieved by data and technologies has mostly been taken for granted, and the articulation of how technological forces and socioeconomic forms shape one another has seldom been studied in detail.

In the literature on platform architectures, there are scholarly areas in which technology is problematized and the modular constitution of digital artifacts and digital infrastructures thoroughly analyzed and linked to economic action and organizations. Some of that work (e.g., Lyytinen 2022; Yoo 2013; Yoo et al. 2010), briefly reviewed earlier in this chapter, goes far toward unpacking the forces of structural economic change and show how economic action and technological architectures essentially mingle with one another and redefine the perception of economic opportunities and the ways that these are addressed. Yet even in that literature, the many and complex bonds that link digital technologies to data are largely overlooked. A fundamental reason for that state of affairs is the conflation of digital technology with data and the failure to see and analyze the relatively independent dynamics by which data shape social interaction and communication, the making of knowledge, and by extension, structure economic exchanges (Alaimo, Kallinikos, & Aaltonen 2020). Digital data are widely diffuse means for organizing cognition, ordering the perception of events, and shaping communication. The lack of reflection on data and data objects and the ways that they are involved in the shaping of interaction and communication processes is therefore striking. Even more regretful, although barely surprising, is the lack of reflection on the social foundations of economics, the social and communicative roots of network effects, and the current invasion and remaking of economic transactions by social interactions that we analyzed in this discussion (for similar points, see also Ekbia & Nardi 2017; Granovetter 2017).

There is certainly some gain to be obtained by studying complex developments such as those with which the diffusion of platforms and ecosystems are associated from a narrow perspective that allows for making selective observations and exploring continuities with other similar theories and empirical studies. But there is also a high risk, particularly in times of radical change, of self-fulfilling prophecies that reinforce established expectations and remain within the bounds of the familiar. In the next chapter, we further develop the theoretical ideas put forward in this chapter and provide empirical illustrations that show what the study of data and data objects can contribute to our understanding of socioeconomic change and the diffusion of platforms and ecosystems.

8   DATA AND ECOSYSTEMS

Borrowing from the sentence that Karl Polanyi once used to react to the predominant ideas concerning the emergence of the market economy, we could say that the prevailing approaches on platforms and ecosystems misunderstand the nature of transformation they refer to, which is essentially a transformation of society and social relations (Polanyi 1944/2001). The ideas we have put forward so far indicate that these approaches to platforms and ecosystems fail to recognize the diffusion of data as a premium mark of a far-reaching sociocultural change. It is within this context that data as medium of social relations assume a variety of semiotic, epistemic, and communicative functions that alter the rules by which goods are made and exchanged, and innovation and value creation are pursued.

Data as elements of work and administration have historically been coupled to expertise, the performance of tasks, and the making of organizations (see, e.g., Beniger 1986; Chandler 1977). However, the characteristics of digital technology and its transformative capacity have triggered, and continue to do so, a change of an entirely different scale. Once digital, data cease to be limited to performing well-defined administrative tasks and functions. Instead, data enter the core of organizational operations, redefine critical functions and processes, unbundle existing knowledge, and bring about novel patterns of organizing within and across settings. In this process, data become new objects of knowledge and, therefore, novel objects of work and exchange. Because of their rendition into data, relations of production, consumption, and exchange[1] can no longer be foregrounded by existing economic frameworks or coordinated and controlled by the familiar organizational, institutional, or market dynamics.

Classic market coordination based on pricing (Arrow 1974) is now a lesser feature of big online marketplaces that are largely run by a variety of hardwired technological operations that optimize exchanges, constantly responding to novel conditions of knowledge, shifting signals and economic states, technological innovations, and criteria of organizational efficiency (much to Friedrich Hayek's dismay, we assume). Take the massive real-time bidding happening in the already mentioned programmatic advertising ecosystem. A vast ecosystem made by data objects, platforms, and bidding algorithms emerges from a marketplace made of thousands of automated microexchanges that happen on demand every time an individual user's browser opens a publisher website and triggers a real-time request for an ad. Price is only one (admittedly important) data element, among many others, encoded into those data objects that coordinate the exchange via their soft standards, hard parameters, and real-time data on individual user behavior (Alaimo 2022a; Alaimo & Kallinikos 2018).[2] The operative logic of markets is heavily overlaid by the *design rules* of the entire system and the *data rules* that increasingly govern the production and use of data within and across various settings. Programmatic advertising is a paradigmatic case of the sweeping changes introduced by data, data objects, platforms, and automation to business relations and interorganizational arrangements. Yet, as financial relations attest to, advertising is not the only sector being transformed (see, e.g., MacKenzie 2021).

As data are diffusing in a variety of sectors, they restructure the ways that organizations relate to each other, redrawing basic rules of membership, competition, and cooperation across the economy and facilitate the emergence of larger aggregates of organizations known as ecosystems (Iansiti & Lakhani 2020; Jovanovic et al. 2021; Kiel, Arnold, & Voigt 2017). When relations are encoded into data, structured by data objects and performed by digital technologies, the possibilities of broadening ecosystem participation and branching out into other economic sectors increase rather substantially. In such settings, data, machines, and data objects shape the relations of production and the mechanisms of coordination, impinging upon the structure and function of ecosystems and prevailing over existing interorganizational dynamics, multilateral interdependencies, or field specializations.

In large, heterogeneous, and dispersed interorganizational arrangements whose connections are mediated by data and the technologies that support data management, existing distinctions such as those of producers versus consumers, sellers versus buyers, complementors, or third parties are far too coarse to capture how such ecosystems work. Despite the heavy legacy of knowledge specialization and the production logic of the industrial age that specialization is inextricably bound up with, what we increasingly observe in such ecosystems is that actors do not predominantly build business relations through preestablished market or industry categories (i.e., supply chains organized under single design hierarchies, as clarified in the previous chapter). Instead, they acquire roles through ecosystem participation and the modalities by which ecosystems define and shape their contributions. When data are the means of participation and the core of value creation, ecosystem dynamics exhibit characteristics and behaviors that are considerably shaped by the patterns by which data structure the relations of ecosystem participants and their actions.

Figure 8.1 portrays the emerging socioeconomic order of which platforms and ecosystems are an integral part as the outcome of the interaction of three systems of rules that derive from (1) the standard functions of the market (and organizations), (2) the structuring role of technology, and (3) the sense making and coordinative performances of data and data objects. The current literature is aware of how market rules interact with design (technology) rules to establish the conditions under which platform and ecosystem configurations emerge (Baldwin & Clark 2000; Cennamo 2021; Gawer 2014; Langlois 2003; Lyytinen 2022; Parker et al. 2016; Yoo et al. 2010). Both the architecture-based view of platforms and the notion of platforms as multisided arrangements of exchange analyzed in the preceding chapter capture the interaction of market rules with design rules and the variable market-organizational configurations such interaction generates. Not surprisingly, the same kind of ideas pervade the explanation of ecosystems in the literature. Value-reinforcing complementarities and the contributions of ecosystem participants emerge at the cross section of market rules and design rules.

Save intermittent associations regarding the role of data, none of these streams of literature confront the transformative repercussions of the data revolution and the emerging rules that govern economic encounters. The ascendance of data to primary means of sense making (i.e., selecting,

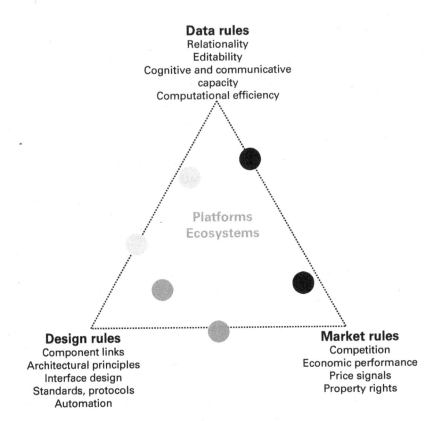

Data rules
Relationality
Editability
Cognitive and communicative
capacity
Computational efficiency

Platforms
Ecosystems

Design rules
Component links
Architectural principles
Interface design
Standards, protocols
Automation

Market rules
Competition
Economic performance
Price signals
Property rights

FIGURE 8.1

How data rules reinvent the market economy.

This drawing represents the new socioeconomic order emerging from the interaction of three systems of rules: (1) the system of *market rules*, with its competition, performance, pricing, and property rights (among others); (2) *design rules*, with its architectural principles, interface design, and component links (among others); and (3) the system of *data rules*, with its principles of relationality, editability, cognitive and communicative functions, and computational efficiency (among others). The three systems of rules interact differently across industries and economic sectors (i.e., the interaction of market rules and data rules may be predominant in one sector at one stage), giving rise to specific platform and ecosystem configurations. This variety is captured by the dots in the picture, which stand for individual platforms and ecosystems.[3]

representing, knowing), action, and coordination establishes a novel regime that overlays a new system of rules upon those of markets and technologies. The individual ecosystem configurations that result from the dynamic interaction of data rules with market rules and design rules may reflect the preeminence of one system of rules over the others (represented by the dots positioned toward the sides of the triangle in figure 8.1) or otherwise exhibit a temporary balance of forces (represented by dots positioned in the middle area of the triangle in figure 8.1).

In the rest of this chapter, we provide theoretical arguments and empirical illustrations in support of these ideas. We start this by inquiring on how data and data technologies mediate the type of relations that lie at the core of ecosystem structure and transform ecosystem dynamics (Iansiti & Levien 2004; Iansiti & Richards 2006). In the first section, we deal with data complementarities. As indicated, value-reinforcing complementarities are constitutive of ecosystems (Jacobides et al. 2018). Yet, complementarities built from data exhibit different characteristics from, say, product, resource, or output complementarities. The granular and homogenizing nature of data (chapter 3) make it possible to forge relations that transcend product, resource and output boundaries and are characterized by a higher degree of dynamism. Such conditions are conducive to the continuous reshuffling of existing roles, activity or resource patterns and the making of complementarities that are qualitatively different from the traditional systems of relations upon which organizations and markets are based (i.e., market rules). We illustrate the features of value-reinforcing complementarities made by data with the cases of TripAdvisor and Flowe (an Italian fintech start-up) and the ecosystems in which they are embedded.

In the second section, we focus on the process by which such complementarities are forged. We show how value-reinforcing data relations are constantly being made rather than being predetermined by preexisting resources and operations. In the Facebook (Meta) ecosystem, for instance, there is no such thing as a direct exchange between participants (e.g., end users do not interact directly with game developers and advertisers), but a rather complex and dynamic interlocking of relations among actors who interact via data, exchanging data with data objects (i.e., user objects, video objects), participating via application programming interfaces (APIs), data dashboards, or other technologies (see also Alaimo 2022a, 2022b; Van der

Vlist & Helmond 2021; Van der Vlist, Helmond, Burkhardt & Seitz 2022). Data objects and technologies such as APIs actively shape (i.e., execute and perform) how data types relate to each other, continuously modulating the possibilities of value-reinforcing relations. Data objects are the key cognitive and functional entities of ecosystems. They structure the variety of data intake and give actors the incentives and tools that they need to act. At the same time, data objects remain undetermined and open to accommodate change, as explained in chapters 4 and 6.

It is important to remark that ecosystems are not empowered by established social actors that interact directly, but by data objects that interact with each other via data and data technologies, bringing about novel social entities that refashion the economic role and position of existing social actors (i.e., organizations, users, and so on). Those new versions of customers, marketers, advertisers, and other users define the ecosystem participants, their roles, and their interdependencies. In addition, the relations between customers, marketers, advertisers, and other users are constantly optimized by interaction data in a dynamic two-way constitutive relation. Viewing ecosystems as "designed" top-down by key actors, or shaped by their strategies appears out of tune with the reality of digital ecosystems, formed by thousands of data objects interacting with each other via layers of technologies and producing value via constant real-time flows of miscellaneous masses of data provided by hugely heterogeneous populations of actors. Equally, reducing ecosystems' emergence to relations orchestrated by platform leaders in a marketlike exchange where roles are predetermined and interaction fixed over time risks constraining the analysis of ecosystems to categories that no longer fit reality.

Novel organizational and interorganizational formations such as platforms and ecosystems emerge to overcome existing arrangements, as these become increasingly dysfunctional in dealing with the data-based infrastructuring of social and economic relations. We conclude the chapter by taking some of these ideas further. As all systems, ecosystems are more than the sum of their parts. To understand how data reinvent the market economy, we must investigate how data, data objects, and digital technologies help establish a novel shared cognitive space that allows novel forms of knowledge and organized action, including new patterns and forms of innovation and value creation, to emerge.

DATA COMPLEMENTARITIES

A recurrent idea in the ecosystem literature is that specific types of complementarities drive the actions and eventual alignment of the productive capacities of various actors (Adner 2017; Jacobides et al. 2018; Shipilov & Gawer 2020). This idea has been applied to resources, activities, and outputs such as physical products or software. As the number of organizations that operate and forge productive alliances through data increases and data become the cognitive means for building and maintaining relations, it becomes relevant to understand the characteristics of complementarities that can be built around and through data.

As distinct from existing definitions of complementarities, value-reinforcing data complementarities can be forged among any kind of resources or activities that have been rendered as data, regardless of sector or industry. As indicated in chapter 3 and throughout this book, the agnostic and homogenizing characteristics of data make the resources and activities that they encode relatable to any other resources and activities captured as data, in principle if not in practice. Specific qualities of data such as their content (e.g., customer data, health data, and traffic data) can limit their relevance to other activities but do not rule out their reusability, which is in fact a pervasive practice in the current economy and society, regularly extending the meaningfulness and relevance of one type of data for others (e.g., the relevance of social and networking data for credit scoring). The relatability of such entities makes the distinctions between "generic-specific" and "part-whole" relationships, which Jacobides et al. (2018) draw heavily upon to explain the formation of ecosystems, less relevant.[4] Data complementarities reframe the generic-specific distinction as they cut across the functional, physical, or cognitive makeup of existing resources, activities, or outputs, and instead work under the logic that governs the production, circulation, and use of data that we reviewed in chapters 3 and 4.[5] Nor can data items be productively understood as complements, if complements are considered, as they should be, as an assembly of several elements and functions. In this regard, data reframe even the very idea of modularity and the pivotal role that it has been accorded to the making of complementarities, and by implication, ecosystems.

Data-based complementarities, we suggest, do not form under the rules of product design (Baldwin & Clark 2000) and the architectural principles reviewed in the preceding chapter. Their capacity to produce value remains underdetermined from existing sector knowledge and operational specificities. The interdependencies that are at the core of data complementarities can be very dynamic and unstable, subject to a high level of generality, newness, and unpredictability. Much of data-based value-reinforcing patterns have an emerging status. Digital technologies and data are underlain by generative characteristics that are tied to the heterogeneity of actors participating in the ecosystem (Zittrain 2008), the partially unspecified nature of ecosystem participation, and the editability and malleability of data (Kallinikos, Aaltonen, & Márton 2013; Lyytinen 2022; Swanson 2022; Yoo et al. 2010). Data-based value-reinforcing complementarities can form *despite* existing resources, activities, or outputs.

Consider TripAdvisor, a well-known social media platform in the travel and hospitality industry. We have reported the detailed history of the platform elsewhere (Alaimo, Kallinikos, & Valderrama 2020). It may be instructive here to briefly describe the transformations that TripAdvisor has undergone over the years to demonstrate how data complementarities form and redefine the relationships between tasks, technologies, processes, and actors and lead to the emergence of an ecosystem. TripAdvisor started as a travel content search engine and advertising company in 2000 before it transitioned a few years later to an influential social media platform dedicated to travel. From 2013 onward, the platform has progressively become part of a rich service ecosystem that provides content to users; data analytics to hotels and partners; advertising; price comparison services; hotel, restaurant, and tour booking services; personalization services; and a range of other services. In each of the three stages of TripAdvisor's evolution, the relations that the platforms maintained with its users and customers have been mediated and managed via data and data technologies. As these relations evolved, however, they became the primary sources of novel data and data-based services and the means of novel value-reinforcing relations that gradually led to the emergence of the complex service ecosystem in which TripAdvisor is currently embedded.

The transformation of TripAdvisor over its life course can be told as a story of corporate strategy and the key decisions that have made it a successful platform in the travel and hospitality sector. There are certainly lessons to be drawn from such a story. Yet this transformation is also the story of the Internet evolution, of the advent of social media platforms, the diffusion of light technologies (smart phones and tablets), and the technologies by which data have been increasingly made available across different types of activities. The story of TripAdvisor's evolution is marked by all these forces and the modalities by which they have given rise to different economic functions and shaped novel business roles and undertakings. The ecosystem in which the platform is currently embedded defies the industry rule book and the proactive outlook of strategy, as most of the data and the data complementarities that have made this ecosystem possible arose along the way (Alaimo & Aaltonen 2023). The ecosystem formed as the outcome of the interplay of technological innovations, business decisions, and other forces that can be attributed only to a limited extent to TripAdvisor itself and to its undeniably successful management.

A closer look at the broader systems of relations and functions that underlie the ecosystem in which TripAdvisor is embedded shows the relevance of these observations and further explicates the ways in which data complementarities provide the backbone of ecosystem formation. Via TripAdvisor, hotels can subscribe to marketing services (targeting, data analytics solutions, content solutions, and other offerings) and room-booking automated services or buy advertising spaces. End users and travelers can browse content; book tours, restaurants, or hotel rooms; take an Uber drive; comment on or post pictures of an establishment; gain badges for their online activities; learn about culture and tradition; and engage in other activities. All these services are the outcomes of specific interdependencies that have emerged and crystallized around patterns of value-reinforcing data relations among several actors that have shifted positions and activities constantly. Despite many of these actors, such as online travel agencies and Internet booking engines, have been the same throughout TripAdvisor's evolution, their roles in the ecosystem have evolved, expanded, or shrunk as the result of fluctuating ecosystem relations. While many ecosystem players remain invisible to end users, they are essential to the constitution of novel types of socioeconomic interdependencies that emerge under the dynamics of data rules.

Where data are involved as key media and pervasive resources of ecosystem relations, the alignment of ecosystem participants is a much more dynamic and unstable enterprise than what is commonly been admitted (Adner 2017). In ecosystems in which data rules prevail, the actors of the ecosystem participate largely interchangeably as data producers and as data-service consumers across several layers of functionalities and services. Interdependencies based on data are thus trickier than part-whole relations and frequently shifting. In these cases, when platforms constantly develop new features and interactions and ecosystems admit new actors, the role and position of a good deal of ecosystem participants are reconfigured as a result. Because of the dynamicity, largely enabled by the editability of digital data and data objects, ecosystem actors and their roles cannot be captured by the standard definitions of partners, clients, competitors, or complementors. Emerging from heterogeneous and real-time data, such interdependent relationships are dynamic, multilateral, and multidimensional, and thus demand novel shared cognitive practices and innovative managerial approaches.

The cognitive and communicative dimensions of data seldom enter into the analysis of ecosystems in managerial economics and strategy fields that dominate the literature on ecosystems. Yet they constitute the building blocks upon which novel productive arrangements can be agreed upon and collectively built when the old ones cease to be effective. In the space created by the hybridization of banking services and digital technologies, called "fintech," there are several interesting examples of ecosystems that are emerging as data help extend and redefine the relevance of finance for other interests and activities. The ecosystem of which Flowe is part is one of them. Flowe is an Italian start-up owned by Banco Mediolanum Spa and founded in June 2020,[6] which offers the common financial and payment services of a payment account, therefore allowing users to initiate online payments, send money to other users, and process payments. As a native digital payment account provider, Flowe furthermore offers user-friendly tools to manage personal savings through the functionality of Drops, digital boxes that create a separate saving account wherein users can allocate financial savings. In addition, Flowe provides a user-friendly service for splitting group expenses among participants. Users can also request a physical debit card that is issued in partnership with Mastercard and is made of 85 to 90 percent wood. Thanks to the relationship that Flowe has built over time with the Italian start-ups ZeroCO2 and Doconomy, by using the card, users can plant trees to contribute to reforestation efforts in Guatemala and offset carbon dioxide (CO_2) emissions from their transactions. Users are notified about their CO_2 footprint through a service named Ecobalance, provided by Doconomy, whose data management systems can convert a transaction in euros to an estimated emission of CO_2. Here, too, the platform not only operates passively but also offers users the opportunity to offset these emissions by planting more trees to support Guatemala's reforestation.

The value-reinforcing patterns of data relations running between Flowe, ZeroCO2, Doconomy, and end users is a telling example of the innovative cognitive space opened by data complementarities. The fact that the case could be narrated as a smart marketing strategy does not invalidate the essential role of data in forging relations among actors, knowledge, and resources that were not possible or tenable before. The interdependence runs between data produced by financial transactions, data produced by the conversion of transactions in CO_2 emissions, and data produced by the planting of a tree (see figure 8.2). It is only because those interactions are made into data that diverse activities such as payment transactions, CO_2 emissions, and the planting of a tree can relate to one another. The nature of data as cognitive (semiotic, epistemic) artifacts, together with their editability, enable novel possibilities of creating services that are breaking the boundaries of traditional knowledge, organizations, industries, and social practices, and that consequently lead to the formation of new socioeconomic spaces. The innovativeness of these spaces, made possible by data

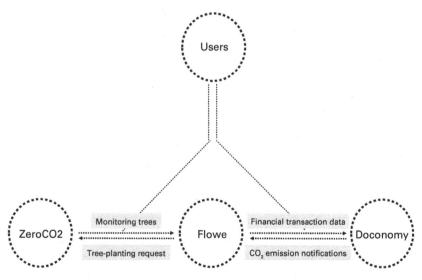

FIGURE 8.2

Illustration of the data flow making value-reinforcing complementarities among Flowe, ZeroCO2, Doconomy, and users. *Source*: Alaimo, Kallinikos, and Sannino (2022).

mediation, is that different economic and social activities are made inter-dependent along several coexisting paths of various kinds such as learning, playing, consuming content, and other actions.

This example well indicates how the transformative power of data cannot be captured by simplistic ideas framing data as mere economic resources or items of exchange (Shapiro & Varian 1998). By the same token, innovative ecosystems do not mechanically emerge when data resources are pooled in or out of organizations by technological connectivity provided by APIs or other boundary-management technologies (Zachariadis & Ozcan 2017). As they connect domains of knowledge and activities that were not perceived as relevant and not connected in any way before, data open novel cognitive spaces that shape innovation possibilities and value creation and, ultimately, reinvent the market economy. None of the elements that make Flowe's service offering would have worked or made sense together under previous market arrangements, knowledge specialization, and industrial practices. Yet because of the cognitive and material infra-structure created by data, such novel data patterns can form new interdependencies and create alternative patterns of living (and, ultimately, value) for different stakeholders. It is because of data production, structuration, and exchange that Flowe can produce value out of activities, cognitive resources, and knowledge domains that have been previously unrelated or not connected, and at the same time offer people alternative visions of finance. Innovation in an ecosystem such as that in which Flowe is embed-ded does not come from the alignment of actors to a set of well-established activities within an industry domain. Rather, interdependencies run across a variety of data patterns that are aggregated and recombined via emergent practices, leading to the establishment of new roles that dynamically align around a shared vision. The world of financial services is made broader as it becomes loosely coupled from existing knowledge, organizational prac-tices, and industry perceptions and classifications. Clearly, there are several downsides to this newly acquired freedom, which are becoming urgent to address now that the first wave of datafication has swept through industries and sectors with little guidance and rules. How to regulate a novel space of interaction that has no tight links with existing procedures, institutions, and routines is a complex issue, of course, and one that we cannot address here. We can stress, however, that current regulatory approaches do little to reveal the central role of data and follow the trend of considering data only as economic resources or technical inputs with questionable results (recall chapter 5; see also Cennamo et al. 2023).

DATA OBJECTS AND THE FORGING OF DATA COMPLEMENTARITIES

The cases that we have just reviewed are indicative of the novelty brought about by data in ecosystem emergence and structuration. The homogenizing, nonneutral, and agnostic character of data mediate and structure relations among heterogeneous actors, tasks, and processes. Actors that did not have reasons to connect before form value-reinforcing complementarities based on patterns of data making, circulation, and use. The ecosystem in which Flowe is embedded is made by actors, tasks, and operations contributing expertise that had not been linked to banking or financial service offerings before. It is the combination of knowledge domains, enabled by the cognitive and technological infrastructure of data, that gives that ecosystem its unique identity and newness.

Heterogeneity has been viewed in the literature mostly as a fixed variable that captures the variety of all the actors involved, usually cataloged under preestablished and fixed roles (i.e., complementors, end users, and marketers). Yet heterogeneity in data-based ecosystems has a more profound and disruptive meaning. Under data rules, ecosystems are comprised of actors that do not belong to the same industrial sectors, are not bound by existing relations of production (i.e., single design hierarchies), and may not have the same knowledge base or specialization. In many ecosystems, actors are composed of social entities as different as corporations, start-ups, individuals, public organizations, professionals, and communities. In addition, as already indicated, actors form heterogeneous relations that do not preexist ecosystem formation and emerge from novel value-reinforcing patterns of data-based exchanges. Those relations remain complex (i.e., show a high degree of interconnection), unstable, and often short-lived and reconfigurable.

Consider again the case of programmatic advertising, where there are literally thousands of heterogeneous actors interacting in real time across a dispersed and fragmented space. The entire ecosystem's exchange, with its massive numbers, operates on demand every time a user's browser opens a publisher's website and triggers a real-time request for an ad. As one user's view of an ad may trigger multiple auctions, millions of data exchanges take place every millisecond. The number of services and actors that have emerged around this apparently simple transaction is mind blowing, as it comprises validation or measurement agencies, complex legal services, data brokers or intermediaries, sophisticated AI companies that offer optimization strategies, and other agents. How can value-reinforcing interdependencies be forged out of this miscellaneous, massive, and real-time flux of data? The role of data objects and technologies, such as the Real-Time Bidding (RTB) protocol,[7] is key to unpacking ecosystem dynamics in such settings. Without their work, no exchange can take place and the space of innovation and value creation of the ecosystem would be considerably truncated.

Let us restate that in ecosystems, there is often no direct interaction between actors such as data brokers, end users, publishers, marketers, and other participants. The ecosystem described here illustrates a complex interlocking of streams of data that are produced en masse, structured by objects interacting with each other under the rules of protocols, and made accessible to participants for several different tasks and operations through APIs, dashboards, and other technologies. In the programmatic advertising ecosystem, data objects, among which the bid requests and bid responses are the central entities, have dimensions and parameters about the available and sellable ad unit inventory that is assumed to be viewed by users in real time.[8] Objects provide the cognitive grid that actors need to participate in the exchange and, at the same time, they function as behavioral scripts, embedding the rules of interaction. They structure the variety of data circulating in the exchange and furnish actors with the incentives and tools that they need to act. Bid request objects, for instance, embed key parameters of the exchange such as viewability,[9] which sets the price of the exchange by computing the likelihood that the ad slot will be viewable by the end user based on a range of indicators.[10] Figure 8.3 shows an example of a bid request object operating in the Google marketplace.

Participation in the ecosystem is made possible by the functioning of the protocol, data objects, and other technologies. However, these objects do more than implement rules for the automation of exchanges. Data objects and their data attributes, structure, and schemas maintain a core knowledge and semiotic function that is consistently shaped by the history and institutional path dependencies of the sector. At the same time, they also remain open, unspecified, and editable to accommodate new uses linked to the epistemic novelty of massive amounts of data generated in real time. As we have seen in chapter 4, data objects are the digital format of basic

AdX <u>bid request</u> for a New York Times article:

BidRequest:id: "Y\032@\207\000\017\a\347\n\033\247C\222\006(\226" ip:
"V\257D" user_agent: "Mozilla/5.0 (Window
s NT 10.0; Win64; x64) AppleWebKit/537.36 (KHTML, like Gecko)
Chrome/58.0.3029.110 Safari/537.36" url:
"https://www.nytimes.com/2017/05/15/business/media/mika-joe-kellyanne-
conway.html" detected_language: "
en" detected_vertical { id: 396 weight: 0.3686498 } detected_vertical {
id: 398 weight: 0.35702515 } detected_vertical { id: 1048 weight:
0.27432504 } detected_vertical { id: 408 weight: 1.0 } detected_vert
ical { id: 1209 weight: 0.75 } adslot { id: 1 width: 300 height: 77
excluded_attribute: 22 excluded_attribute: 32 excluded_attribute: 34
excluded_attribute: 30 excluded_attribute: 7 excluded_attribute: 13 e
xcluded_attribute: 14 excluded_attribute: 15 excluded_attribute: 16
excluded_attribute: 70 excluded_attribute: 48 excluded_attribute: 26
excluded_attribute: 95 excluded_attribute: 18 excluded_attribute: 28
excluded_attribute: 17 excluded_attribute: 20 excluded_attribute: 19
excluded_attribute: 13 excluded_attribute: 14 excluded_attribute: 15
excluded_attribute: 16 excluded_attribute: 17 excluded_attribute: 18
 excluded_attribute: 19 excluded_attribute: 20 excluded_attribute: 26
excluded_attribute: 13 excluded_attribute: 14 excluded_attribute: 15
excluded_attribute: 16 excluded_attribute: 17 excluded_attribute: 1
8 excluded_attribute: 19 excluded_attribute: 20 excluded_attribute: 26
allowed_vendor_type: 10 allowed_vendor_type: 42 allowed_vendor_type: 56
allowed_vendor_type: 94 allowed_vendor_type: 130 allowed_vendor
_type: 132 allowed_vendor_type: 144 allowed_vendor_type: 145
allowed_vendor_type: 182 allowed_vendor_type: 204 allowed_vendor_type:
225 allowed_vendor_type: 233 allowed_vendor_type: 237
allowed_vendor_type:
 238 allowed_vendor_type: 242 allowed_vendor_type: 255
allowed_vendor_type: 260 allowed_vendor_type: 267 allowed_vendor_type:
284 allowed_vendor_type: 303 allowed_vendor_type: 331
allowed_vendor_type: 332 allowed_vendor_type: 334 allowed_vendor_type:
342 allowed_vendor_type: 395 allowed_vendor_type: 414
allowed_vendor_type: 432 allowed_vendor_type: 441 allowed_vendor_type:
445 allowed_vendor_type: 472 allowed_vendor_type: 474
allowed_vendor_type: 476 allowed_vendor_type: 477 allowed_vendor_type:
481 allowed_vendor_type: 485 allowed_vendor_type: 486
allowed_vendor_type: 489 allowed_vendor_type: 490 allowed_vendor_type:
497 allowed_vendor_type: 529 allowed_vendor_type: 537
allowed_vendor_type: 538 allowed_vendor_type: 542 allowed_vendor_type:
543 allowed_vendor_type: 550 allowed_vendor_type: 551
allowed_vendor_type: 562 allowed_vendor_type: 564 allowed_vendor_type:
572 allowed_vendor_type: 573 allowed_vendor_type: 575
allowed_vendor_type: 577 allowed_vendor_type: 606 allowed_vendor_type:
615 allowed_vendor_type: 616 allowed_vendor_type: 618
allowed_vendor_type: 623 allowed_vendor_type: 698 allowed_vendor_type:
704 allowed_vendor_type: 713 allowed_vendor_type: 724
allowed_vendor_type: 743 allowed_vendor_type: 745 allowed_vendor_type:
767 allowed_vendor_type: 776 allowed_vendor_type: 780
allowed_vendor_type: 785 allowed_vendor_type: 793 allowed_vendor_type:
797 allowed_vendor_type: 798 allowed_vendor_type: 808
allowed_vendor_type: 813 allowed_vendor_type: 814 allowed_vendor_type:
815 allowed_vendor_type: 818 allowed_vendor_type: 826
allowed_vendor_type: 828 allowed_vendor_type: 832 allowed_vendor_type:
864 allowed_vendor_type: 874 allowed_vendor_type: 880
allowed_vendor_type: 884 allowed_vendor_type: 885 allowed_vendor_type:
886 allowed_vendor_type: 888 allowed_vendor_type: 889
excluded_sensitive_category: 19 excluded_sensitive_category: 4
excluded_sensitive_category: 23 excluded_sensitive_category: 30
excluded_sensitive_category: 10 excluded_sensitive_category: 3
excluded_sensitive_category: 31 excluded_sensitive_category: 5
excluded_sensitive_category: 8 excluded_sensitive_category: 18

FIGURE 8.3

A screenshot of an AdX Bid Request object for a *New York Times* article for the Google Ad Exchange (called AdX). Viewability can be seen in the 13th line of the second column.

matching_ad_data { billing_id: 44193563514 minimum_cpm_micros: 72680000
pricing_rule { minimum_cpm_micros: 72680000 } } slot_visibility:
NO_DETECTION excluded_product_category: 10031 excluded_product_category:
10048 excluded_product_category: 10050 excluded_product_category: 10085
excluded_product_category: 10127 excluded_product_category: 10299
excluded_product_category: 10454 excluded_product_category: 10584
excluded_product_category: 11669 excluded_product_category: 11772
excluded_product_category: 12865 excluded_product_category: 13422
excluded_product_category: 13536 ad_block_key: 361006263
publisher_settings_list_id: 3444293677936173152
publisher_settings_list_id: 1129425920034446512
allowed_restricted_category: 33 iframing_state: UNKNOWN_IFRAME_STATE
viewability: 60 allowed_restricted_category_for_deals: 33 31: "" 36:
"\000" } is_test: false cookie_version: 1 google_user_id:
"CAESEPGREhUZCsoxgUgBu-Ef8hs" timezone_offset: 60
detected_content_label: 26 detected_content_label: 120
detected_content_label: 40 cookie_age_seconds: 0 geo_criteria_id:
1006886 encrypted_hyperlocal_set:
"Y\032@\207\000\017\a\347\n\033\247C\002\006(\226\273\366}\000\343\031\3
64\310Q\036\001\326\276\357L/\340\245\002p\303\302\301\343\\Y\332?\375\2
54\002\225\2463YI9\362b\216m/j\243~xM@\032g.v=\026\322\"<\005Am\312K<\37
7\206\257" seller_network_id: 1251 publisher_type:
ADX_PUBLISHER_OWNED_AND_OPERATED hyperlocal_set { hyperlocal { corners {
latitude: 51.490345 longitude: -0.2034498 } corners { latitude:
51.490345 longitude: -0.0907036 } corners { latitude: 51.560493
longitude: -0.0907036 } corners { latitude: 51.560493 longitude: -
0.2034498 } } center_point { latitude: 51.525417 longitude: -0.1470767 }
} device { device_type: PERSONAL_COMPUTER platform: "Windows"
screen_pixel_ratio_millis: 1000 } 55: "US"

FIGURE 8.3
(continued)

entities of a given sector, such as goods, tasks, users, marketers, customers, suppliers, advertisements, and music tracks (Rosch et al. 1976). They can be the digital rendition of social roles and entities, physical machinery such as engines in manufacturing plants, or stuff that does not exist outside the ecosystem in which they operate.

Data objects aren't digitized versions of existing entities. An ad impression object, for instance, does not represent a social entity whose existence can be referred to anywhere outside programmatic advertising. It rather reconstructs an *editable* and *executable* version of the rules and behavior of ad impressions. Such a version remains linked to what already operated as a weak or soft standard in the advertising industry but is now based on data and methods that weren't available before. Interactions of a certain kind happen because data objects execute several basic functions and because actors implement automatic responses (via other objects, APIs, and algorithms) to object rules and behaviors.[11]

The rules of such interactions embedded in data objects constitute the basis of actors' exchanges. At the same time, objects are editable. The digital nature of such entities allows for accommodating the constant change that occurs across the heterogeneity of actors, actor roles, tasks, and resources and the variety of situations involved in the ecosystem exchange. Objects are routinely updated in terms of properties and parameters, fields are deprecated, access to them is restricted, and the interactive properties of objects with other objects are endlessly optimized. Much of this regulates how specific categories of actors access objects (and their data) via a thick infrastructure of data technologies such as algorithms, APIs, and other interfaces. As certain interactions are structured by the work of data objects and related technologies and stabilized into patterns, they come to be crystallized into roles with their own set of specific resources, permissions, and tools. Data objects take part in reframing the knowledge, soft standards, and behavioral scripts of actors, allowing novel modalities through which different types of data are produced and relate to one another.

Data objects and the sociotechnical resources that regulate patterns of data exchange become essential to understanding how certain types of interdependency emerge and evolve and how others decay. As ecosystem actors predominantly interact with objects rather than with each other, data objects acquire a powerful role in shaping novel forms of organizational and institutional agency. It is important to consider that data objects are neither technological devices nor simply goods or resources that are produced and exchanged. They are rather the new social entities that structure certain conditions of production and exchange in vast, agnostic, and dispersed data spaces. Data objects embed agreed-upon rules and accommodate change by executing functions on behalf of users. In doing so, they structure the possibilities of creating value-reinforcing complementarities for different categories of actors. These new, data-based versions of users, impressions, marketers, and publishers define ecosystem roles, interactions, and interdependencies in a dynamic, recursive, and constitutive relation.

SUMMARY AND IMPLICATIONS

After more than two decades of nonintervention politics, there has recently been a shift in the public perception and political discourse concerning the necessity of regulating platform ecosystems. As noted in chapter 5, the European Union (EU) recently introduced the Digital Services Act (DSA) and the Digital Markets Acts (DMA) as part of a wider legislative effort aimed at ensuring the proper function of the digital economy. The DMA focuses on issues of competition and innovation in digital markets and is particularly relevant to platform ecosystems.

Beyond the specificities of the DMA, which are addressed elsewhere (see, e.g., Colangelo 2023; Jacobides & Lianos 2021; Larouche & de Streel 2021), what remains still largely absent from the current debate on regulation is an assessment of the validity of the premises and assumptions upon which such regulatory efforts are predicated (with few exceptions, such as Cennamo et al. 2023; Cioffi, Kenney, & Zysman 2022; Jenny 2021). We are not referring to principles or social values, which would still be interesting to discuss from time to time, but rather to something more primary, relating to the knowledge assumptions upon which the regulatory interventions are erected. The first set of assumptions concern the notion of data and what data are. The relevant issues have been thoroughly discussed throughout the book, specifically in chapter 5.

Rather than reiterating them here, we would like to draw attention to several important implications that stem from the misperception of data and weigh heavily on the current regulatory approach to digital platforms and ecosystems. If data are considered as input to algorithmic systems, the only option left to regulators is to regulate algorithmic systems. This misstep may have costly unintended consequences as regulators would find themselves chasing individual technological developments rather than producing frameworks within which individual technologies can develop. The difference is well exemplified by the approach to tracking in the General Data Protection Regulation (GDPR). It poorly defines personal data and badly regulates cookies (one of the many tracking technologies) rather than producing a strong legal framework that regulates behavioral advertising. One of the many unintended consequences of the GDPR has been to make competition worse in some cases, as end users tend to trust large providers (see, e.g., Peukert et al. 2022); meanwhile, in the behavioral advertising sector, the rich become richer. Data assumptions may trigger conflicting rules and the overstepping of obligations from one jurisdictional sector to the other (Obendiek 2023). A clear example is the trade-off implied between sharing end-user data versus protecting end-user data safety and security.

If data are considered fixed items, ready-made resources kept in some of the silos (repositories) of large data infrastructures, then platform ecosystems are virtually economic actors that extract those resources only by exploiting users, while withholding them by blocking fair access to competitors. Aligned with those assumptions, regulation maintains its traditional approach, applying existing competition law recipes to regulate the access or accumulation of such resources. Such an approach sidesteps the distinct nature of data as resources and the specificities of data production processes, including the knowledge and technical capabilities that the approach requires and the variety of institutional contexts in which it takes place. In addition, it completely overlooks the character of platforms and ecosystems as novel economic actors whose positions in the digital economy sit uncomfortably in the conceptual cages of markets and bounded (or traditional) organizations (see chapter 6 in this regard, as well as figure 8.1). This is the problem with the DMA and the current approach to competition in digital markets. In this case, wrong assumptions mostly concern the relation between data (poorly defined) and innovation, and by extension, value creation.

The assumption that data are ready-made resources extracted in ways analogous to physical resources has far-reaching implications for the perception of the contribution of the main actors dealing with data (i.e., platforms and ecosystems) that cascade across the processes that underlie data-based innovation and value creation. Data are never found, and even if they are not costly to reproduce, their production costs may be far from negligible. In fact, so far, data production costs have not been properly accounted for, partially because of the misrepresentation of data as ready-made resources resting idle somewhere. Yet, particularly when data are innovative or significant for developing highly specialized knowledge, they are far from cheap to produce (as any researcher should know). The mechanical and automated operations by which they are often generated foster the illusion that data are cheap to produce, as they make it easy to conflate high fixed costs with low variable costs. Clicks and other anonymous acts such as scrolling, swiping, or tapping are only the last moments of a long process that, as seen in chapter 4, involves a variety of cognitive, economic, and technological steps and resources. A click becomes possible thanks to a complex and ramified set of technological operations and should make sense within a system of communication where it works as a sign of approval, preference, or any other type of signification that it performs. Within the gears of the digital economy, a click can become many other things (e.g., data objects, data doubles, or data twins). This too, involves several infrastructures, actors, and technological capabilities. In the end, part of the output of this process is fed back to users as innovative data-based services, while another part is opened to third parties for further and often complementary innovations. The common misperception of data as fixed and ready-made items discounts the fact that data are always outputs of a complex process before being inputs for others.

In this respect, the hard-to-die motto "More data, better products" does not go far in acknowledging the complexities, interrelations, and feedback loops of the digital economy. Similarly, the regulatory efforts that find their point of departure on assumptions such as "more data leads to more market power" fall short of understanding that the power of big players does not come only from access to data, but from access to means of data production. Access to vast quantities of data with no institutional, technical, or cultural capacity to work with those data may lead nowhere.

In current attempts, the process of innovating with data is left black-boxed, with legislators cherry-picking a few of its operations, isolating them, and issuing a set of obligations. The complex and reciprocal entanglements of actors participating in the innovation process are left unacknowledged. Issues such as competition across different ecosystems are not addressed (see Cennamo & Santalò 2022). The natural trade-offs arising from picking up only one stick in a massive Mikado game are not discussed.

Besides the points already raised and other shortcomings of the DMA (for more, see Cennamo et al. 2023; Colangelo 2023), a few more abstract questions arise on the scope and aims of a general approach to regulating the digital economy that does not consider the complex interdependencies between data, the economy, and society. The ideas put forward in this chapter debunk this approach. Ecosystems have mostly been studied through the lens of preconceived categories such as types of actors (i.e., complementors, developers, users, or buyers), established notions of complementarities (i.e., specific versus generic), and a limited view of the heterogeneity of the actors, actor roles, tasks, and processes that underlie the economic functions that ecosystems perform.

Even more regretful seem to be the limited attention that research on ecosystems has paid to the technological upheavals that over the course of several decades have redefined the texture of the economy and society touched upon chapters 5 and 6. It wouldn't be an exaggeration to argue that save a few exceptions (e.g., Márton 2022; Wang 2021), the literature on ecosystems overlooks the technological processes that make current business ecosystems novel compared to existing interorganizational networks. Ecosystems become widespread interorganizational arrangements thanks to the variety of functions that they perform in the current economy and society beyond familiar business affiliations. Such functions, we have argued, are marked by the critical role that data and data technologies assume as diffuse artifacts of cognition and knowledge. These ideas should make regulators cautious when seeking to apply existing approaches to ecosystems.

An important claim we make throughout this chapter connects to the emerging nature of complementarities and, by extension, the data-based processes by which complementarities are sustained and managed. In this hypertechnological age, complementarities are not given in advance. They do not inhere to the specific nature of resources and the ways that actors can manipulate these resources to forge complementarities. Rather, complementarities are constantly made and remade under data rules (i.e., by how data encode economic and social facts), and data management technologies dynamically reweave the fabric of economic relations and, by doing this, extend the semantic horizon against which new relations are perceived and built. Conceived in more abstract terms, the ways that we treat complementarities suggest that relations rather than actors/resources should become the primary unit of ecosystem analysis (Abdelnour et al. 2017; Abbott 1995; Bailey et al. 2022; Bateson 1972/2000; Hanseth 2022; Kempton 2022; Star 1995; Star & Griesemer 1989; Star & Ruhleder 1996; Wang 2021). The structure of relations that is the ecosystem, we claim, does not derive from the alignment of actors and the resources that they command (e.g., Adner 2017), but rather from the much more complex, insidious, and dynamic character of structural conditions and processes that link tasks, functions, technologies, data, data structures, and ultimately, organizations and actors (Kallinikos 2007).

Making relations and the ways that they form and dissolve the focus of analysis in ecosystems amounts to a call to address the technological dynamics that rule and dissolve ecosystem structures and investigate the causes and modalities of ecosystem emergence and evolution (Iansiti & Levien 2004). The central role that we accord to relations in this context should not be understood as a claim to the ontological primacy of relations vis-à-vis entities, but rather as a methodological principle for investigating a world in constant flux. Relations are of entities as much as entities are of relations (Abbott 1995); that is, relations are made of entities that pre-exist them as much as they may help bring about entities that were not there before. It is the position of entities within a network of relations that defines their function (Faulkner & Runde 2013; Kempton 2022).

Shifting positions may bring about new relations epistemically (the perception of new things) and can ultimately arrive at constructing new entities, as architecture qua field often illustrates. The structure of relations that decree the making of complementarities attests to the fundamental fact that the complexity of ecosystems and the many things and relations that they are made of usually develop beyond the limited horizon of willful actors and their decisions. Focusing on the structuring of relations holds the promise of disclosing how different types of complementarities lead to different forms and degrees of interdependency (Wang 2021). A better appreciation of these interdependencies within and across ecosystems in turn may help bring back the "eco" in "ecosystems" (Iansiti & Levien 2004; Márton 2021; Phillips & Ritala 2019; Ritala & Almpanopoulou 2017; Shipilov & Gawer 2020) and avoid the fallacy of studying ecosystems as functional networks, created and managed to serve the pecuniary and political objectives of specific actors. As the empirical illustrations in this chapter suggest, value-reinforcing relations are seldom the outcome of deliberate planning alone.

Such a focus may contribute to the public discourse on platform and ecosystem regulation by inserting data and their rules at the center of ecosystem formation and evolution.

9 EPILOGUE

REINVENTING THE MARKET ECONOMY

Throughout the pages of this book, we have traced the system of forces and operations with which the diffusion of digital data is associated and explored the critical role that data and data objects assume in the technological, social, and economic transformations that mark our times. Data perform functions critical to the current economy and its institutions. As tools of cognition and knowledge, data enable marking, encoding, inventing, calculating, and establishing diverse facets of reality that in turn furnish the ground upon which much of new organizational and economic relations are built, including the making and exchanging of data commodities. The diversified system of operations and relations in which digital data are embedded makes them ubiquitous elements of the current economy and society, as well as a critical frontier of new practice formation and socioeconomic restructuring.

The scale of these transformations is clearly shown in the rise of new enterprise forms such as those exemplified by digital platforms. In a rather short period of time, digital platforms have grown into pervasive providers of goods and services that result from how they mediate the contributions and pursuits of diverse and often populous types of actors. The economic functions that platforms perform cross the traditional divide of production and intermediation and reconfigure the institutional settings in which organizations and markets have traditionally been embedded (Arrow 1974). Throughout this volume, we have shown that platforms are underlain by a pronounced outbound orientation that repositions the focus of organizational operations from the resource conversion process itself to the system of rules and technological facilities that mediate the economic exchanges and relationships of platform participants. Viewed in this light, platforms are conspicuously different beasts from the bounded and concentrated forms of organization that dominated the production of goods and services during large parts of the industrial age and the early information economy. It is perhaps the most emblematic organizational form of the age and a clear indicator of wider technological, economic, and social transformations that call for and enable new patterns of producing and delivering goods and services.

These transformations are forcefully shown in the complex machinery of data operations that register, process, carry out, aggregate, and variously compute the actions of hugely diversified and distributed populations of users (e.g., producers, consumers, financial institutions, regulators, and third parties). The scale, complexity, and sophistication of these data operations, often performed on the fly, grant platforms a functional profile that distinguishes them from earlier forms of intermediation. The distribution of knowledge and the processing capacity of markets that arguably made them superior coordination mechanisms vis-a-vis centralized systems (Hayek 1945) are dwarfed compared to the distribution, dynamic character, and scale of knowledge (data) operations that underlie the operations of platforms. In this regard, platforms are more than just enterprise forms. They are the organizational format of an age in which the functions and boundaries of central modern institutions such as organizations versus markets are redefined, along with many of the distinctions that they have occasioned, such as those of private versus public life, internal organizational operations versus external events, concentration versus distribution of activities, and social versus economic relevance.

The rise of platforms coincides with the formation of broader arrangements of economic exchanges and operations that have often been referred to in the literature as "ecosystems." In some ways, platforms cannot exist without ecosystems. Ecosystems are essential to platforms insofar as platform operations entail the tuning and coordination of the resources and operations of different types of participants in large numbers. At the same time, the structuring of such business relationships by means of data enables the pursuit of value-reinforcing synergies or complementarities that stretch beyond individual platforms and frequently alternate between several platforms. The boundaries distinguishing platforms from ecosystems are undeniably fluid and often hard to draw. It is nonetheless important to remind that platforms remain enterprise forms, legal sites of rent extraction and capital accumulation. By contrast, digital ecosystems are better seen as collective arrangements of coordination that enable the exploration and building of economic relationships across the boundaries of familiar activities and business affiliations that would have remained unfulfilled in their absence. Looked at this way, platforms and ecosystems could be seen as structurally equivalent to firms and industries.

These remarks should make evident that the mediating functions of platforms and the type of complementarities characteristic of ecosystems are heavily reliant on data and the rules that dictate the functions that data perform. None of the operations of platforms and ecosystems could ever be imagined, let alone performed, without the liquefaction of the real (Leonardi 2012; Monteiro 2022; Monteiro & Parmiggiani 2019) that data afford and the mediation, continuous monitoring, and assessment of means/ends sequences that they enable. The scope, geographical expansion, and distribution of platforms and ecosystems make the functional tasks achieved by data essential to the building of ties that platforms and ecosystems instantiate. In this regard, data and platforms/ecosystems presuppose and reinforce one another.

The theorization of data and their placement at the center of these transformations distinguish our own contribution from the overwhelming part of the literature on these subjects. Data are conspicuously absent and undertheorized in much of the current body of literature on platforms and ecosystems or, in the best case, are considered as assets and treated in terms of the functions that they assume as nonrival and nondepletable resources (see, e.g., Adner 2017; Brynjolfsson & McAfee 2014; Jacobides et al. 2018; McIntyre & Srinivasan 2017; McIntyre et al. 2020; Parker et al. 2016). We have time and again stressed the variety of functions that data perform beyond those traditionally associated with assets and resources. Data, we claimed, are instruments of marking and world-making, tools of knowledge development, and media of communication that essentially transcribe the obstinate relations of the economic order to the revocable order of signs (i.e., data tokens) (Knorr-Cetina 1999). This massive rendition of things and situations into data provides the basis for reimagining, rehearsing, and reconfiguring the social and technical constraints that have traditionally accommodated the operations of markets and organizations in modern times (Arrow 1974).

Left on their own, these developments might seem limited to the economic sphere and the restructuring of its institutions (i.e., markets and organizations). The advent of platforms as enterprise forms and ecosystems as coordinative arrangements, however, transcends the orbit of economy alone and carries wider societal implications, which have been analyzed throughout this book. This should hardly come as a surprise to students of the social embedment of economy and the variety of links that bind economy to society (Couldry & Mejias 2019, 2020; Granovetter 1985; Heller 1999; Polanyi 1944/2001; Luhmann 1982, 1995). Yet data, we have claimed, take the social embedment of economy to new directions and dissolve critical boundaries that once kept economy and society at arm's length from one another. The rendition of economic and social facts into data enables commensuration (Alaimo & Kallinikos 2017, 2022; Espeland & Stevens 1998; Espeland & Sauder 2007) or otherwise transcends the intrinsic differences underlying the varying regions of reality and transcribes and reduces these differences to common metrics. The philosophical assumptions upon which data societies are predicated are reflected in the often-unspoken belief that all things in life can be rendered as data and managed accordingly (see, e.g., Pentland 2014).

These trends show themselves with unusual evocation in the developments that challenge the characteristically modern separation of transactions from social interactions. Modernity singled out economic transactions from the wider context of social interaction and gave economic encounters distinct and functionally narrower attributes (Luhmann 1982). Even though that separation remained a problematic achievement (Zelizer 2005) throughout modern times, it is currently rehearsed along several frontiers and in ways that question whatever distinctive connotations have been attached to them. Data and the technologies with which they are closely related make it possible to overlay the data footprint of social interaction and communication (social and networking data) on the narrower spectrum of economic exchanges. The outcome, characteristic of the operations of platforms, is to merge and compare transaction exchanges and social interaction without regard to their conspicuously diverse origins and the varying life orders that they once served. It is not by accident that a key challenge confronting commercial, innovation, and social media platforms is building, maintaining, and governing diverse and shifting crowds, communities, or networks that perform a variety of functions and tasks beyond those linked with the familiar roles of clients, buyers, or employees. It is in this context that the economic notion of network effects should be read as an indirect measure of the sociality of goods and the value-building functions that social relationships confer on such goods.

Placed against this backdrop, the rules that dictate the generation, distribution, and use and reuse of data described in this book reposition the role of the economy vis-à-vis other social functions (e.g., education, health care, politics, and entertainment) and the wider society (Heller 1999). The economic, personal, and societal functions of data and the advance of platforms and ecosystems are thus indicative of a change of far-larger proportions (see, e.g., Greenfield 2017; Hildebrandt 2015) than what is commonly admitted by the instrumental and managerial reading of these developments, which are widespread in most of the platform and ecosystems literature.

Crowd participation and network building on platforms are characteristic of a new social architecture—a novel, as it were, social contract—whereby atomized actions and aggregate outcomes are brought together in ways hitherto unknown. Riding on the infrastructural affordances of digital technologies, such an architecture essentially refigures the modern social contract itself and the modes through which individuals qua sovereign subjects (Hildebrandt 2015; Hildebrandt & Rouvroy 2011) have so far been linked to stable and clearly bounded social and economic institutions. The distinctive flavor of this book and the major arguments put forward in its pages are closely linked to such a wider understanding of data and their socioeconomic implications. The making of platforms to diffuse enterprise/organizational forms and the advent of ecosystems to widespread arrangements of cooperation (and competition) are inconceivable without data. Both platforms and ecosystems presuppose and reinforce the reconfiguration of the borders that have separated economy from society, forms of interaction and engagement that are characteristic of daily life from the institutional order and the functions of institutions.

The market economy, of course, is a complex and multidimensional order itself that includes financial institutions and legal systems, along with the critical operations of the state without which the market economy probably would have remained a disembodied ideal (Polanyi 1944/2001). We have said very little in this book about these fundamental aspects of the market economy and the social order with which it is associated. We are keenly aware of these limitations. On the other hand, we have assumed throughout the book that an essential frontier along which the modern social order and its market economy are rehearsed coincides with the central place of formal organizations in the modern industrial society (Weber 1947/2012, 1978/2019). The bounded and concentrated form that such organizations have assumed throughout modern industrial history articulated the relationship between economy and society, markets as exchanged systems and organizations as sites of production (Kallinikos 2003, 2004). The ways that platforms and ecosystems challenge and redefine the patterns by which formal organizations have been implicated in these operations suggest to us that a change of major proportions is unfolding in front of our eyes. It is this change that we refer to as "the reinvention of the market economy." It is obvious that much more work is needed in this direction.

TOWARD A SOCIAL SCIENCE OF DATA

The far-reaching economic restructuring and social engineering that we attribute to data stand at the opposite end of a widespread perception across the management and social sciences literature that continues to consider data an appendix of the transformations that mark our times.

The common view of data across much of the social sciences is mostly as a by-product or supportive element of other operations that reflect the functions of social, economic, or political institutions and the rationalities governing them. In this view, data matter only to the degree that they serve the institutional orders in which they are embedded and the interests and preoccupations of the social actors that dominate them. While seemingly reasonable, such a view has little space for the unintended consequences of social action and no recognition for the forces that undo and elude established orders, social actors, and their pursuits (Kallinikos 2007; Knorr Cetina 1999; March & Olsen 1976, 1989). It critically lacks the conceptual apparatus for confronting and analyzing the structural grid into which data are embedded and the fascinating dynamics (i.e., the data rules) through which that grid reshapes the ends or objectives that purportedly data are called upon to serve. Some of these widely dispersed academic predilections are reinforced by the diffuse misperception of data as technological items and the conflation of the operations that we classified as semiotic, epistemic, and communication-based with the state of the art of the computational technologies from which data derive (recall chapters 3 and 4).

Contrary to these views, we consider data and the socioeconomic relations that keep on morphing around their production and use as establishing, as it were, its own gravity field, a new system of rules that qualify the operations of markets, organizations, and the modern institutional order. As data diffuse throughout the socioeconomic fabric, they become indispensable means by which the world is perceived, filtered, and understood, and productive relations instrumented, performed, and assessed. It is rather unlikely that the diversified operations that stem from this complex and evolving system of rules can solely be attributed to causes that are exogenous to it, driven by economic or political rationalities or institutional inertia. The semiotic, epistemic, and communication functions that this complex system of rules performs calls for explanation in terms that can do justice to its distinct profile and the processes and dynamics that it helps set in motion. Accounting for the workings of this system of rules by recourse to omniscient economic agents or the inertia of institutions are long-driven and unproductive simplifications of the far-reaching developments that unfold right in front of our eyes.

Once formed, this system of rules sets in motion dynamics (i.e., adjustments, incompatibilities, and path dependencies) that are endogenous to it. Data records in one area, for instance, may call for data records in adjacent areas that may illuminate a further lack of data and suitable arrangements in other areas, which may in turn generate further institutional setups and drive new cycles of development, and on and on (Arthur 2009; Bowker 2005; Hanseth 2022; Kallinikos 2007). While certainly punctuated by decisions derived from the institutional relations to which it is embedded, the workings of these data rules exhibit endogenous dynamics (specific to these rules), in which exogenous forces (political or economic decisions) have secondary significance. We have associated the formation of this system of rules with the functions that data perform as pervasive artifacts of cognition and knowledge and media of communication, the formation of new economic practices, the historical decline of the bounded and concentrated form of organization, and the rise of digital platforms and ecosystems. These changes are not mechanically installed, of course. The conditions underlying these changes frame what is perceived as possible or relevant, contribute to defining the nature of social and economic objectives, and ultimately shape the constitution of agency and modes of acting and evaluating (Abdelnour et al. 2017; Meyer & Jepperson 2000).

Approaching these multifaceted historic processes in terms of economic rationality (the prevailing view of platforms) alone unduly simplifies the structural composition of socioeconomic change and black-boxes the layered and sedimented patterns of solutions (e.g., the installed base) through which data processes and practices acquire their causal tenor (Arthur 2009; Hanseth 2022; Swanson 2022). The work of data rules is never a straightforward derivative of the rationalities, practices, and institutions with which it is associated. Rather, as these rules diffuse throughout the socioeconomic order, they acquire a sui generis existence that qualifies, annuls, extends, or modifies established rationalities, practices, and institutions (Winner 1978, 1986/2010, 1993). Or to put things more mildly, economic rationality, with or without the system of rules and its underlying data machinery (e.g., the variety of records, data management techniques, technological systems, and devices) that we expose in this book, is not the same thing. Finding out the differences by looking at both sides of the equation would seem critical.

There is currently a growing scholarship on the impact of data on such diverse areas as smart cities and traffic monitoring, science making, medicine and health care, law and police work, managerial strategy, industrial platforms and manufacturing, politics and justice, and social and commercial media, among other topics (see, e.g., Greenfield 2017). At the same time, ongoing research in each of these areas is uncertain with respect to the causal status of data and ambiguous with regard to the value of employing data as a lens for studying social and economic practices and institutions.

What is often missing is an outlook or approach that understands data as pervasive and distinct artifacts of knowledge, cognition, and communication and investigates the analytic paths along which the rules that they establish are involved in the restructuring of socioeconomic operations and the change of established institutions. To our knowledge, there is no systematic or coherent narrative in the current literature concerning how and why data matter beyond the specific areas or contexts in which their impact is investigated. But can there ever be such a narrative? Would it ever be possible to cross the intrinsic differences of the areas in which data perform their functions? Most critically, would it make sense to transcend the varying circumstances that each of these areas confronts and the particular social practices and technologies with which they are associated? And, if so, what purpose is served?

These are no doubt tantalizing questions that do not admit conclusive answers. Yet they are essential to raise, as they are closely associated with the difficulties of conjecturing the work of data rules and the range of semiotic, epistemic, and communication operations that data perform across the diverse areas of socioeconomic life. Some of these difficulties are certainly associated with the specific nature of the social and economic areas that are selected for study and the specific functions that data perform in these areas (e.g., health data, traffic data, data in education, and law enforcement and justice). Others reflect the prevailing division of labor in social sciences, along with the process of academic socialization that discourage perspective crossing and the adoption of new frames of reference. These difficulties are aggravated, as suggested, by the widespread misperception of data as mostly inputs to quantitative modeling that serve established fields of knowledge or practice (recall chapters 3 and 4). Such an understanding of data, it should be acknowledged, has a longer and undeniably productive line of descent. It is linked with the recording, interpretation, and management of a large number of contingent events of variable likelihood (probability) that are historically connected with the rise and significance of statistics and the modern social project (Hacking 1983, 1990).

The contingent empiricism of statistics and the capturing of miscellaneous events that intrinsically have no bounds (Rosch 1975; Rosch et al. 1976) as discrete and standardized tokens (data points) is a straightforward predecessor to current data science. Out of this grows the pervasive belief that sufficiently large numbers of tiny, rather insignificant, and properly standardized events can be made the stuff of which the leitmotifs and patterns of persons and institutions are inferred and physical processes and mechanical operations reconstructed. The road from statistics to data science is certainly more ambiguous and circuitous than these brief remarks suggest. However, the widespread and rather narrow perception of data as technical elements, devoid of meaning and causal tenor and assessed only in terms of their frequency or prevalence, is closely associated with the establishment and institutional success of statistics as the science of the probable and contingent.

The ideas put forward in this book represent a counterpoint but also a complement to the data perspectives and practices developing at the crossroads of statistics with engineering (i.e., artificial intelligence/AI) that characterizes current data science. In one way or another, these ideas work as signposts for rediscovering the semiotic, communication, and knowledge trajectories of data and the role that they play as active forces of the social and economic transformations that characterize our time. Such a perspective on data enables linking data to the study of culture and cognition and their significance across time (Tomasello 1999). Throughout the chapters of this book, we have repeatedly critiqued the narrow perception of data as just inputs to quantitative modeling and showed the paths along which such a limited outlook can be transcended. The character of data as artifacts of cognition and knowledge and communication media cannot be undone by the technological circuits in which they are inscribed, and the role reserved to them by statistics and data science. Semantics precedes counting, as Frege (1964) put it some time ago. Counting is inexorably applied to some aspect of the world that has been lifted out of its dense background through intelligible operations and accordingly established as separate from others to admit enumeration and any other operations that enumeration affords, including inference (Kallinikos 2010; Porter 1995, Rose 1991). Selecting an aspect of the real is always a meaningful operation that transcends counting and, also, an operation (as noted several times) that could have produced other results had it been predicated on other assumptions or outlooks.

Conceived along these lines, data are important social and cultural artifacts through which aspects of the intelligibility of the current world are perceived and understood, and the actions of social and economic institutions organized, performed, and assessed. Such a conception of data as multifaceted artifacts of meaning and communication that affect the social and economic world in ways that are not reducible to exogenous forces justifies putting forward the quest for a social science of data, distinct and different from the methods and techniques of data science (Couldry & Kallinikos 2017). By a social science of data, we envision an analytic project that reconceives data as cultural records and artifacts of cognition and unpacks the fabric of operations by which the social and economic objects of the current world are generated and managed through data. This is obviously an intellectual undertaking that surpasses the confines of engineering, statistics, and economics and the understanding of data in sheer technical or economic (i.e., assets or resources) terms. It is an undertaking that requires the conceptual resources of social science and the ways that it has in the past helped us comprehend the broader social contours of such fields as statistics and mathematics (Desrosiéres 1998; Hacking 1990; Porter 1995) and sociocultural developments such as the rise and diffusion of numeracy (Cline-Cohen 1982; Hopwood 1987; Miller 2004; Rose 1991) and the management of uncertainty and risk in modern times (Graeber 2011; Power 2007; Zelizer 2005).

It is reasonable to wonder what types of problems a social science of data should study and what kind of knowledge it is likely to promote. Following the ideas that we have put forward in this book, we can claim that a social science of data carries the promise of unpacking the predilections through which data are generated and disclose the partial, fallible, and transient relationships their aggregation and computation occasion. Such a science can also entail research on the practices of calibration and negotiation through which data contribute to the construction of local orders, much in the spirit of what has over the last few decades came to be widely known by the abbreviation STS (which stands for "science and technology studies").

Placed against this background, a social science of data may be interpreted as a mode of engagement that is no longer concerned with basic or foundational issues but rather with the dynamics of the transient events that are characteristic of our world and the local practices to which these dynamics give rise. The reorientation away from substantial or foundational issues and toward small events of provisional and revocable status engulfed in limited enclaves of the social world fits, perhaps, what Knorr Cetina (1999), in a rather different context, referred to as "negative knowledge." That is, a knowledge that unfolds around the limits of knowing, its temporal and transitive nature, its inherent fallibility, and the practices of calibration, revision, restoring, and repair of the social or economic areas that it addresses (see also Monteiro 2022). To a certain extent, the ideas put forward in this book fit this picture.

There is, however, another sense in which data and the technological and institutional relations that they form transcend the data practices of restoration, revision, and calibration that are linked to the workings of negative knowledge. In this book, we have described data and the network of relations in which they are embedded as a system of rules that are centrally implicated in, and to a certain degree govern, the broader social and economic transformations of our times. The functions that data perform across social and economic settings conjure up a system of forces that redefine long-standing patterns of producing goods and services and restructure the operations of markets and organizations along with the links that these institutions have maintained with the wider society. Rather than considering the spread of data only as an index of negative knowledge, we view the developments that they are part of as characteristic of an emerging socioeconomic order in which the representational, performative, and evaluative functions of data increasingly move to the center stage of the operations of its institutions.

NOTES

CHAPTER 1

1. The focus of this book is on digital data. As in most of the ongoing discourse on digital data, we often use the term "data" rather than "digital data." There are, however, several occasions where we use "data" to encompass the antecedents of digital technologies and digital data and others where we use it to refer to data as a generic label that includes both digital and nondigital tokens. The difference, we hope, will be evident from the context. When this is not obvious, we use the qualifier "digital" to forestall misunderstanding.

2. See chapter 3 for a more elaborate discussion of the formal attributes of digital data.

3. Such a statement should not be understood as a claim along conventionalist lines, a kind of "anything goes" so far as a community decides it to be. We view the understanding of data along the terms expounded here as being broadly compatible with realism (see Hacking 1982, 1999; Searle 1995, 2010).

CHAPTER 2

1. However, a bone marked with tally and used as an early counting device was found and dated to more than 30,000 years ago. Tally sticks as a form of receipt for government income were used by the British government until 1826 (see Agar 2003).

2. Very interesting in this regard is the recent special issue edited by Aronova, von Oertzen, and Sepkoski, who consider "big data" as a chapter in a "longer history of observation, quantification, statistical methods, models and computing technologies" (2017, 6).

3. This is, as Jack Goody (1986, xiv) reminds us, a form of inquiry with a respectable lineage that is very much used across a broad spectrum of social science to discuss

the effect of a major shift in social practice such as the implication of printing, personal computers, and writing. (See also, for instance, Eisenstein 1979; Turckle 1984.)

4. Hal Varian (2010) starts with clay tokens to lay the groundwork for his conceptualization of computer-mediated transactions, which will be later operationalized by his work as the chief economist of Google.

5. Records are defined as "information or data on a specific subject collected methodically over a long period" (https://www.collinsdictionary.com/dictionary /english/records). They are always embedded in a format (i.e., marks, written text, and pictures) and are supported by physical carriers or bearers (i.e., stone, wood, paper, and film). Writing, as such, is just one of the formats (codes or languages) in which record keeping can occur.

6. As Bowker (2005) suggested, the database, far from being an invention of the computer era, preexisted the computer revolution and indeed led to it.

7. This was done by Christopher Wood, a professor at the University of Chicago's Oriental Institute, as reported in Owen (2013).

8. According to Schmandt-Besserat, who dedicated her life to the study of clay tokens, "the invention of the [clay] envelopes seems to have been stimulated by the need to confer an official character on certain transactions by the means of seals" (Schmandt-Besserat 1980, 366); see also MacGinnis et al. (2010, 291) and Oppenheim (1959).

9. As we will see in the next sections, the practice bears a close resemblance with that of creating social objects out of statistical regularities that emerged prominently during modernity and the several accounting devices or knowledge objects that accompanied the birth of modern corporations. In the next chapters, we will refer again to clay envelopes, as their cognitive function is somehow mirrored by one of the most relevant contemporary data work practices that can create novel social objects out of data aggregation and structuration.

10. It is now generally accepted that writing was initially established to support accounting and record-keeping systems rather than, as previously believed, to transcribe oral communications (Ong 1982). See also Goody (1986, 49).

11. See also Beniger (1986); Kallinikos (2001, 23–35).

12. We are suggesting that writing can be included in a larger family of technologies of recording and representing that, even with significant differences, presents strong commonalities in the making of "signifying entities" that become independent from what they communicate, represent, or inform about (see, e.g., Eisentein 1979; Poovey 1998 and her account of numbers as epistemological units; Havelock 1986).

13. Clay tokens have been found in association with several other accounting devices within a building, on the site of Ziyaret Tepe on the river Tigris (in what today is in southeastern Turkey), which unambiguously served economic and administrative functions. Together with tokens, archaeologists have found tablets concerned with transactions of grain, receipts of barley, loans of barley, and payments for rations.

They also found a stone duck weighing 30 kilograms corresponding to one of the Assyrian talents (unity of measure), which would have been used in the weighing of metal, textiles, and bitumen. Archaeologists are certain that tokens from the site were used to monitor commodities (or animals) or information concerning them, such as keeping track of livestock holding or the management of grain stores. Also, they were used in administering accounts, where tokens were placed in leather or textile bags prior to the recording of the entries in waxed tables or in conjunction to them, or to recording transactions that could not be recorded by written means. See MacGinnis et al. (2014).

14. As Havelock himself suggested, the matter was first noted by Plato in his *Phaedrus* (Havelock 1963).

15. The expression "Given this, then," which in common language does not refer to something but rather initiates an argument, comes much closer to the original meaning and use of "datum" and "data" than the forced interpretation of data as facts (Rosenberg 2013).

16. In her beautiful epistemological history of facts, Poovey also well illustrates the connections between the rise of numerical representations as facts and what happens afterward:

After the late nineteenth century, at least in the natural and social sciences, expert knowledge producers sought not to generate knowledge that was simultaneously true to nature and systematic but to model the range of the normal or sometimes simply to create the most sophisticated models from available data, often using mathematical formulas. As the units of such models, postmodern facts are not necessarily observed particulars, instead, as digital "bits" of information, the "phenomenological laws" of physics, or poststructuralist signifiers with no referent, they are themselves already modeled and thus exist at one remove from what the eye can see, although they are no less the units by which we make what counts as knowledge about our world. (Poovey 1998, 3–4).

17. As Foucault (1963/2012) remarks, "Analysis was defined according to the epistemological model of mathematics and the instrumental structure of ideology. As an instrument, it served to define the system of implications in its complex totality" (105). The very idea of modern medical knowledge was constructed and operated on the basis of its links with measure both in the sense of standard model of knowledge and public action.

18. This is so much the case that Nikolas Rose called them the "technology of the soul" (quoted in Porter 1995).

CHAPTER 3

1. Even Hollerith's invention has its own predecessors in the work of Charles Babbage, and several important inventions and technological developments are disseminated

in the work of computer pioneers Alan Turing, Konrad Zouse, and John von Neumann. However, it is with Hollerith, and later with IBM, that machines enter into businesses and organizations. For a history of computers, see Agar (2017), Campbell-Kelly, Aspray, Yost, Tinn, & Díaz (2023), Ceruzzi (2012), and Cortada (2019), among others.

2. Already by 1955, for instance, SHARE, one of the biggest IBM user communities, had been established with the purpose of suggesting improvements and giving feedback to the technology giant (Cortada 2016, 180–181). Cortada also illustrates many other examples of continuous feedback that took place either directly, through official channels, or indirectly, through the nascent ecosystem of expert publications, magazines, and conferences.

3. Later, when computers eventually displaced tabulating equipment in the 1960s, the centrality of data over computational features was reasserted by the implementation and diffusion of Common Business-Oriented Language (COBOL), a high-level programming language for business applications based on data and file structures, which prevailed over FORTRAN (whose name stands for "FORmula TRANslation"), a language developed for scientific computing (Swanson 2022, 2).

4. We refer here to just one approach of defining information that keeps data and information separate based on their semantic properties. Albeit very diffuse, this approach is not the only one. Although we are aware that addressing the conceptual dispute over what distinguishes data from information would require another tack altogether, this is not the task of this chapter. Here, we merely point toward the *artificial* separation between the two that was introduced at some point in history when machines took over information-related tasks. As for the discussion about definitions and approaches to these vexed matters, others have done a much more thorough job (see, e.g., Borgmann 1999; Eco 1976; Floridi 2010, 2013; Swanson 2022).

5. It is very important to stress that the "communication" aspect of Claude Shannon's *Mathematical Theory of Communication* is a "transmission," as communication is a much more complex endeavor than transmission is (see also Floridi 2013, 46; Shannon & Weaver 1949).

6. There are a few notable exceptions, of course. One is represented by the scholarly tradition that has narrated and documented the history of the Internet and the web, focusing on communities and individuals. Within this tradition, several significant contributions have shed light on the social and cultural consequences of computer-mediated interactions (see, e.g., Nardi 1996; Turkle 1984, 1995, 2011); however, very few have focused on the role of data and information as complex and dynamic cognitive artifacts that link technological implementations to social change (see, e.g., Borgmann 1999; Carr 2009, 2010; Manovich 2002; Nardi & O'Day 2000; Turow & Tsui 2008).

7. In 2015, Zuboff published a very well received piece in which she criticizes Varian's points, specifically on the new forms of contract established by computer-mediated

transactions. Zuboff argues that when surveillance technology is in place, there is no trust, and therefore no contract. Even if we take her point, this does not invalidate the fact that computer-mediated transactions give rise to new forms of social exchange. Although the idea of surveillance capitalism (Zuboff 2015, 2019) has been successful in many respects, it has also glossed over some of the most complex aspects of how data are connected to social interaction, new forms of sociality, and economic value. We will take on and explain this topic in the remaining chapters of this book.

CHAPTER 4

1. There is a quite common misunderstanding of data as being the first step in a pyramid that leads to information, knowledge, and wisdom. The data-knowledge life cycle, in other words, is generally seen as a linear progression from bits to wisdom. Yet data cannot be produced out of thin air, nor can they blossom out of real-life events. The data life cycle is a process of worldmaking that starts from selecting events, stimuli, or properties that will be encoded into digital data. Selection is always based on knowledge. See, for instance, Tuomi (1999) and Kallinikos (2007, chap. 3).

2. See Dourish (2017) for a telling example.

3. Although it is not immediate, it is important to think that a playback signal may be sent by a streaming device and taken as the indication of an event, even if the event has not occurred. For instance, a signal may be sent even when users skip a track. The decision and design of which kind of signal should be taken as the indication of a listening event are part of the process of data making.

4. The illustration shows also how the road to data, data objects, and recommendations is littered with errors. The concept of errors and the active role that they play in data making and algorithmic systems would require a more ample reflection than what it is usually dedicated to them in the literature. Some scholars are starting to tackle these relevant issues (see, e.g., Hand 2020; Thylstrup, Agostinho, Ring, D'Ignazio, & Veel 2021).

5. See, for instance, Iqbal (2019).

6. CPM, together with cost per click, are the main standards of the industry.

CHAPTER 5

1. Cambridge Analytica used personal data from millions of Facebook users without their consent to provide analytic support to the targeting strategies of the 2016 electoral campaign of President Donald Trump.

2. GDPR came to replace the Data Protection Directive, which had been in place in the European Union since 1995. Economic firms and other institutions were given a two-year window to make their practices and policies conform to GDPR.

3. The DMA and the DSA are part of the sustained effort of the European Union to regulate the digital economy. The GDPR (2018), the Open Data Directive (2019), the European Data Act (2022), the Data Governance Act (2022), and the Artificial Intelligence Act (still being considered) represent other relevant initiatives. All these acts are centrally concerned with data. Although the list of such laws is much longer, from the examples given here, it is perhaps already apparent how the proliferation of legislation on data creates a complex tangle of hardly enforceable rules by referring to distinct law traditions and overstepping on different jurisdictions.

4. The GDPR, for instance, must be understood in such a context.

CHAPTER 6

1. The establishment of firms and organizations as bounded and concentrated systems should not be conflated with what in the past has been referred to as "closed systems." Bounded and concentrated organizations interact and communicate with their environments on a regular basis. They do so along paths that are largely premeditated and controlled, even though none of them offers a guarantee against uncertainty and unpredictability.

2. The conflation of jurisdictional responsibility with the structural and functional makeup of the firm represents a widespread source of confusion with respect to the kind of organizations that platforms are and the ways that they differ from standard firms. We will explore this topic more in this chapter and the remaining chapters of this book.

3. An exception should perhaps be made for Castells (1996, 2000, 2001).

4. It is worth pointing out that we deal here with the factors that shape institutional units, not with processes of control and coordination. The two are related, but they are also separate, in the sense that more or fewer decentralized and distributed forms of coordination may still be compatible with the bounded and concentrated institutional forms (see, e.g., Chesbrough 2003; Chesbrough, Vanhaverbeke, & West 2006).

5. As a matter of fact, the key specializations of the field of management taught in education still reecho the key groups of internal operations of the modern business enterprise. Marketing is an internal operation as far as its outgoing activities make sense only from the point of view of internal conditions, problems, and circumstances.

6. See Power (2007) for an exception.

CHAPTER 7

1. That is, backstage technologies of data management and frontage technologies of interfacing and hardware.

2. Smart phones, email accounts and social media accounts represent typical examples.

3. We illustrate such connections by referring to three different ecosystems in chapter 8.

4. By "value-reinforcing complementarities," we refer to the value of resource or activity combinations that accrues in ways other than additive and thus considerably enhance the value of the final outcome. Jacobides et al. (2018) describe them formulaically as "more of A makes B more valuable and vice versa." The case of operating systems and apps is a clear example.

CHAPTER 8

1. This increasingly includes all social relations, as seen in chapter 4.

2. In 2021, the share of programmatic advertising in digital display advertising spending in the US was projected to stand at 86.5 percent, attesting to the rapid diffusion and adoption of automated exchange across the industry. Acontecendo Aqui (2021).

3. We are indebted to Carmelo Cennamo for an original discussion of this matter.

4. Jacobides et al. (2018) refer to the distinction of generic versus specific to mark relations that cannot be taken care of by market mechanisms and therefore lead to ecosystem formation. As these distinctions do not apply to data, they will likely cease to be a determinant of market coordination versus ecosystem formation. Already the hybrid nature of digital platform ecosystems puts hard-boundary approaches to the test. What we are arguing here is that the proliferation of data ecosystems will likely lift prior boundaries and define new ones in ways that are bound to be transient and refigurable.

5. Data production is agnostic, nonneutral, and homogenizing and opens up possibilities of building relations across most regions of life transcending economic or productive domains and crisscrossing existing social divisions such as private versus public. At the same time, data keep their editability, portability, and recontextualizability for much of their value journey. This means that relations formed via data and because of data outputs are unstable, as we will see later in this chapter (also see chapters 3 and 4).

6. See Alaimo, Kallinikos, and Sannino (2022).

7. The RTB protocol derives from a concerted effort undertaken by a group of demand-side and supply-side platforms in 2010 (Alaimo 2022a). Under the supervision of the Interactive Advertising Bureau (IAB), these platforms started to lay down the standards for the programmatic exchange. JavaScript Object Notation (JSON) is the suggested format for bid request and bid response data payloads, but not the only one adopted. Google Ad Exchange (AdX), for instance, offers three protocol options: (1) Google Ad Exchange protocol; (2) Open RTB protobuf (a protocol buffer,

which is a free, open-source cross-platform data format used to serialize structured data); and (3) Open RTB JSON.

8. Similarly, the bid responses that are sent back to the AdX for impressions that fit a campaign's criteria (like match score, geolocation, ad-unit size) will carry objects and parameters to define the bid. Objects will include advertiser name, creative size, Cost per Mille (CPM) bid, impression-tracking Uniform Resource Locator (URL), and other information. The impression-tracking URL is an object utilized to track the transaction and the spending of the budget through AdX. If the bidder's bid response wins the auction, then the impression-tracking URL indicates the victory and triggers the CPM transaction that will then occur (Alaimo 2022a).

9. See Google, "OpenRTB Integration" (https://developers.google.com/ad-exchange /rtb/openrtb-guide). (The description is based on the 2018 version of the documentation; see Alaimo 2022a).

10. This is expressed as a percentage and calculated by considering historical data on user behavior and ad slot attribute data such as certain pixel and exposure thresholds, usually counting a minimum of 50 percent of the ad's pixel exposure for one or two continuous seconds. MRC and IAB (2017).

11. It contains different attributes that may refer to the type of ad (banner, video, native) subordinated to the impression object, size, price such as bid floor (if any), modality of exchange, such as if the object is exchanged through private marketplace, the expected time lag between bid winning and effective ad delivery, and an array of metrics. Google's AdX supplies three metrics for the ad impression object: viewability, click-through rate, and video completion rate. See Google, "OpenRTB Integration."

REFERENCES

Aaltonen, A., Alaimo, C., & Kallinikos, J. (2021). The making of data commodities. Data analytics as embedded process, *Journal of Management of Information Systems*, *38*(2), 401–429.

Abbate, J. (2000). *Inventing the Internet*. Cambridge, MA: MIT Press.

Abbott, A. (1995). Things of boundaries. *Social Research*, *62*(4), 857–882.

Abdelnour, S., Hasselbladh, H., & Kallinikos, J. (2017). Agency and institutions in organization studies. *Organization Studies*, *38*(12), 1775–1792.

Acontecendo Aqui. (2021). Share of programmatic in digital display advertising spending in the United States from 2019 to 2022 [Graph]. *Statista*, January 20. Retrieved April 7, 2021, from https://www.statista.com/statistics/311403/share-program matic-display-ad-spend-usa/.

Adner, R. (2017). Ecosystem as structure: An actionable construct for strategy. *Journal of Management*, *43*(1), 39–58.

Adner, R., & Levinthal, D. (2001). Demand heterogeneity and technology evolution: Implications for product and process innovation. *Management Science*, *47*(5), 611–628.

Agar, J. (2003). *The government machine: A revolutionary history of the computer*. Cambridge, MA: MIT Press.

Agar, J. (2006). What difference do computers make? *Social Studies of Science*, *36*(6), 869–907.

Agar, J. (2017). *Turing and the universal machine: The making of the modern computer*. London: Icon Books.

Ahonen, P. (Ed.). (1993). *Tracing the semiotic boundaries of politics*. Berlin: Walter de Gruyter.

Alaimo, C. (2022a). From people to objects: The digital transformation of fields. *Organization Studies*, *43*(7), 1091–1114.

Alaimo, C. (2022b). *The role of boundary resources in ecosystem innovation: A study of Facebook's evolution.* Available at SSRN: https://ssrn.com/abstract=4026712; http://dx.doi.org/10.2139/ssrn.4026712.

Alaimo, C., & Aaltonen, A. (2023). Data and strategy. In C. Cennamo, G. Dagnino, & F. Zhu (Eds.), *Research handbook on digital strategy* (pp. 239–254). Cheltenham, UK: Edward Elgar.

Alaimo, C., & J. Kallinikos (2016). Encoding the everyday: The infrastructural apparatus of social data. In C. Sugimoto, H. Ekbia, & M. Mattioli (Eds.), *Big data is not a monolith: Policies, practices, and problems* (pp. 77–90). Cambridge, MA: MIT Press.

Alaimo, C., & Kallinikos, J. (2017). Computing the everyday: Social media as data platforms. *The Information Society, 33*(4), 175–191.

Alaimo, C., & Kallinikos, J. (2018). Objects, metrics, and practices: An inquiry into the programmatic advertising ecosystem. In U. Schultze, M. Aanestad, M. Mähring, C. Østerlund, & K. Riemer (Eds.), *Living with monsters? Social implications of algorithmic phenomena, hybrid agency, and the performativity of technology* (pp. 110–126). Cham, Switzerland: Springer.

Alaimo, C., & Kallinikos, J. (2019). Social media and the infrastructuring of sociality. *Research in the Sociology of Organizations, 62,* 289–306.

Alaimo, C., & Kallinikos, J. (2020). Recommender systems. In T. Beyes, R. Holt, & C. Pias (Eds.), *Oxford handbook of media, technology, and organization studies* (pp. 401–411). Oxford: Oxford University Press.

Alaimo, C., & Kallinikos, J. (2021). Managing by data: Algorithmic categories and organizing. *Organization Studies, 42*(9), 1385–1407.

Alaimo, C., & Kallinikos, J. (2022). Organizations decentered: Data objects, technology, and knowledge. *Organization Science, 33*(1), 19–37.

Alaimo, C, Kallinikos, J., & Aaltonen, A. (2020). Data and value. In S. Nambisan, K. Lyytinen, & Y. Yoo (Eds.), *Handbook of digital innovation* (pp. 162–178). Cheltenham, UK: Edward Elgar Publishing.

Alaimo, C., Kallinikos, J., & Sannino, F. (2022). *The platformization of banking: The case of Flowe.* LUISS teaching cases. Rome: LUISS University Press. https://luissuniversitypress.it/wp-content/uploads/2022/03/Alaimo_Kallinikos_Sannino_case.pdf.

Alaimo, C., Kallinikos, J., & Valderrama, E. (2020). Platforms as service ecosystems: Lessons from social media. *Journal of Information Technology, 35*(1), 25–48.

Aldrich, H. E., & Pfeffer, J. (1976). Environments of organizations. *Annual Review of Sociology, 2*(1), 79–105.

Appadurai, A. (Ed.). (1988). *The social life of things: Commodities in cultural perspective.* Cambridge, MA: Cambridge University Press.

Arendt, H. (1959/2013). *The human condition.* Chicago: University of Chicago Press.

Argyres, N. S., & Zenger, T. R. (2012). Capabilities, transaction costs, and firm boundaries. *Organization Science, 23*(6), 1643–1657.

Aronova, E., von Oertzen, C., & Sepkoski, D. (Eds.). (2017). Data histories. *Osiris, 32*/1.

Arrow, K. J. (1974). *The limits of organization.* New York: W. W. Norton & Company.

Arthur, W. B. (1994). *Increasing returns and path dependence in the economy.* Ann Arbor: University of Michigan Press.

Arthur, W. B. (2009). *The nature of technology: What it is and how it evolves.* New York: Simon and Schuster.

Aspray, W. (Ed.). (1990). *Computing before computers.* Ames: Iowa State University Press.

Aspray, W., & Ceruzzi, P. E. (Eds.). (2008). *The Internet and American business.* Cambridge, MA: MIT Press.

Autio, E., & Thomas, L. (2014). Innovation ecosystems. In M. Dodgson, D. M. Gann, & N. Phillips (Eds.), *Oxford handbook of innovation management* (pp. 204–228). Oxford: Oxford University Press.

Ayres, I. (2006). *Super crunchers: Why thinking-by-numbers is the new way to be smart.* New York: Bantam Books.

Bailey, D. E., Faraj, S., Hinds, P. J., Leonardi, P. M., & von Krogh, G. (2022). We are all theorists of technology now: A relational perspective on emerging technology and organizing. *Organization Science, 33*(1), 1–18.

Bailey, D. E., Leonardi, P. M., & Barley, S. R. (2012). The lure of the virtual. *Organization Science, 23*(5), 1485–1504.

Bailey, D. E., Leonardi, P. M., & Chong, J. (2010). Minding the gaps: Understanding technology interdependence and coordination in knowledge work. *Organization Science, 21*(3), 713–730.

Baldwin, C. Y., & Clark, K. B. (2000). *Design rules: The power of modularity.* Vol. 1. Cambridge, MA: MIT Press.

Baldwin, C. Y., & Woodard, C. J. (2009). The architecture of platforms: A unified view. In A. Gawer (Ed.), *Platforms, markets and innovation* (pp. 19–44), Cheltenham, UK: Edward Elgar.

Barley, S. R. (1986). Technology as an occasion for structuring: Evidence from observations of CT scanners and social order of radiology departments. *Administrative Science Quarterly, 31*(1), 78–108.

Barley, S. R. (2015). Anticipatory work: How the need to represent knowledge across boundaries shapes work practices within them. *Organization Science, 26*(6), 1612–1628.

Barley, S. R., Leonardi, P. M., & Bailey, D. E. (2012). Engineering objects for collaboration: Strategies of ambiguity and clarity at knowledge boundaries. *Human Communication Research, 38*(3), 280–308.

Barney, J., Wright, M., & Ketchen D. J. (2001), The resource-based view of the firm: Ten years after 1991. *Journal of Management, 27*(6), 625–641.

Barrett, M., Oborn, E., Orlikowski, W. J., & Yates, J. (2012). Reconfiguring boundary relations: Robotic innovations in pharmacy work. *Organization Science, 23*(5), 1448–1466.

Bateson, G. (1972). *Steps to an ecology of mind*. New York: Ballantine.

Beaulieu, A., & Leonelli, S. (2021). *Data and society: A critical introduction*. London: Sage.

Bechmann, A., & Bowker, G. C. (2019). Unsupervised by any other name: Hidden layers of knowledge production in artificial intelligence on social media. *Big Data & Society*, *6*(1), 2053951718819569.

Bechmann, A., & Lomborg, S. (2013). Mapping actor roles in social media: Different perspectives on value creation in theories of user participation. *New Media & Society*, *15*(5), 765–781.

Beniger, J. (1986). *The control revolution: Technological and economic origins of the information society*. Cambridge, MA: Harvard University Press.

Beyes, T., Chun, W. H. K., Clarke, J., Flyverbom, M., & Holt, R. (2022). Ten theses on technology and organization: Introduction to the special issue. *Organization Studies*, *43*(7), 1001–1018

Beyes, T., Holt, R., & Pias, C. (Eds.). (2020). *Oxford handbook of media, technology, and organization studies*. Oxford: Oxford University Press.

Bogost, I. (2015), The cathedral of computation. We're not living in an algorithmic culture so much as a computational theocracy. *The Atlantic*. Retrieved from https://www.theatlantic.com/technology/archive/2015/01/the-cathedral-of-computation/384300/.

Boland, R. J. Jr., & Hirschheim, R. A. (Eds.). (1987). *Critical issues in information systems research*. New York: Wiley.

Borgmann, A. (1999). *Holding onto reality: The nature of information at the end of the millennium*. Chicago: University of Chicago Press.

Borgmann, A. (2010). Orientation in technological space. *First Monday*, *15*(6–7).

Borgmann, A. (2012). Matter matters: Materiality in philosophy, physics, and technology. Leonardi, Nardi & Kallinikos (eds.), *Materiality and Organizing: Social Interaction in a Technological World*, 335–347, Oxford: Oxford University Press.

Boudreau, K. J., & Hagiu, A. (2009). Platform rules: Multisided platforms as regulators. *Platforms, Markets and Innovation*, *1*, 163–191.

Bouk, D. (2015). *How our days became numbered*. Chicago: University of Chicago Press.

Bowker, G. C. (2005). *Memory practices in the sciences*. Cambridge, MA: MIT Press.

Bowker, G. C. (2014). The theory/data thing: Commentary. *International Journal of Communication*, *8*(2043), 1795–1799.

Bowker, G., & Star, S. L. (1999). *Sorting things out: Classification and its consequences*. Cambridge, MA: MIT Press.

boyd, D. (2015). Social media: A phenomenon to be analyzed. *Social Media + Society*, *1*(1), 2056305115580148.

boyd, D., & Crawford, K. (2012). Critical questions for big data: Provocations for a cultural, technological, and scholarly phenomenon. *Information, Communication & Society*, *15*(5), 662–679.

boyd, D., & Ellison, N. (2008). Social network sites: Definition, history, and scholarship. *Journal of Computer-Mediated Communication*, 13, 210–230.

Bratton, B. H. (2016). *The stack: On software and sovereignty*. Cambridge, MA: MIT Press.

Brown, J. S., & Duguid, P. (2000). *The social life of information*. Boston: Harvard Business School Press.

Brusoni, S., & Prencipe, A. (2001). Unpacking the black box of modularity: Technologies, products and organizations. *Industrial and Corporate Change*, 10(1), 179–205.

Brusoni, S., & Prencipe, A. (2006). Making design rules: A multidomain perspective. *Organization Science*, 17(2), 179–189.

Brusoni, S., Prencipe, A., & Pavitt, K. (2001). Knowledge specialization, organizational coupling, and the boundaries of the firm: Why do firms know more than they make? *Administrative Science Quarterly*, 46(4), 597–621.

Brynjolfsson, E., & McAfee, A. (2014). *The second machine age: Work, progress, and prosperity in a time of brilliant technologies*. New York: W. W. Norton & Company.

Buckland, M. (1991). *Information and information systems*. Westport, CT: Praeger Publishers.

Buckland, M. (2017). *Information and society*. Cambridge, MA: MIT Press.

Burchell, G., Gordon, C., & Miller, P. (1991). *The Foucault effect: Studies in governmentality*. Chicago: University of Chicago Press.

Burton-Jones, A. (2014). What have we learned from the Smart Machine? *Information and Organization*, 24(2), 71–105.

Campbell-Kelly, M., Aspray, W. F., Yost, J. R., Tinn, H., & Díaz, G. C. (2023). *Computer: A history of the information machine*. London: Routledge.

Carr, N. (2008). *The big switch: Rewiring the world, from Edison to Google*. New York: W. W. Norton & Company.

Carr, N. (2010). *The shallows: How the Internet is changing the way we think, read, and remember*. Berkeley, CA: Atlantic Books.

Castells, M. (1996). *The information age: Economy, society and culture. Volume 1: The rise of the network society*, Cambridge, MA: Blackwell.

Castells, M. (2000). Materials for an exploratory theory of the network society. *British Journal of Sociology*, 51(1), 5–24.

Castells, M. (2001). *The Internet galaxy: Reflections on the Internet, business, and society*. Oxford: Oxford University Press.

Cennamo, C. (2021). Competing in digital markets: A platform-based perspective. *Academy of Management Perspectives*, 35(2), 265–291.

Cennamo, C., Kretschmer, T., Constantinides, P., Alaimo, C., & Santalò, J. (2023). Digital platforms regulation: An innovation-centric view of the EU's Digital Markets Act. *Journal of European Competition Law & Practice*, 14(1), 44–51.

Cennamo, C., & Santaló, J. (2022). *Value in digital platforms: The choice of tradeoffs in the Digital Markets Act*. Available at SSRN: https://ssrn.com/abstract=4152113

Ceruzzi, P. E. (2012). *Computing: A concise history.* Cambridge, MA: MIT Press.

Ceruzzi, P. E. (2003). *A history of modern computing.* Cambridge, MA: MIT Press.

Chandler, A. D. (1977). *The visible hand. The managerial revolution in American business.* Cambridge, MA: Harvard University Press.

Chandler, A. D. (1990). *Scale and scope: The dynamics of industrial capitalism.* Cambridge, MA: Harvard University Press.

Chandler, A. D., & Cortada, J. W. (Eds.). (2000). *A nation transformed by information: How information has shaped the United States from colonial times to the present.* Oxford: Oxford University Press.

Chesbrough, H. W. (2003). *Open innovation: The new imperative for creating and profiting from technology.* Cambridge, MA: Harvard Business Press.

Chesbrough, H., Vanhaverbeke, W., & West, J. (Eds.). (2006). *Open innovation: Researching a new paradigm.* Oxford: Oxford University Press.

Ciborra, C. U. (1996). The platform organization: Recombining strategies, structures, and surprises. *Organization Science, 7*(2), 103–118.

Cioffi, J. W., Kenney, M. F., & Zysman, J. (2022). Platform power and regulatory politics: Polanyi for the twenty-first century. *New Political Economy, 27*(5), 820–836.

Clarke, R. (1988). Information technology and dataveillance. *Communications of the ACM, 31*(5), 498–512.

Clarke, R. (2019). Risks inherent in the digital surveillance economy: A research agenda. *Journal of Information Technology, 34*(1), 59–80.

Clarysse, B., Wright, M., Bruneel, J., & Mahajan, A. (2014). Creating value in ecosystems: Crossing the chasm between knowledge and business ecosystems. *Research Policy, 43*(7), 1164–1176.

Clegg, S. R., Pitsis, T. S., & Mount, M. (2021). *Managing and organizations: An introduction to theory and practice.* London: Sage.

Cline-Cohen, P. (1982). *A calculating people: The spread of numeracy in early America.* Chicago: University of Chicago Press.

Cluley, R. (2018). The construction of marketing measures: The case of viewability. *Marketing Theory, 18*(3), 287–305.

Coase, R. H. (1937). The nature of the firm. *Economica, 4*(16), 386–405.

Cohen, W. M., & Levinthal, D. A. (1990). Absorptive capacity: A new perspective on learning and innovation. *Administrative Science Quarterly, 35*(1), 128–152.

Colangelo, G. (2023). DMA begins. *Journal of Antitrust Enforcement, 11*(1), 116–122.

Corallo, A., Passiante, G., & Prencipe, A. (Eds.). (2007). *The digital business ecosystem.* Cheltenham, UK: Elgar.

Cortada, J. W. (2000). *Before the computer: IBM, NCR, Burroughs, and Remington Rand and the industry they created, 1865–1956.* Princeton, NJ: Princeton University Press.

Cortada, J. W. (2011). *Information and the modern corporation.* Cambridge, MA: MIT Press.

Cortada, J. W. (2016). *All the facts: A history of information in the United States since 1870*. Oxford: Oxford University Press.

Cortada, J. W. (2019). *IBM: The rise and fall and reinvention of a global con*. Cambridge, MA: MIT Press.

Couldry, N., & Kallinikos, J. (2017). Ontology. In J. Burgess, T. Poell, & A. E. Marwick (Eds.), *SAGE handbook of social media*. 146–159, London: Sage.

Couldry, N., & Mejias, U. A. (2019). Data colonialism: Rethinking big data's relation to the contemporary subject. *Television & New Media, 20*(4), 336–349.

Couldry, N., & Mejias, U. A. (2020). *The costs of connection. How data are colonizing human life and appropriating it for capitalism*. Stanford, CA: Stanford University Press.

Cyert, R. M., & March, J. G. (1963). *A behavioral theory of the firm*. New York: Wiley.

Daston, L. (2022). *Rules: A short history of what we live by*. Princeton, NJ: Princeton University Press.

Daston, L., & Galison P. (2007). *Objectivity*. Princeton, NJ: Princeton University Press.

Dean, M. M. (1999). *Governmentality: Power and rule in modern society*. London: Sage.

Demsetz, H. (1988). The theory of the firm revisited. *Journal of Economics and Organization, 4*(1), 141.

De Reuver, M., Sørensen, C., & Basole, R. C. (2018). The digital platform: A research agenda. *Journal of Information Technology, 33*(2), 124–135.

Desrosières, A. (1998). *The politics of large numbers: A history of statistical reasoning*. Cambridge, MA: Harvard University Press.

DiMaggio, P. (Ed.). (2001). *The twenty-first-century firm: Changing economic organization in international perspective*. Princeton, NJ: Princeton University Press.

DiMaggio, P. J., & Powell, W. W. (1983). The iron cage revisited: Institutional isomorphism and collective rationality in organizational fields. *American Sociological Review*, 48/2, 147–160.

Donzelot, J. (2008). Michel Foucault and liberal intelligence. *Economy and Society, 37*(1), 115–134.

Dosi, G., Nelson, R. R., Winter, S. G., & Winter, S. G. (Eds.). (2000). *The nature and dynamics of organizational capabilities*. Oxford: Oxford University Press.

Dourish, P. (2016). Algorithms and their others: Algorithmic culture in context. *Big Data & Society, 3*(2), 205395171666512.

Dourish, P. (2017). *The stuff of bits: An essay on the materialities of information*. Cambridge, MA: MIT Press.

Dreyfus, H. L. (2001). *On the Internet*. London: Routledge.

Dreyfus, H. L., & Rabinow, P. (1982). *Michel Foucault: Beyond structuralism and hermeneutics*. London: Routledge.

Eco, U. (1976). *A theory of semiotics*. Bloomington: Indiana University Press.

Eco, U. (1986). *Semiotics and the philosophy of language* (Vol. 398). Bloomington: Indiana University Press.

Eco, U. (2000). *Kant and the platypus: Essays on language and cognition*. Orlando, FL: HMH.

Eco, U. (2014). *From the tree to the labyrinth*. Cambridge, MA: Harvard University Press.

Edwards, P. N. (2010). *A vast machine: Computer models, climate data, and the politics of global warming*. Cambridge, MA: MIT Press.

Eisenhardt, K. M., & Martin, J. A. (2000). Dynamic capabilities: What are they? *Strategic Management Journal, 21*(10–11), 1105–1121.

Eisenstein E. L. (1979). *The printing press as an agent of change*. Cambridge: Cambridge University Press.

Ekbia, H. R. (2009). Digital artifacts as quasi-objects: Qualification, mediation, and materiality. *Journal of the American Society for Information Science and Technology, 60*(12), 2554–2566.

Ekbia, H., Mattioli, M., Kouper, I., et al. (2015). Big data, bigger dilemmas: A critical review. *Journal of the Association for Information Science and Technology, 66*, 1523–1545. doi: 10.1002/asi.23294.

Ekbia, H. R., & Nardi, B. A. (2017). *Heteromation, and other stories of computing and capitalism*. Cambridge, MA: MIT Press.

Espeland, W. N., & Sauder, M. (2007). Rankings and reactivity: How public measures recreate social worlds. *American Journal of Sociology, 113*(1), 1–40.

Espeland, W. N., & Stevens, M. L. (1998). Commensuration as a social process. *Annual Review of Sociology, 24*(1), 313–343.

Espeland, W. N., & Stevens, M. L. (2008). A sociology of quantification. *European Journal of Sociology/Archives Européennes de Sociologie, 49*(3), 401–436.

Esposito, E. (2011). *The future of futures: The time of money in financing and society*. Cheltenham, UK: Edward Elgar.

Eubanks, V. (2018). *Automating inequality: How high-tech tools profile, police, and punish the poor*. New York: St. Martin's Press.

Evans, D., & Schmalensee, R. (2005). The industrial organization of markets with two-sided platforms. *NBER* working paper 11603. *National Bureau of Economic Research*. doi: 10.3386/w11603.

Ewenstein, B., & Whyte, J. (2009). Knowledge practices in design: The role of visual representations as 'epistemic objects'. *Organization Studies, 30*(1), 07–30.

Faraj, S., Jarvenpaa, S. L., & Majchrzak, A. (2011). Knowledge collaboration in online communities. *Organization Science, 22*(5), 1224–1239.

Faraj, S., Pachidi, S., & Sayegh, K. (2018). Working and organizing in the age of the learning algorithm. *Information and Organization, 28*(1), 62–70.

Faraj, S., von Krogh, G., Monteiro, E., & Lakhani, K. R. (2016). Online community as space for knowledge flows. *Information Systems Research, 27*(4), 668–684.

Faulkner, P., & Runde, J. (2013). Technological objects, social positions, and the transformational model of social activity. *MIS Quarterly, 37*(3), 803–818.

Faulkner, P., & Runde, J. (2019). Theorizing the digital object. *MIS Quarterly, 43*(4), 1279–1302.

Fligstein, N. (1990). *The transformation of corporate control.* Cambridge, MA: Harvard University Press.

Floridi, L. (2010). *Information: A very short introduction.* Oxford: Oxford University Press.

Floridi, L. (2013). *The philosophy of information.* Oxford: Oxford University Press.

Flyverbom, M. (2019). *The digital prism.* Cambridge: Cambridge University Press.

Flyverbom, M., & Murray, J. (2018). Datastructuring—Organizing and curating digital traces into action. *Big Data & Society, 5*(2), 2053951718799114.

Foucault, M. (1963/2012). *The birth of the clinic.* London: Routledge.

Foucault, M. (1970). *The order of things.* London: Tavistock.

Foucault, M. (1977). *Discipline and punish: The birth of prison.* New York: Random House.

Foucault, M. (1980). *Power/knowledge.* Edited by Colin Gordon. New York: Pantheon.

Foucault, M. (1988). Technologies of the self. In L. Martin, H. Gutman, & P. Hutton (Eds.), *Technologies of the self.* London: Tavistock.

Foucault, M. (1990). *The history of sexuality: The will to knowledge.* London: Penguin.

Foucault, M. (1997). *The politics of truth.* Los Angeles: Semiotext.

Frege, G. (1964). *The basic laws of arithmetic.* Berkeley: University of California Press.

Garud, R., & Kumaraswamy, A. (1995). Technological and organizational designs for realizing economies of substitution. *Strategic Management Journal, 16*(S1), 93–109.

Gavetti, G., Greve, H. R., Levinthal, D. A., & Ocasio, W. (2012). The behavioral theory of the firm: Assessment and prospects. *Academy of Management Annals, 6*(1), 1–40.

Gavetti, G., Levinthal, D., & Ocasio, W. (2007). Perspective—neo-Carnegie: The Carnegie school's past, present, and reconstructing for the future. *Organization Science, 18*(3), 523–536.

Gawer, A. (Ed.). (2009). *Platforms, markets and innovation.* Cheltenham, UK: Edward Elgar.

Gawer, A. (2014). Bridging differing perspectives on technological platforms: Toward an integrative framework. *Research Policy, 43*(7), 1239–1249.

Gebru, T., Morgenstern, J., Vecchione, B., et al. (2021). Datasheets for datasets. *Communications of the ACM, 64*(12), 86–92.

Gerlitz, C., & Helmond, A. (2013). The like economy: Social buttons and the data-intensive web. *New Media & Society, 15*(8), 1348–1365.

Giddens, A. (1990). *The consequences of modernity.* Stanford, CA: Stanford University Press.

Gillespie, T. (2014). The relevance of algorithms. In T. Gillespie, P. J. Boczkowski, & K. A. Foot (Eds.), *Media technologies: Essays on communication, materiality, and society* (pp. 167–194). Cambridge, MA: MIT Press.

Gilmore, J. H., & Pine, B. J. (1997). The four faces of mass customization. *Harvard Business Review, 75*(1), 91–102.

Gitelman, L. (2013). *Raw data is an oxymoron.* Cambridge, MA: MIT Press.

Gitelman, L. (2014). *Paper knowledge: Toward a media history of documents.* Durham, NC: Duke University Press.

Glaser, V. L., Pollock, N., & D'Adderio, L. (2021). The biography of an algorithm: Performing algorithmic technologies in organizations. *Organization Theory, 2*(2), 26317877211004609.

Gleick, J. (2011). *The information: A history, a theory, a flood.* New York: Vintage.

Goodman, N. (1976). *Languages of art: An approach to a theory of symbols.* Indianapolis: Hackett Publishing.

Goodman, N. (1978). *Ways of worldmaking.* Indianapolis: Hackett Publishing.

Goody, J. (1986). *The logic of writing and the organization of society.* Cambridge, MA: Cambridge University Press.

Graeber, D. (2011). *Debt: The first 5,000 years.* London: Melville House.

Granovetter, M. (1985). Economic action and social structure: The problem of embeddedness. *American Journal of Sociology, 91*(3), 481–510.

Granovetter, M. (2017). *Society and economy: Framework and principles.* Cambridge, MA: Harvard University Press.

Granovetter, M., & Swedberg, R. (2018). *The sociology of economic life.* London: Routledge.

Gray, G., & Benning, B. (2019). Crowdsourcing criminology: Social media and citizen policing in missing person cases. *Sage Open, 9*(4), 2158244019893700.

Greenfield, A. (2017). *Radical technologies: The design of everyday life.* New York: Verso Books.

Grisot, M., Moltubakk Kempton, A., Hagen, L., & Aanestad, M. (2019). Data-work for personalized care: Examining nurses' practices in remote monitoring of chronic patients. *Health Informatics Journal, 25*(3), 608–616.

Habermas, J. (1985). *The theory of communicative action. Volume 1: Reason and the rationalization of society.* Boston: Beacon Press.

Hacking, I. (1983). *Representing and intervening: Introductory topics in the philosophy of natural science.* Cambridge: Cambridge University Press.

Hacking, I. (1986). Making up people. In T. C. Heller and C. Brooke-Rose (Eds.), *Reconstructing individualism: Autonomy, individuality, and the self in Western thought* (pp. 161–171). Stanford, CA: Stanford University Press.

Hacking, I. (1990). *The taming of chance.* Cambridge: Cambridge University Press.

Hacking, I. (1999). *The social construction of what?* Cambridge, MA: Harvard University Press.

Hagiu, A., & Wright, J. (2015). Multi-sided platforms. *International Journal of Industrial Organization, 43*, 162–174.

Hand, D. J. (2020). *Dark data: Why what you don't know matters*. Princeton, NJ: Princeton University Press.

Hannan, M. T., & Freeman, J. (1977). The population ecology of organizations. *American Journal of Sociology, 82*(5), 929–964.

Hannan, M. T., & Freeman, J. (1986). Where do organizational forms come from? In *Sociological Forum*, 1: 50–72.

Hansen, K. B., & Borch, C. (2022). Alternative data and sentiment analysis: Prospecting non-standard data in machine learning-driven finance. *Big Data & Society, 9*(1), 20539517211070701.

Hanseth, O. (2000). The economics of standards. In C. Ciborra (Ed.), *From control to drift: The dynamics of corporate information infrastructures* (pp. 56–70). Oxford: Oxford University Press.

Hanseth, O. (2022). When stars align: The interactions and transformations of e-Health infrastructure regimes. *Historical Social Research/Historische Sozialforschung, 47*(3/181), 40–80.

Hanseth, O., & Ciborra, C. (Eds.). (2007). *Risk, complexity and ICT*. Cheltenham: Edward Elgar Publishing.

Hanseth, O., & Lyytinen, K. (2010). Design theory for dynamic complexity in information infrastructures: The case of building Internet, *Journal of Information Technology, 25*(1), 1–19.

Hanseth, O., Monteiro, E., & Hatling, M. (1996). Developing information infrastructure: The tension between standardization and flexibility. *Science, Technology, & Human Values, 21*(4), 407–426.

Hasselbladh, H., & Kallinikos, J. (2000). The project of rationalization: A critique and reappraisal of neo-institutionalism in organization studies. *Organization Studies, 21*(4), 697–720.

Havelock, E. A. (1963). *Preface to Plato*. Cambridge, MA: Harvard University Press.

Havelock, E. A. (1986). *The muse learns to write: Reflections on orality and literacy from antiquity to the present*. New Haven, CT: Yale University Press.

Hawley, A. H. (1986). *Human ecology: A theoretical essay*. Chicago: University of Chicago Press.

Hayek, F. (1945). The use of knowledge in society. *American Economic Review, 35*(4), 519–530.

Heller, A. (1999). *A theory of modernity*. New York: Wiley.

Helmond, A. (2015). The platformization of the web: Making web data platform ready. *Social Media+ Society, 1*(2), 2056305115603080.

Henderson, K. (1991). Flexible sketches and inflexible data bases: Visual communication, conscription devices, and boundary objects in design engineering. *Science, Technology, & Human Values, 16*(4), 448–473.

Henderson, R. M., & Clark, K. B. (1990). Architectural innovation: The reconfiguration of existing product technologies and the failure of established firms. *Administrative Science Quarterly, 35*(1), 9–30.

Henfridsson, O., Nandhakumar, J., Scarbrough, H., & Panourgias, N. (2018). Recombination in the open-ended value landscape of digital innovation. *Information and Organization, 28*(2), 89–100.

Hicks, M. (2017). *Programmed inequality: How Britain discarded women technologists and lost its edge in computing.* Cambridge, MA: MIT Press.

Hildebrandt, M. (2015). *Smart technologies and the end(s) of law: Novel entanglements of law and technology.* Cheltenham, UK: Edward Elgar.

Hildebrandt, M. (2019). Privacy as protection of the incomputable self: From agnostic to agonistic machine learning. *Theoretical Inquiries in Law, 20*(1), 83–121.

Hildebrandt, M., & Gutwirth, S. (2008). *Profiling the European citizen.* Dordrecht, Netherlands: Springer.

Hildebrandt, M., & Rouvroy, A. (Eds.). (2011). *Law, human agency and autonomic computing: The philosophy of law meets the philosophy of technology.* London: Routledge.

Hirschman, A. O. (1977). *The passions and the interests: Political arguments for capitalism before its triumph.* Westport, CT: Greenwood Publishing Group.

Hirschman, A. O. (1982). *Shifting involvements: Private interest and public action.* Princeton, NJ: Princeton University Press.

Holmstrom, B. R., & Tirole, J. (1989). The theory of the firm. *Handbook of Industrial Organization, 1*, 61–133.

Hopwood, A. G. (1987). The archaeology of accounting systems. *Accounting, Organizations and Society, 12*(3), 207–234.

Hoskin, K. W., & Macve, R. H. (1986). Accounting and the examination: A genealogy of disciplinary power. *Accounting, Organizations and Society, 11*(2), 105–136.

Hui, Y. (2016). *On the existence of digital objects. Vol. 48.* Minneapolis: University of Minnesota Press.

Iansiti, M., & Lakhani, K. R. (2020). *Competing in the age of AI: Strategy and leadership when algorithms and networks run the world.* Boston: Harvard Business Press.

Iansiti, M., & Levien, R. (2004). *The keystone advantage: What the new dynamics of business ecosystems mean for strategy, innovation, and sustainability.* Boston: Harvard Business Press.

Iansiti, M., & Richards, G. L. (2006). The information technology ecosystem: Structure, health, and performance. *Antitrust Bulletin, 51*(1), 77–110.

Iliadis, A. (2023). *Semantic media. Mapping meaning on the Internet.* New York: Wiley.

Iliadis, A., & Russo, F. (2016). Critical data studies: An introduction. *Big Data & Society, 3*(2), 205395171667423.

Iqbal, N. (2019). Forget the DJs: Spotify playlists are the new musical starmakers, *The Guardian,* https://www.theguardian.com/music/2019/apr/28/streaming-music-algorithms-spotify.

Jacobides, M. G., Cennamo, C., & Gawer, A. (2018). Towards a theory of ecosystems. *Strategic Management Journal, 39*(8), 2255–2276.

Jacobides, M. G., & Lianos, I. (2021). Regulating platforms and ecosystems: An introduction. *Industrial and Corporate Change, 30*(5), 1131–1142.

Jarvenpaa, S. L., & Markus, M. L. (2020). Data sourcing and data partnerships: Opportunities for IS sourcing research. In *Information systems outsourcing* (pp. 61–79). Heidelberg, Germany: Springer.

Jenny, F. (2021), Competition law and digital ecosystems: Learning to walk before we run. *Industrial and Corporate Change, 30*(5), 1143–1167.

Jones, M. (2019). What we talk about when we talk about (big) data. *Journal of Strategic Information Systems, 28*(1), 3–16.

Jonsson, K., Holmström, J., & Lyytinen, K. (2009). Turn to the material: Remote diagnostics systems and new forms of boundary-spanning. *Information and Organization, 19*(4), 233–252.

Jovanovic, M., Sjödin, D., & Parida, V. (2022). Co-evolution of platform architecture, platform services, and platform governance: Expanding the platform value of industrial digital platforms. *Technovation, 118*, 102218.

Kallinikos, J. (1995). The architecture of the invisible: Technology is representation. *Organization, 2*(1), 117–140.

Kallinikos, J. (1996). Predictable worlds: On writing, accountability and other things. *Scandinavian Journal of Management, 12*(1), 7–24.

Kallinikos, J. (1999). Computer-based technology and the constitution of work: A study on the cognitive foundations of work. *Accounting, Management and Information Technologies, 9*(4), 261–291.

Kallinikos J. (2001). *The age of flexibility. Managing organizations and technology.* Lund, Sweden: Academia Adacta.

Kallinikos, J. (2003). Work, human agency and organizational forms: An anatomy of fragmentation. *Organization Studies, 24*(4), 595–618.

Kallinikos, J. (2004). The social foundations of the bureaucratic order. *Organization, 11*(1), 13–36.

Kallinikos, J. (2007). *The consequences of information: Institutional implications of technological change.* Cheltenham, UK: Edward Elgar Publishing.

Kallinikos, J. (2009a). On the computational rendition of reality: Artefacts and human agency. *Organization, 16*(2), 183–202.

Kallinikos, J. (2009b). The making of ephemeria: On the shortening life spans of information. *International Journal of Interdisciplinary Social Sciences, 4*(3), 227–236.

Kallinikos, J. (2010). *Governing through technology: Information artefacts and social practice.* New York: Springer.

Kallinikos, J. (2012). Form, function, and matter: Crossing the border of materiality. In P. Leonardi, B. Nardi, & J. Kallinikos (Eds.), *Materiality and organizing: Social interaction in a technological world* (pp. 67–87). Oxford: Oxford University Press.

Kallinikos, J., Aaltonen, A., & Márton, A. (2013). The ambivalent ontology of digital artifacts. *MIS Quarterly, 37*(2), 357–370.

Kallinikos, J., & Constantiou, I. D. (2015). Big data revisited: A rejoinder. *Journal of Information Technology, 30*(1), 70–74.

Kallinikos, J., & Hasselbladh, H. (2009). Work, control and computation: Rethinking the legacy of neo-institutionalism. *Research in the Sociology of Organizations, 27,* 257–282.

Kallinikos, J., Hasselbladh, H., & Márton, A. (2013). Governing social practice. *Theory and Society, 42*(4), 395–421.

Kallinikos, J., & Mariátegui, J. C. (2011). Video as digital object: Production and distribution of video content in the Internet media ecosystem. *The Information Society, 27*(5), 281–294.

Kallinikos, J., & Tempini, N. (2014). Patient data as medical facts: Social media practices as a foundation for medical knowledge creation. *Information Systems Research, 25*(4), 817–833.

Kellogg, K. C., Valentine, M. A., & Christin, A. (2020). Algorithms at work: The new contested terrain of control. *Academy of Management Annals, 14*(1), 366–410.

Kempton, A. M. (2022). The digital is different: Emergence and relationality in critical realist research. *Information and Organization, 32*(2), 100408.

Kiel, D., Arnold, C., & Voigt, K. I. (2017). The influence of the Industrial Internet of Things on business models of established manufacturing companies–A business level perspective. *Technovation, 68,* 4–19.

Kitchin, R. (2014). *The data revolution: Big data, open data, data infrastructures and their consequences.* London: Sage.

Kittler, F. A. (1985). *Gramophone, film, typewriter.* Stanford, CA: Stanford University Press.

Kittler, F. (1996). The history of communication media. *CTheory,* 7–30.

Kittler, F. A. (1997). *Literature, media, information systems.* London: Routledge.

Kling, R. (Ed.). (1996). *Computerization and controversy: Value conflicts and social choices.* San Diego: Morgan Kaufmann.

Knorr Cetina, K. (1981). *The manufacture of knowledge: An essay on the constructivist and contextual nature of science.* Oxford, UK: Pergamon Press.

Knorr Cetina, K. (1999). *Epistemic cultures.* Cambridge, MA: Harvard University Press.

Knorr Cetina, K. (2001). Objectual practice. In K. K. Knorr Cetina, T. R. Schatzki, & E. Von Savigny (Eds.), *The practice turn in contemporary theory* (pp. 175–188). London: Routledge.

Knorr Cetina, K., & Bruegger, U. (2002). Global microstructures: The virtual societies of financial markets. *American Journal of Sociology, 107*(4), 905–950.

Kornberger, M., Pflueger, D., & Mouritsen, J. (2017). Evaluative infrastructures: Accounting for platform organization. *Accounting, Organizations and Society, 60,* 79–95.

Kretschmer, T., Leiponen, A., Schilling, M., & Vasudeva, G. (2022). Platform ecosystems as meta-organizations: Implications for platform strategies. *Strategic Management Journal, 43*(3), 405–424.

Labatut, J., Aggeri, F., & Girard, N. (2012). Discipline and change: How technologies and organizational routines interact in new practice creation. *Organization Studies, 33*(1), 39–69.

Lampel, J., & Mintzberg, H. (1996). Customizing customization. *Sloan Management Review, 38*(1), 21–30.

Langlois, R. N. (2003). The vanishing hand: The changing dynamics of industrial capitalism. *Industrial and Corporate Change, 12*(2), 351–385.

Langlois, R. N., & Robertson, P. L. (1995). *Firms, markets and economic change: A dynamic theory of business institutions.* London: Routledge.

Larouche, P., & de Streel, A. (2021). The European Digital Markets Act: A revolution grounded on traditions. *Journal of European Competition Law & Practice, 12*(7), 542–560.

Latour, B. (1986). Visualization and cognition. *Knowledge and Society, 6*(6), 1–40.

Latour, B. (1987). *Science in action: How to follow scientists and engineers through society.* Cambridge, MA: Harvard University Press.

Lebovitz, S., Lifshitz-Assaf, H., & Levina, N. (2022). To engage or not to engage with AI for critical judgments: How professionals deal with opacity when using ai for medical diagnosis. *Organization Science, 33*(1), 126–148.

Lemke, T. (2015). *Foucault, governmentality, and critique.* London: Routledge.

Leonardi, P. M. (2012). *Car crashes without cars: Lessons about simulation technology and organizational change from automotive design.* Cambridge, MA: MIT Press.

Leonardi, P. M. (2014). Social media, knowledge sharing, and innovation: Toward a theory of communication visibility. *Information Systems Research, 25*(4), 796–816.

Leonardi, P. M. (2020). COVID-19 and the new technologies of organizing: Digital exhaust, digital footprints, and artificial intelligence in the wake of remote work. *Journal of Management Studies, 58*(1), 249–253.

Leonardi, P. M., Nardi, B. A., & Kallinikos, J. (Eds.) (2012). *Materiality and organizing: Social interaction in a technological world.* Oxford: Oxford University Press.

Leonardi, P. M., & Treem, J. W. (2012). Knowledge management technology as a stage for strategic self-presentation: Implications for knowledge sharing in organizations. *Information and Organization, 22*(1), 37–59.

Leonardi, P. M., & Treem, J. W. (2020). Behavioral visibility: A new paradigm for organization studies in the age of digitization, digitalization, and datafication. *Organization Studies, 41*(12), 1601–1625.

Leonelli, S. (2014). What difference does quantity make? On the epistemology of big data in biology. *Big Data & Society.* doi: 10.1177/2053951714534395.

Leonelli, S. (2015). "What counts as scientific data? A relational framework. *Philadelphia Scientific, 82*, 810–821.

Leonelli, S. (2019). Data governance is key to interpretation: Reconceptualizing data in data science. *Harvard Data Science Review, 1*(1). doi: 10.1162/99608f92.17405bb6.

Lessig, L. (2001). *Code and other laws of cyberspace.* New York: Basic Books.

Levinthal, D. A., & March, J. G. (1993). The myopia of learning. *Strategic Management Journal, 14*(S2), 95–112.

Lévi-Strauss, C. (1966). *The savage mind.* Chicago: University of Chicago Press.

Levy, K. (2015). The contexts of control: Information, power, and truck-driving work. *The Information Society 31*(2), 160–174.

Levy, K. (2023). *Data driven: Truckers, technology, and the new workplace surveillance.* Princeton, NJ: Princeton University Press.

Lindgren, S., & Holmström, J. (2020). A social science perspective on Artificial Intelligence: Building blocks for a research agenda. *Journal of Digital Social Research (JDSR), 2*(3), 1–15.

Lomborg, S. (2013). *Social media, social genres: Making sense of the ordinary.* London: Routledge.

Loukissas, Y. A. (2019). *All data are local: Thinking critically in a data-driven society.* Cambridge, MA: MIT Press.

Lounsbury, M., & Crumley, E. T. (2007). New practice creation: An institutional perspective on innovation. *Organization studies, 28*(7), 993–1012.

Luhmann, N. (1982). *The differentiation of society.* New York: Columbia University Press.

Luhmann, N. (1990). *Essays on self-reference.* New York: Columbia University Press.

Luhmann, N. (1995). *Social systems.* Stanford, CA: Stanford University Press.

Luhmann, N. (2002/2017). *Risk: A sociological theory.* New York: Routledge.

Luhmann, N. (2002). *Theories of distinction: Redescribing the descriptions of modernity.* Stanford, CA: Stanford University Press.

Lyon, D. (2001). *Surveillance society.* London: McGraw-Hill Education (UK).

Lyon, D. (2007). *Surveillance studies: An overview.* Cambridge, MA: Polity Press.

Lyytinen, K. (2022). Innovation logics in the digital era: A systemic review of the emerging digital innovation regime. *Innovation, 24*(1), 13–34.

Lyytinen, K., Nickerson, J. V., & King, J. L. (2021). Metahuman systems = humans + machines that learn. *Journal of Information Technology, 36*(4), 427–445.

Lyytinen, K., & Yoo, Y. (2002). Ubiquitous computing. *Communications of the ACM, 45*(12), 63–96.

MacGinnis, J., Monroe, M. W., Wicke, D., & Matney, T. (2014). Artifacts of cognition: The use of clay tokens in a Neo-Assyrian provincial administration. *Cambridge Archaeological Journal, 24*(2), 289–306.

Macintosh, N. B., & Quattrone, P. (2010). *Management accounting and control systems: An organizational and sociological approach.* New York: John Wiley & Sons.

MacKenzie, D. (2021). *Trading at the speed of light.* Princeton, NJ: Princeton University Press.

Manovich, L. (2001). *The language of new media.* Cambridge, MA: MIT Press.

March, J. G. (1994). *Primer on decision making: How decisions happen.* New York: Simon and Schuster.

March, J. G. (2006). Rationality, foolishness, and adaptive intelligence. *Strategic Management Journal, 27*(3), 201–214.

March, J. G., & Olsen, J. P. (1976). *Ambiguity and choice in organizations.* Bergen, Norway: Universitetsforlaget.

March, J. G., & Olsen, J. P. (1989). *Rediscovering institutions.* New York: Simon and Schuster.

Markus, M. L. (1983). Power, politics, and MIS implementation. *Communications of the ACM, 26*(6), 430–444.

Markus, M. L. (2001). Toward a theory of knowledge reuse: Types of knowledge reuse situations and factors in reuse success. *Journal of Management Information Systems, 18*(1), 57–93.

Markus, M. L., Majchrzak, A., & Gasser, L. (2002). A design theory for systems that support emergent knowledge processes. *MIS Quarterly,* 179–212.

Martin, K. E. (2015) Ethical issues in the big data industry. *MIS Quarterly Executive, 14*(2), 67–85.

Márton, A. (2022). Steps toward a digital ecology: Ecological principles for the study of digital ecosystems. *Journal of Information Technology, 37*(3), 250–265.

Mayer-Schönberger, V. (2009). *Delete: The virtue of forgetting in the digital age.* Princeton, NJ: Princeton University Press.

McIntyre, D. P., & Srinivasan, A. (2017). Networks, platforms, and strategy: Emerging views and next steps. *Strategic Management Journal, 38*(1), 141–160.

McIntyre, D., Srinivasan, A., Afuah, A., Gawer, A., & Kretschmer, T. (2020). Multi-sided platforms as new organizational forms. *Academy of Management Perspectives, 35*(4), 566–583.

McLuhan, M. (1964). *Understanding media: The extensions of man.* Cambridge, MA: MIT Press.

Media Rating Council (MRC) and Interactive Advertising Bureau (IAB), (2017). *Digital audience-based measurement standards,* v5.1. Public Comment Draft. http://mediaratingcouncil.org/MRC%20Digital%20Audience-Based%20Public%20Comment%20Draft.pdf.

Mennicken, A., & Salais, R. (2022). *The new politics of numbers: Utopia, evidence and democracy.* New York: Palgrave Mcmillian.

Meyer, J. W., & Jepperson, R. L. (2000). The "actors" of modern society: The cultural construction of social agency. *Sociological Theory, 18*(1), 100–120.

Miettinen, R., & Virkkunen, J. (2005). Epistemic objects, artefacts and organizational change. *Organization, 12*(3), 437–456.

Miller, P. (2004). Governing by numbers: Why calculative practices matter. In A. Amin and N. Thrift (Eds.), *Blackwell Cultural Economy Reader* (pp. 179–189). Malden, MA: Blackwell Publishing.

Miller, P., & O'Leary, T. (1987). Accounting and the construction of the governable person. *Accounting, Organizations and Society, 12*(3), 235–265.

Mingers, J., & Willcocks, L. (2014). An integrative semiotic framework for information systems: The social, personal and material worlds. *Information and Organization, 24*(1), 48–70.

Mintzberg, H. (1979). *The structuring of organization: A synthesis of the research*. Englewood Cliffs, NJ: Prentice-Hall.

Monteiro, E. (2022). *Digital oil: Machineries of knowing*. Cambridge, MA: MIT Press.

Monteiro, E., & Parmiggiani, E. (2019). Synthetic knowing: The politics of the Internet of Things. *MIS Quarterly, 43*(1), 167–184.

Moore, J. F. (1993). Predators and prey: A new ecology of competition. *Harvard Business Review, 71*(3), 75–86.

Moore, J. F. (2006). Business ecosystems and the view from the firm. *Antitrust Bulletin, 51*(1), 31–75.

Muller, J. Z. (2019). *The tyranny of metrics*. Princeton, NJ: Princeton University Press.

Mumford, L. (1934/2010). *Technics and civilization*. Chicago: University of Chicago Press.

Napoli, P. M. (2003). *Audience economics: Media institutions and the audience marketplace*. New York: Columbia University Press.

Napoli, P. M. (2011). *Audience evolution: New technologies and the transformation of media audiences*. New York: Columbia University Press.

Nardi, B. A. (Ed.). (1996). *Context and consciousness: Activity theory and human-computer interaction*. Cambridge, MA: MIT Press.

Nardi, B. A., & O'Day, V. (2000). *Information ecologies: Using technology with heart*. Cambridge, MA: MIT Press.

Nelson, R. R., & Winter, S. G. (1982). *An evolutionary theory of economic change*. Cambridge, MA: Harvard University Press.

Nissenbaum, H. (2004). Privacy as contextual integrity. *Washington Law Review, 79*, 119.

Nissenbaum, H. (2010). *Privacy in context*. Stanford, CA: Stanford University Press.

Nissenbaum, H. (2011). A contextual approach to privacy online. *Daedalus, 140*(4), 32–48.

Noble, S. U. (2018). *Algorithms of oppression: How search engines reinforce racism*. New York: New York University Press.

Nohria, N., Eccles, R. G., & Press, H. B. (Eds.). (1992). *Networks and organizations: Structure, form, and action* (Vol. 367). Boston: Harvard Business School Press.

Norberg, A. L. (1990). High-technology calculation in the early 20th century: Punched card machinery in business and government. *Technology and Culture, 31*(4), 753–779.

Norberg, A. L., O'Neill, J. E., & Freedman, K. (1996). *Transforming computer technology: Information processing for the Pentagon, 1962–1986*. Baltimore: Johns Hopkins University Press.

North, D. C. (1984). Transaction costs, institutions, and economic history. *Zeitschrift für die gesamte Staatswissenschaft/Journal of Institutional and Theoretical Economics*, (H. 1), 7–17.

Obendiek, A. S. (2023). *Data governance. Value orders and jurisdictional conflicts*. Oxford: Oxford University Press.

O'Neil, C. (2016). *Weapons of math destruction: How big data increases inequality and threatens democracy*. New York: Broadway Books.

Ong, W. J. (1982). *Orality and literacy*. London: Routledge.

Oppenheim, A. L. (1959). On an operational device in Mesopotamian bureaucracy. *Journal of Near Eastern Studies, 18*(2), 121–128.

Orlikowski, W. J., & Scott S. V. (2014). What happens when evaluation goes online? Exploring apparatuses of valuation in the travel sector. *Organization Science, 25*(3), 868–891.

Østerlie, T., & Monteiro, E. (2020). Digital sand: The becoming of digital representations. *Information and Organization, 30*(1). doi: 100275.

Owen, J. (2013). Balls of clay could have provided prehistoric data storage, *NBC News*, Retrieved from https://www.nbcnews.com/sciencemain/balls-clay-could-have -provided-prehistoric-data-storage-8C11380771.

Pachidi, S., Berends, H., Faraj, S., & Huysman, M. (2021). Make way for the algorithms: Symbolic actions and change in a regime of knowing. *Organization Science, 32*(1), 18–41.

Parker, G. G., Van Alstyne, M., & Choudary, S. P. (2016). *Platform revolution: How networked markets are transforming the economy—and how to make them work for you*. New York: Norton.

Parker, G., Van Alstyne, M., & Jiang, X. (2017). Platform ecosystems: How developers invert the firm. *MIS Quarterly, 41*(1), 255–266.

Parmiggiani, E., Østerlie, T., & Almklov, P. G. (2022). In the backrooms of data science. *Journal of the Association for Information Systems, 23*(1), 139–164.

Passi, S., & Jackson, S. J. (2018). Trust in data science: Collaboration, translation, and accountability in corporate data science projects. *Proceedings of the ACM on Human-Computer Interaction, 2*(CSCW), 136.

Paullada, A., Raji, I. D., Bender, E. M., Denton, E., & Hanna, A. (2021). Data and its (dis)contents: A survey of dataset development and use in machine learning research. *Patterns, 2*(11), 100336.

Penrose, E., & Penrose, E. T. (1959/2009). *The theory of the growth of the firm*. Oxford: Oxford University Press.

Pentland, A. (2014). *Social physics: How good ideas spread-the lessons from a new science*. London: Penguin.

Perrow, C. (1986). *Complex organizations: A critical essay.* 3rd ed. New York: McGraw-Hill.

Perrow, C. (2002). *Organizing America.* Princeton, NJ: Princeton University Press.

Peukert, C., Bechtold, S., Batikas, M., & Kretschmer, T. (2022). Regulatory spillovers and data governance: Evidence from the GDPR. *Marketing Science, 41*(4), 746–768.

Phillips, M. A., & Ritala, P. (2019). A complex adaptive systems agenda for ecosystem research methodology. *Technological Forecasting and Social Change, 148,* 119739.

Pine, B. J. (1991). *Paradigm shift—From mass production to mass customization.* Doctoral dissertation, Massachusetts Institute of Technology, Cambridge, MA.

Piore, M. J., & Sabel, C. F. (1984). *The second industrial divide: Possibilities for prosperity.* New York: Basic Books.

Polanyi, K. (1944/2001). *The great transformation: The political and economic origins of our time.* Boston: Beacon Press.

Poon, M. (2009). From New Deal institutions to capital markets: Commercial consumer risk scores and the making of subprime mortgage finance. *Accounting, Organizations and Society, 34*(5), 654–674.

Poovey, M. (1998). *A history of the modern fact: Problems of knowledge in the sciences of wealth and society.* Chicago: University of Chicago Press.

Porter, T. M. (1995). *Trust in numbers: The pursuit of objectivity in science and public life.* Princeton, NJ: Princeton University Press.

Power, M. (1997). *The audit society: Rituals of verification.* Oxford: Oxford University Press.

Power, M. (2000). The audit society—second thoughts. *International Journal of Auditing, 4*(1), 111–119.

Power, M. (2007). *Organized uncertainty: Designing a world of risk management.* Oxford: Oxford University Press.

Power, M. (2022). Theorizing the economy of traces: From audit society to surveillance capitalism. *Organization Theory, 3,* 1–19.

Quattrone, P. (2009). Books to be practiced: Memory, the power of the visual, and the success of accounting. *Accounting, Organizations and Society, 34*(1), 85–118.

Rammert, W., Windeler, A., Knoblauch, H., & Hutter, M. (2018). *Innovation society today: Perspectives, fields and cases.* Wiesbaden, Germany: Springer.

Rawls, A. W., & Mann, D. (2015). Getting information systems to interact: The social fact character of "object" clarity as a factor in designing information systems. *The Information Society, 31*(2), 175–192.

Redström, J., & Wiltse, H. (2015). Press play: Acts of defining (in) fluid assemblages. In M. Tham, H. Edeholt, & M. Ávila (Eds.), *Nordes 2015: Design ecologies,* June 7–10, Konstfack, Stockholm, Sweden. doi: 10.21606/nordes.2015.018.

Redström, J., & Wiltse, H. (2018). *Changing things: The future of objects in a digital world.* London: Bloomsbury Publishing.

Ritala, P., & Almpanopoulou, A. (2017). In defense of "eco"in innovation ecosystem. *Technovation, 60*, 39–42.

Robertson, C. (2021). *The filing cabinet: A vertical history of information.* Minneapolis: University of Minnesota Press.

Rochet, J. C., & Tirole, J. (2003). Platform competition in two-sided markets. *Journal of the European Economic Association, 1*(4), 990–1029.

Rochet, J. C., & Tirole, J. (2006). Two-sided markets: A progress report. *RAND Journal of Economics, 37*(3), 645–667.

Rosch, E. (1975). Cognitive reference points. *Cognitive Psychology, 7*(4), 532–547.

Rosch, E., Mervis, C. B., Gray, W. D., Johnson, D. M., & Boyes-Braem, P. (1976). Basic objects in natural categories. *Cognitive Psychology, 8*(3), 382–439.

Rose, N. (1991). Governing by numbers: Figuring out democracy. *Accounting, Organizations and Society, 16*(7), 673–692.

Rosenberg, D. (2013). Data before the fact. In L. Gitelman (Ed.), *Raw data is an oxymoron* (pp. 15–40). Cambridge, MA: MIT Press.

Rosenberg, D. (2018). Data as word. *Historical Studies in the Natural Sciences, 48*(5), 557–567.

Ryan, J. (2010). *A history of the Internet and the digital future.* Chicago: University of Chicago Press..

Santos, F. M., & Eisenhardt, K. M. (2005). Organizational boundaries and theories of organization. *Organization Science, 16*(5), 491–508.

Saura, J. R., Ribeiro-Soriano, D., & Palacios-Marqués, D. (2021). Setting privacy "by default" in social IoT: Theorizing the challenges and directions in big data research. *Big Data Research, 25*, 100245.

Schilling, M. A. (2000). Toward a general modular systems theory and its application to interfirm product modularity. *Academy of Management Review, 25*(2), 312–334.

Schmandt-Besserat, D. (1980). The envelopes that bear the first writing. *Technology and Culture, 21*(3), 357–385, 358.

Schmandt-Besserat, D. (2010). *How writing came about.* Austin: University of Texas Press.

Schultze, U., & Boland Jr, R. J. (2000). Knowledge management technology and the reproduction of knowledge work practices. *Journal of Strategic Information Systems, 9*(2–3), 193–212.

Schwartz, P. M. (2019). Global data privacy: The EU way. *New York University Law Review, 94*, 771.

Scott, W. R., & Meyer, J. W. (1994). *Institutional environments and organizations: Structural complexity and individualism.* London: Sage.

Searle, J. R. (1995). *The construction of social reality.* New York: Simon and Schuster.

Searle, J. (2010). *Making the social world: The structure of human civilization.* Oxford: Oxford University Press.

Sepkoski, D. (2017). The database before the computer? *Osiris, 32*(1), 175–201.

Shannon, C. E., & Weaver, W. (1949). *The mathematical theory of communication.* Chicago: University of Illinois Press.

Shapiro, C. S., & Varian, H. R. (1998). *Information rules: A strategic guide to the network economy.* Cambridge, MA: Harvard Business Press.

Shipilov, A., & Gawer, A. (2020). Integrating research on interorganizational networks and ecosystems. *Academy of Management Annals, 14*(1), 92–121.

Simon, H. A. (1997). *Models of bounded rationality: Empirically grounded economic reason.* Vol. 3. Cambridge, MA: MIT Press.

Simons, R. (1994). *Levers of control: How managers use innovative control systems to drive strategic renewal.* Boston: Harvard Business School Press.

Sismondo, S. (1993). Some social constructions. *Social Studies of Science, 23*(3), 515–553.

Smith, G. (2020). Data mining fool's gold. *Journal of Information Technology, 35*(3), 182–194.

Sontag, S. (1966/2009). *Against interpretation: And other essays.* London: Macmillan.

Srnicek, N. (2017). *Platform capitalism.* New York: John Wiley & Sons.

Star, S. L. (Ed.). (1995). *Ecologies of knowledge: Work and politics in science and technology.* New York: New York University Press.

Star, S. L. (2010). This is not a boundary object: Reflections on the origin of a concept. *Science, Technology, & Human Values, 35*(5), 601–617.

Star, S. L., & Griesemer, J. R. (1989). Institutional ecology, translations, and boundary objects: Amateurs and professionals in Berkeley's Museum of Vertebrate Zoology, 1907–39. *Social Studies of Science, 19*(3), 387–420.

Star, S. L., & Ruhleder, K. (1996). Steps toward an ecology of infrastructure: Design and access for large information spaces. *Information Systems Research, 7*(1), 111–134.

Stark, D., & Pais, I. (2020). Algorithmic management in the platform economy. *Sociologica, 14*(3), 47–72.

Strasser, B. J., & Edwards, P. N. (2017). Big data is the answer . . . but what is the question? *Osiris, 32*(1), 328–345.

Swanson, E. B. (2020). How information systems came to rule the world: Reflections on the information systems field. *The Information Society, 36*(2), 109–123.

Swanson, E. B. (2021). When data becomes infrastructure and our lives depend on it. *European Conference on Information Systems,* https://aisel.aisnet.org/ecis2021_rp/10/.

Swanson, E. B. (2022). *How information systems came to rule the world: And other essays.* London: Routledge.

Teece, D. J. (2018). Business models and dynamic capabilities. *Long Range Planning, 51*(1), 40–49.

Thompson, J. D. (1967/2003). *Organizations in action.* New York: McGraw Hill.

Thylstrup, N. B., Agostinho, D., Ring, A., D'Ignazio, C., & Veel, K. (Eds.). (2021). *Uncertain archives: Critical keywords for big data*. Cambridge, MA: MIT Press.

Tilly, C. (1984). *Big structures, large processes, huge comparisons*. New York: Russell Sage Foundation.

Tilly, C. (2001). Welcome to the seventeenth century. In P. DiMaggio (Ed.), *The twenty-first-century firm: Changing economic organization in international perspective* (pp. 200–209). Princeton, NJ: Princeton University Press.

Tilson, D., Lyytinen, K., & Sørensen, C. (2010). Research commentary—Digital infrastructures: The missing IS research agenda. *Information Systems Research, 21*(4), 748–759.

Timmermans, S., & Berg, M. (1997). Standardization in action: Achieving local universality through medical protocols. *Social Studies of Science, 27*, 273–305.

Timmermans, S., & Berg, M. (2010). *The gold standard: The challenge of evidence-based medicine*. Philadelphia: Temple University Press.

Tiwana, A. (2014). *Platform ecosystems: Aligning architecture, governance, and strategy*. Waltham, MA: Morgan Kaufmann.

Tiwana, A. (2015). Evolutionary competition in platform ecosystems. *Information Systems Research, 26*(2), 266–281.

Tiwana, A., Konsynski, B., & Bush, A. A. (2010). Research commentary—Platform evolution: Coevolution of platform architecture, governance, and environmental dynamics. *Information Systems Research, 21*(4), 675–687.

Tomasello, M. (1999). *The cultural origins of human cognition*. Cambridge, MA: Harvard University Press.

Tuomi, I. (1999). Data is more than knowledge: Implications of the reversed knowledge hierarchy for knowledge management and organizational memory. *Journal of Management Information Systems, 16*(3), 103–117.

Turkle S. (1984). *The second self: Computers and the human spirit*. Cambridge, MA: MIT Press.

Turkle, S. (1995). *Life on the screen*. New York: Simon and Schuster.

Turkle, S. (2011). *Alone together: Why we expect more from technology and less from each other*. New York: Basic Books.

Turow, J. (2011). *The daily you: How the new advertising industry is defining your identity and your worth*. New Haven, CT: Yale University Press.

Turow, J., & Couldry, N. (2018). Media as data extraction: Towards a new map of a transformed communications field. *Journal of Communication, 68*(2), 415–423.

Turow, J., & Tsui, L. (Eds.) (2008). *The hyperlinked society: Questioning connections in the digital age*. Ann Arbor: University of Michigan Press.

Ulrich, K. (1995). The role of product architecture in the manufacturing firm. *Research Policy, 24*(3), 419–440.

Uzzi, B. (1997). Social structure and competition in interfirm networks: The paradox of embeddedness. *Administrative Science Quarterly*, 35–67.

Uzzi, B., & Gillespie, J. J. (2002). Knowledge spillover in corporate financing networks: Embeddedness and the firm's debt performance. *Strategic Management Journal*, 3(7), 595–618.

Van Alstyne, M. W., Parker, G. G., & Choudary, S. P. (2016). Pipelines, platforms, and the new rules of strategy. *Harvard Business Review*, 94(4), 54–62.

Van der Vlist, F. N., & Helmond, A. (2021). How partners mediate platform power: Mapping business and data partnerships in the social media ecosystem. *Big Data & Society*, 8(1), 205395172110250.

Van der Vlist, F. N., Helmond, A., Burkhardt, M., & Seitz, T. (2022). API governance: The case of Facebook's evolution. *Social Media+ Society*, 8(2), 20563051221086228.

Van Dijck, J. (2013). *The culture of connectivity: A critical history of social media*. Oxford: Oxford University Press.

Varian, H. R. (2010). Computer mediated transactions. *American Economic Review*, 100(2), 1–10.

Varian, H. R. (2014). Big data: New tricks for econometrics. *Journal of Economic Perspectives*, 28(2), 3–28.

Visnjic, I., Jovanovic, M., & Raisch, S. (2022). Managing the transition to a dual business model, *Organization Science*, 33(5), 1964–1989.

Voigt, P., & Von dem Bussche, A. (2017). *The EU General Data Protection Regulation (GDPR)*. Cham, Switzerland: Springer.

Von Krogh, G. (2018). Artificial intelligence in organizations: New opportunities for phenomenon-based theorizing. *Academy of Management Discoveries*, 4(4), 404–409.

Von Krogh, G., Roos, J., & Slocum, K. (1994). An essay on corporate epistemology. *Strategic Management Journal*, 15(2), 53–71.

Von Oertzen, C. (2017). Machineries of data power: Manual versus mechanical census compilation in nineteenth-century Europe. *Osiris*, 32(1), 129–150.

Waardenburg, L., Huysman, M., & Sergeeva A. V. (2022). In the land of the blind, the one-eyed man is king: Knowledge brokerage in the age of learning algorithms. *Organization Science*, 33(1), 59–82.

Walzer, M. (1983). *Spheres of justice: A defense of pluralism and equality*. New York: Basic Books.

Wang, P. (2021). Connecting the parts with the whole: Toward an information ecology theory of digital innovation ecosystems. *MIS Quarterly*, 45(1), 397–422.

Weaver, W. (1949). The mathematics of communication. *Scientific American*, 181(1), 11–15.

Weber, M. (1947/2012). *The theory of social and economic organization*. New York: Free Press.

Weber, M. (1978/2019). *Economy and society: A new translation.* Cambridge, MA: Harvard University Press.

Weber, R. A. (1998). *Information systems control and audit.* Upper Saddle River, NJ: Pearson Education.

Wegner, P. (1997). Why interaction is more powerful than algorithms. *Communications of the ACM, 40*(5), 80–91.

Weick, K. E. (1979). *The social psychology of organizing.* Boston: Addison-Wesley.

Weinberger, D. (2007). *Everything is miscellaneous: The power of the new digital disorder.* New York: Macmillan.

Wernerfelt, B. (1984), A resource-based view of the firm. *Strategic Management Journal, 5/2,* 171–180.

Williamson, O. E. (1975). *Markets and hierarchies: Analysis and antitrust implications: A study in the economics of internal organization.* New York: Free Press.

Winner, L. (1978). *Autonomous technology: Technics-out-of-control as a theme in political thought.* Cambridge, MA: MIT Press.

Winner, L. (1986/2010). *The whale and the reactor: A search for limits in an age of high technology.* Chicago: University of Chicago Press.

Winner, L. (1993). Upon opening the black box and finding it empty: Social constructivism and the philosophy of technology. *Science, Technology, & Human Values, 18*(3), 362–378.

Winter, S. G. (2003). Understanding dynamic capabilities. *Strategic Management Journal, 24*(10), 991–995.

Winter, S., Berente, N., Howison, J., & Butler, B. (2014). Beyond the organizational "container": Conceptualizing 21st century sociotechnical work. *Information and Organization, 24*(4), 250–269.

Winter, S. G., & Szulanski, G. (2001). Replication as strategy. *Organization Science, 12*(6), 730–743.

Winter, S. J., & Taylor, S. L. (1996). The role of IT in the transformation of work: A comparison of post-industrial, industrial, and proto-industrial organization. *Information Systems Research, 7*(1), 5–21.

Wu, T. (2016). *The attention merchants: The epic scramble to get inside our heads.* New York: Alfred A. Knopf.

Yates, J. (1989). *Control through communication: The rise of system in American management.* Baltimore: Johns Hopkins University Press.

Yoo, Y. (2010). Computing in everyday life: A call for research on experiential computing. *MIS Quarterly, 34*(2), 213–231.

Yoo, Y. (2013). The tables have turned: How can the information systems field contribute to technology and innovation management research? *Journal of the Association for Information Systems, 14*(5), 227.

Yoo, Y., Henfridsson, O., & Lyytinen, K. (2010). Research commentary—The new organizing logic of digital innovation: An agenda for information systems research. *Information Systems Research, 21*(4), 724–735.

Zachariadis, M., & Ozcan, P. (2017). *The API economy and digital transformation in financial services: The case of open banking.* SWIFT Institute working paper no. 2016–001. Available at SSRN: https://ssrn.com/abstract=2975199 or http://dx.doi.org/10.2139/ssrn.2975199.

Zelizer, V. A. (2005). *The purchase of intimacy.* Princeton, NJ: Princeton University Press.

Zittrain, J. (2008). *The future of the Internet—and how to stop it.* New Haven, CT: Yale University Press.

Zuboff, S. (1988). *In the age of the smart machine: The future of work and power.* New York: Basic Books.

Zuboff, S. (2015). Big other: Surveillance capitalism and the prospects of an information civilization. *Journal of Information Technology, 30*(1), 75–89.

Zuboff, S. (2019). *The age of surveillance capitalism: The fight for the future at the new frontier of power.* London: Profile Books.

INDEX

Page numbers followed by *f* and *t* indicate figures and tables, respectively.

Accounting tools, historical origins
of. *See also* Digital data
revolution
clay tokens and exchange, 21–29, 25*f*,
28*f*, 39, 184n4, 184n13
corporate coordination and control,
33–38
modernity, rise of, 29–33
Adding machines, 41–46
Ad impressions
commodification of, 79*t*, 82–85
as data objects, 71, 164
Administered exchange systems,
platforms as, 137–141
Administrative control, historical
origins of, 33–38
Advertising
ad impressions, 71, 79*t*, 82–85, 164
AdX bid requests, 163–164*f*
audiences, 75–76
commodification of, 82–85
data complementarities, 161–165
programmatic, 82–85, 150, 161–165,
163–164*f*, 189n2
AdX bid request, 163–164*f*

Aggregation
data objects constructed from, 14, 70,
75, 80, 123, 184n9
demand, 127–128, 140–141
politics of data and, 56
in social science of data, 181
Agnostic character of digital data, 14,
48, 55, 59–60, 63, 76, 118
Airbnb, 52
Algorithms
data complementarities, 165
data shaped by, 5–8, 66
ecosystems, 150
machine learning, 69
Alibaba, 138
All-purpose machines, 46, 59
Amazon, 52, 125, 138
Ambiguity of data, 66–67
Apple, 125, 135
Application programming interfaces
(APIs), 17, 75–76, 153, 160, 162,
164
Aqui, Acontecendo, 189n2
Architecture-based view of platforms,
132–137, 151

Architectures of control, 11–12
Archiving, 36–38
Aronova, E., 183n2
Artifacts, cognitive, 21–29, 39, 184n4,
     184n13
Artificial intelligence (AI), 6, 60, 65, 69,
     102, 162, 180
Audiences, advertising, 75–76
Audioscrobbler, 67–68

Babbage, Charles, 46, 55, 185n1
Banco Mediolanum Spa, 158–160
Beniger, J., 36
Berners-Lee, Tim, 50
Bid request objects, 71, 76–77
Big Brother surveillance, 15, 91, 99
Big data, 1, 4, 43, 55, 183n2
Billing machines, 41–46
Bills of lading, clay tokens used as,
     27
Bone tally sticks, 183n1
Bookkeeping, 24, 29, 44, 57, 58t
Bounded systems, organizations as, 15,
     112, 115–118, 188n1
Bowker, G. C., 184n6
Business ecosystems. See Ecosystems

Calculators, 41–46
Cambridge Analytica scandal, 89–90,
     187n1
Carnegie, Andrew, 35
Castells, Manuel, 126, 188n3
Categorical thinking, record-keeping
     systems as basis of, 29
Cave wall markings, 21
Cennamo, Carmelo, 189n3
Centered systems, organizations as, 12,
     16, 112–118
Cetina, Knorr, 67, 181
Chandler, Alfred, 2, 36, 38, 39, 45
Clark, K. B., 134
Classification, making of data and, 30,
     61–63, 68–69

Clay tokens
     clay envelopes, 27, 37, 51, 184n8,
          184n9
     cognitive functions of, 21, 24–29, 28f
     data storage units, 27–29
     format of, 24, 25f, 28f
     protobureaucracies emerging from,
          22–23, 38–39
     significance of, 13, 39, 184n4
     widespread use of, 24, 184n13
Click-through rates, 40, 71
Closed systems, 188n1
Cognition, data and, 13
Cognitive artifacts, 21–29, 25f, 28f, 39,
     184n4, 184n13
Cognitive foundations of data.
     See Epistemic foundations of
     data
Collaboration, in digital ecosystems,
     17–18, 93, 134, 143, 146
Commodities, data, 64f, 78–79t, 81–87
Common Business-Oriented Language
     (COBOL), 186n3
Communication layer, digital data, 54,
     54f
Competition, in digital ecosystems,
     17–18
Complementarities, data. See Data
     complementarities
Computation, history of
     data production, 58t
     data transmission, 46–48, 47f
     digital data, characteristics of, 52–57,
          54f
     implications of, 58–60
     mechanization of records, 41–46, 43f
Computational layer, digital data, 54,
     54f
Computational science, emergence of,
     13–14
Computed sociality, 65, 82
Computer systems, development of,
     41–46

Computing-Tabulating-Recording Company (C-T-R), 42
Concentrated systems, organizations as, 116–118, 188n1
Content-agnosticism, 48, 55, 57, 60, 76, 118
Continuous feedback, 186n2
Control, architectures of, 11–12
Coordination, data, 23, 33–38
Corporations
  mechanization of records in, 41–48, 43f
  role of data in shaping, 23, 33–38, 39
  scientific management, 23, 35, 41
Cortada, J. W., 186n2
Cost per click, 187n6
Cost per Mille (CPM), 83, 187n6
Credit scores, 40, 57, 71, 120
Crime statistics, 13–14, 31–33
Cryptography, 47
Culture of data, 22, 44
Customer profiles, 71

Data aggregation. See Aggregation
Data-as-things, mechanization and, 41–46, 43f
Databases, 24, 184n6
Data commodities, 64f, 81–87
Data complementarities
  characteristics of, 151–161, 159f
  concept of, 159f
  Flowe case study, 153, 158–161
  forging of, 161–165
  implications of, 165–171
  TripAdvisor case study, 52, 153, 156–157
  value-reinforcing, 155, 159f, 189n4
Datafication, socioeconomic transformations resulting from, 1–5, 171–176
Data governance, 89–90, 101, 188n3. See also Surveillance
Data Governance Act, 188n3

Data-knowledge life cycle, 187n1
Data lakes, 75
Data life cycle
  common misunderstandings of, 187n1
  concept of, 61–63, 64f
  data commodities, 81–87
  data making, 63–69, 187n4
  data objects, 69–81, 72–73f, 74f, 78–79t, 80f, 85–86
  implications of, 84–87
Data-made ecosystems, 17
Data making. See also Data life cycle
  agnosticism in, 48, 55, 58t, 59, 60, 76, 118
  ambiguity in, 66–67
  characteristics of, 58t
  data formats for, 68
  data objects versus, 76–77
  errors in, 187n4
  expectations of, 69
  nonneutrality in, 13–14, 55, 58t, 59, 63
  overview of, 14, 64f
  processes underlying, 63–69, 64f
  rise of modern management and, 33–38
  as social inquiry, 9–13
Data mechanization, history of, 41–46, 43f
Data objects. See also Data complementarities
  ad impressions as, 71
  characteristics of, 78–79t
  concept of, 64f, 69–71, 84–86
  data making versus, 76–77
  definition of, 69–70, 78t
  examples of, 71–76, 72–73f, 74f
  form of, 78–79t
  functions of, 70–71, 74, 78–79t
  knowledge and organizational processes of, 77, 78–79t, 80–81
  knowledge management with, 118–123
  software objects versus, 70

Data Protection Directive, 187n2
Data reuse, 6–7, 63–69, 122–123
Data rules
  definition of, 82, 150
  reinvention of market economy and, 151–154, 152*f*
  significance of, 17
Data science, 3, 180
Data transmission, mathematics of, 46–48, 47*f*
Data use, 9–13, 64*f*
Data visualization, 36
Datum, 30, 185n15
Decentering of organizations
  architecture of knowledge in, 118–123
  conditions and processes supporting, 118–123
  environmental changes and, 111–112
  implications of, 128–129
  isotropism and structural change, 123–128
  organizations as centered systems, 12, 16, 112–118
  theory of the firm, 15, 113–115
  unbundling of data collection for, 121–123
Decoupling of data and information, 45–46, 186n4
Demand aggregation, 127
Design rules, 17, 150, 152*f*
Desrosières, Alain, 31
Dial-up Internet, 50–52
Difference, machineries of, 99
Digital business ecosystems.
  See Ecosystems
Digital data, characteristics of, 52–57, 54*f*
Digital data revolution
  agnostic character of, 48, 55, 59, 60, 76, 118
  culture of data and, 44
  data transmission, 46–48, 47*f*
  digital and social media platforms, 48–52

digital data characteristics, 52–57, 54*f*
  homogenizing character of, 13–14, 57, 59, 63, 153
  implications of, 58–60
  mechanization in, 41–46, 43*f*
  nonneutrality in, 55, 58*t*, 59, 63
  PC revolution and, 48–52, 186n6
Digital Markets Act (DMA), 90, 165–168
Digital platforms. *See* Platforms
Digital rendition. *See* Rendition, digital
Digital revolution
  narratives of, 4
  roots of (*see* Historical origins of data)
  socioeconomic transformations resulting from, 1–5, 171–176
Digital Services Act (DSA), 90, 165–166
Digitized sociality, 140
Doconomy, 158–160, 159*f*
Document-handling techniques, 36–38, 41–46

Ecobalance, 158–160
Economic rationality, 104–105, 117, 178
Ecosystems, data and. *See also* Data complementarities
  attributes, 144–145
  collaboration and competition, 17–18
  concept of, 149–154, 152*f*
  ecosystem of knowing, 10
  implications of, 146–149, 165–171
  platforms versus, 141–146, 172–173
  regulation, 165–170
  reinvention of market economy and, 151–154, 152*f*
  research on, 131–132
  structure of, 17
Edgar Thomson steel production plant, 35
Editable objects, 164
Electrical engineering, 46–47
Embedment of data, 12
Empiricism, 30, 179

Endogenous dynamics, 177
Enlightenment, 30
Enterprise forms, 11
Envelopes, clay, 27, 37, 51, 184n8,
    184n9
Epistemic foundations of data
    clay tokens and exchange, 21–29, 25f,
        28f, 39, 184n4, 184n13
    concept of, 13, 17–18
    corporate coordination and control,
        23, 33–39
    historical origins of, 38–39
    implications of, 38–40
    importance of, 2–5, 21–23
    modernity and formation of modern
        social order., 23, 29–33
    as part of ecosystem of knowing, 10
    politics of data and, 23, 29–33, 39–40
Erie railroad company, 35–36
Errors, in making of data, 187n4
European Union
    Data Protection Directive, 187n2
    Digital Markets Act, 90, 165–168
    Digital Services Act, 90, 165–166
    European Data Act, 188n3
    General Data Protection Regulation,
        89–90, 96, 166, 187n2, 188n3
Exchanges
    clay tokens and, 21–29, 25f, 28f, 39
    concept of, 26–27
    platforms as, 137–141
Executable objects, 164
Exogenous forces, 177

Facebook (Meta), 52, 138, 140, 153
Facts, data as, 30–31
Filing
    mechanization of records, 41–46
    rise of modern management and,
        36–38
Fintech apps, 52
Firm, theory of, 15–16, 113–115
Flowe, 153, 158–161, 159f

Forging of data complementarities,
    161–165
Formats, data, 68
FORTRAN, 186n3
Foucault, Michel, 11, 98, 185n17
Frege, G., 180

General Data Protection Regulation
    (GDPR), 89–90, 96, 166, 187n2,
    188n3, 188n4
Gerlitz, C., 140
Goody, Jack, 183n3
Google, 52, 85, 125, 184n4
Granovetter, M., 104
Gross domestic product (GDP), 31–33

Habermas, J., 102
Hacking, Ian, 31, 32, 98–99
Havelock, E. A., 185n14
Hayek, Friedrich, 150
Helmond, A., 140
Henderson, R. M., 134
Hirschman, A. O., 104
Historical origins of data. See also Digital
    data revolution
    cave wall markings, 21
    clay tokens, 21–29, 25f, 28f, 38–39
    corporate coordination and control,
        23, 33–38
    data production, 58t
    data transmission, 46–48, 47f
    implications of, 38–40
    importance of, 21–23
    mechanization of records, 41–46,
        43f
    modernity and formation of modern
        social order, 23, 29–33
    politics of data, 23, 29–33, 39–40
    tally sticks, 21, 50–52, 183n1
    writing, emergence of, 27–28,
        184n10
Hollerith, Herman, 42, 44–46, 185n1.
    See also Punch card tabulators

Homogenizing data, 13–14, 57, 58*t*, 59, 63, 135, 153
"Hostile worlds" argument, 105

IBM, 41–46, 185n1, 186n2
Impressions, ad. *See* Ad impressions
In Action (Thompson), 117
Indexing, 36–38
Industrial Internet of Things (IoT), 145–146
Industrial Revolution, 34
Information, decoupling of data from, 45–46, 186n4
Information theory, 47
Institutional/personal worlds, blurring of boundaries between, 101–107
Interactions
    making of data from, 63–69
    transactions versus, 7–8, 174–175
Internal information, corporate coordination and control through, 36–38
Internet browsing, 48–52, 89–96, 186n6
Internet of Things (IoT), 7–8, 74, 89–96, 145–146
Interpretation, 62–63
Isotropism, 123–128

Jacobides, M. G., 189n4
Jiang, X., 126

Kay, Alan, 50
Knowing, ecosystem of, 10
Knowledge, architecture of, 118–123
Knowledge building
    architecture of knowledge in, 118–123
    in organizations as centered systems, 112–118
    unbundling of data collection for, 121–123
Knowledge objects made of data. *See* Data objects

Labeling, 62–63
Lading, bills of, clay tokens used as, 27
Lakes, data, 75
Last.fm, data life cycle on
    data making, 67–68, 187n3
    data objects, 77, 80–81, 80*f*
Legislation
    Data Governance Act, 188n3
    Data Protection Directive, 187n2
    Digital Markets Act, 90, 165–168
    Digital Services Act, 90, 165–166
    European Data Act, 188n3
    General Data Protection Regulation, 89–90, 96, 166, 187n2, 188n3, 188n4
    Open Data Directive, 188n3
Life cycle, data. *See* Data life cycle
Like economy, 3, 63–69, 140
LinkedIn, 138
Lookalike audiences, 71
Lyytinen, K., 134

MacCallum, Daniel, 35–36
Machineries of difference, 99
Mainframe computers, 41–46
Making of data. *See* Data making
Management, role of data in shaping, 33–38
Market economy, reinvention of commodification in, 82–86
    scale of transformations, 171–176
    systems of rules in, 151–154, 152*f*
Market rules, 16, 17, 85–87, 151–154, 152*f*
Material layer, digital data, 54, 54*f*
Mathematical theory of communication, 47–48
Mathematical Theory of Communication (Shannon), 186n5
Mathematics of data transmission, 46–48
McCallum, B. T., 41

Mechanization of records
   implications of, 58–60
   technical and cultural repercussions
      of, 13–14, 41–47, 43f
Memory, record keeping technology
   for, 26
Metadata, 27, 67–70, 76–77, 78t, 82
Metcalfe, Robert, 35
Modernity. See also Surveillance
   emergence of, 29–31
   formation of modern social order
      and, 29–33, 39
Modern state, birth of, 29–31
Moore, J. F., 142
Mumford, L., 42
Music streaming platforms, data life
   cycle on
   data making, 67–68, 187n3
   data objects, 77, 80–81

Nelson, R. R., 114
Netflix, 52
Nonneutrality in data production,
   13–14, 55, 58t, 59, 63
Norberg, Arthur, 45
Notation technologies
   cave wall markings, 21
   clay tokens, 21–29, 25f, 28f, 39,
      184n4, 184n13
   roots of digital revolution in, 21
   tally sticks, 21, 50–52, 183n1

Objectification, 47, 86
   politics of data, 23, 29–33, 39–40
   social objects constructed by, 11, 26,
      37, 40
Objects, data. See Data objects
Ong, Walter, 27, 29
Online connectivity
   data governance problems resulting
      from, 89–91
   impact on epistemic functions,
      48–52

sociocultural context of data from,
   91–96
Open Data Directive, 188n3
Open-Source Software Development,
   138
Operating ratios, 37, 120
Organizational adaptation, period of, 51
Organizations, decentering of
   architecture of knowledge in,
      118–123
   conditions and processes supporting,
      118–123
   definition of, 12, 16
   environment, 111–112
   implications of, 128–129
   isotropism and structural change,
      123–128
   organizations as centered systems,
      112–118
   theory of the firm, 15, 113–115
   unbundling of data collection for,
      121–123
Organization theory, 15–16
Orwell, George, 99

Parker, G. G., 126–127
Perforations, punch-card tabulator, 46
Personal computers, 48–52, 186n6
Personal/institutional worlds, blurring
   of boundaries between, 101–107
Platforms
   as administered exchange systems,
      137–141
   architecture-based view of, 132–137,
      151
   defined, 132
   diversity of research on, 131–132
   ecosystems versus, 141–146, 172–173
   emergence of, 12–13
   impact on data makeup and epis-
      temic functions, 48–52
   implications of, 38–39, 146–149
   literature on, 147t, 148

Platforms (cont.)
   market economy, reinvention of,
      151–154, 152f
   mediating functions of, 173
   as multisided markets and virtual
      exchange systems, 16–17
   origins of, 16–17
   outbound orientation, 172
   socioeconomic transformations
      resulting from, 171–176
Plato, 185n14
Playcounts, Last.fm, 67–68
Polanyi, Karl, 82, 104, 149
Political artifacts, data as, 9
Politics of data, 23, 29–33, 39–40
Poovey, M., 185n16
Popularity indexes, 31–33
Probabilistic thought, 32–33
Processual thinking, 29
Product and platform architecture, 136
Profiles, 71, 72–73f
Profit/loss data, 37
Programmatic advertising
   AdX bid request, 163–164f
   commodification of, 83–85
   data complementarities, 161–165
   ecosystems, 150
   editable/executable objects, 163–164f
   share of, 189n2
Protobureaucracies, emergence of,
      22–23, 38–39
Punch cards, 43, 47f
Punch card tabulators, 41–46, 43f

Quantification, formation of modern
   social order and, 31–33

Rationality, economic, 104–105, 117,
   178
Rationalization, formation of modern
   social order and, 29–33
Real-Time Bidding (RTB) protocol, 162
Recommender systems, 11, 79, 100

Record keeping, roots of digital revolution in, 2–3
   cave wall markings, 21
   clay tokens, 21–29, 25f, 28f, 38–39
   corporate coordination and control,
      23
   data production, 58t
   data transmission, 46–48, 47f
   digital data characteristics, 52–57, 54f
   implications of, 38–40, 58–60
   mechanization of records, 41–46, 43f
   politics of data and, 23, 29–33, 39–40
   primary epistemic function of, 26
   tally sticks, 21, 50–52, 183n1
   writing, emergence of, 27–28, 184n10
Regulation, challenges of, 89–91,
      161–170. See also Legislation
   personal/institutional worlds, blurring
      of boundaries between, 101–105
   public perception of surveillance
      impacting, 97–101
   sociocultural context of data, 91–96
Relations, structure of, 17
Rendition, digital, 1–5, 13–14, 171–176
Repetitions, in clay tokens, 27–28
Reports, corporate administrative
   control and, 33–38
Repurposing of data. See Data reuse
Resources, data viewed as, 94
Reuse of data, 6–7, 63–69, 122–123
Rochet, J. C., 137
Rosch, Eleanor, 71
Rose, Nikolas, 185n18

Schmandt-Besserat, D., 184n8
Science and technology studies (STS),
   181
Scientific management, 23, 35, 41
Scientific objectivism, 30
Semiotic functions of data, 2, 5, 10,
   17–18, 53, 176–182
Sepkoski, D., 183n2
Shannon, Claude, 46, 186n5

SHARE, 186n2
Signifying entities, 184n12
Slips, production, 35
Social action, data and, 13
Social data
  ambiguity of data, 66–67
  computed sociality, 65, 82
  value of, 66–67
Social inquiry, areas of
  data use, 9–13
  making of, 9–13
Social institutions, social objects and,
  31–33
Sociality, digitized, 140
Social media
  computed sociality, 65, 82
  corporate administrative control and,
  33–38
  data governance problems resulting
  from, 89–91
  formation of modern social order
  and, 29–33
  impact on epistemic functions, 48–52
  like economy on, 3
  making of data in, 63–69
  significance of, 11, 13, 23
  sociocultural context of data, 91–96
Social science of data, 18, 176–182
Socioeconomic transformations
  data at center of, 1–5
  reinvention of market economy and,
  151–154, 152f, 171–176
  scale of, 171–176
  social science of data, need for,
  176–182
Sociotechnical dynamics, 60
Spotify, 52
Standardization, 14, 44, 67, 68–69, 81,
  112, 140
Statistics, 10–11, 31–38
Sticks, tally. See Tally sticks
Structural change, 123–128
Structure of relations, 17

Suicide rates, 31–33, 39
Surveillance
  Big Brother imagery associated with,
  14–15, 91, 99
  Cambridge Analytica scandal, 89–90,
  187n1
  contingencies in, 101
  data governance problems resulting
  from, 89–91
  implications of, 106–107, 186n7
  machineries of difference generated
  by, 100–101
  narratives of, 4
  personal versus institutional worlds
  in, 101–105
  public perception of, 97–101
  sociocultural context of, 4–5, 91–96
Swedberg, R., 104

Tabulating Machine Company, 41–42
Tabulating machines, 41–46, 43f
Tally sticks, 21, 50–52, 183n1
Taylor, Frederic, 35
Technological artifacts, 13–14, 94
Technology, data shaped by, 5–8
Tesla, 125
Theorization of data, 173–174
Theory of the firm, 15, 113–115
Things, records as, 26–29, 39
Thompson, James, 117
Tickets, production, 35
Tilly, C., 104
Tirole, J., 137
Tokens. See Clay tokens
Tracking. See User tracking and
  monitoring
Transactions, interactions versus,
  174–175
TripAdvisor, 52, 153, 156–157
Trump, Donald, 187n1
Turing, Alan, 185n1
Twitter, user objects on, 72–73f
Typewriters, 41–46

Uber, 52, 138
Unbundling of data collection, 121–123
Unemployment rates, 13–14, 31–32, 40
Universal machines, 8, 48, 55
Upper Paleolithic era, record keeping in, 21
User profiles, 71, 72–73*f*
User tracking and monitoring
    Big Brother imagery associated with, 14–15, 91, 99
    Cambridge Analytica scandal, 89–90, 187n1
    contingencies in, 101
    data governance problems resulting from, 89–91
    implications of, 106–107
    machineries of difference generated by, 99
    making of data and, 67–69
    personal versus institutional worlds in, 101–105
    public perception of, 97–101
    role in development of modern corporations, 40
    sociocultural context of, 4–5, 91–96

Value-reinforcing complementarities, 154–161, 159*f*, 189n4
Van Alstyne, M., 126
Varian, Hal, 51, 184n4, 186n7
Viewability metrics, 71
Virtual exchange systems, digital platforms as, 16–17
Virtualization of assets, data objects created by, 71, 74–75, 74*f*
von Neumann, John, 185n1
Von Oertzen, 183n2
Voucher system, 35

Wegner, Peter, 7
Wikipedia, 138
Winter, S. G., 114

Wood, Christopher, 184n7
Writing, emergence of, 27–28, 184n10

Xerox Park, 50

Yates, J., 34
Yoo, Y., 134, 136

Zelizer, V. A., 105
ZeroCO2, 158–160, 159*f*
Zouse, Konrad, 185n1
Zuboff, S., 49, 186n7